KATHMANDU
AND BEYOND
A PHOTOGRAPHIC EXPLORATION

SCOTT SHAW

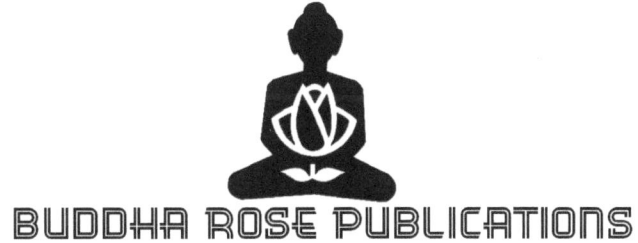

BUDDHA ROSE PUBLICATIONS

Kathmandu and Beyond:
A Photographic Exploration
Copyright © 2016 by Scott Shaw
All Rights Reserved
No part of this publication can be duplicated
in any manner without the expressed written
permission of the publisher.

First Edition 2016

ISBN: 1-877792-90-X
ISBN 13: 978-1-877792-90-8

Printed in the United States of America

10 9 8 7 6 5 4 3 2 1

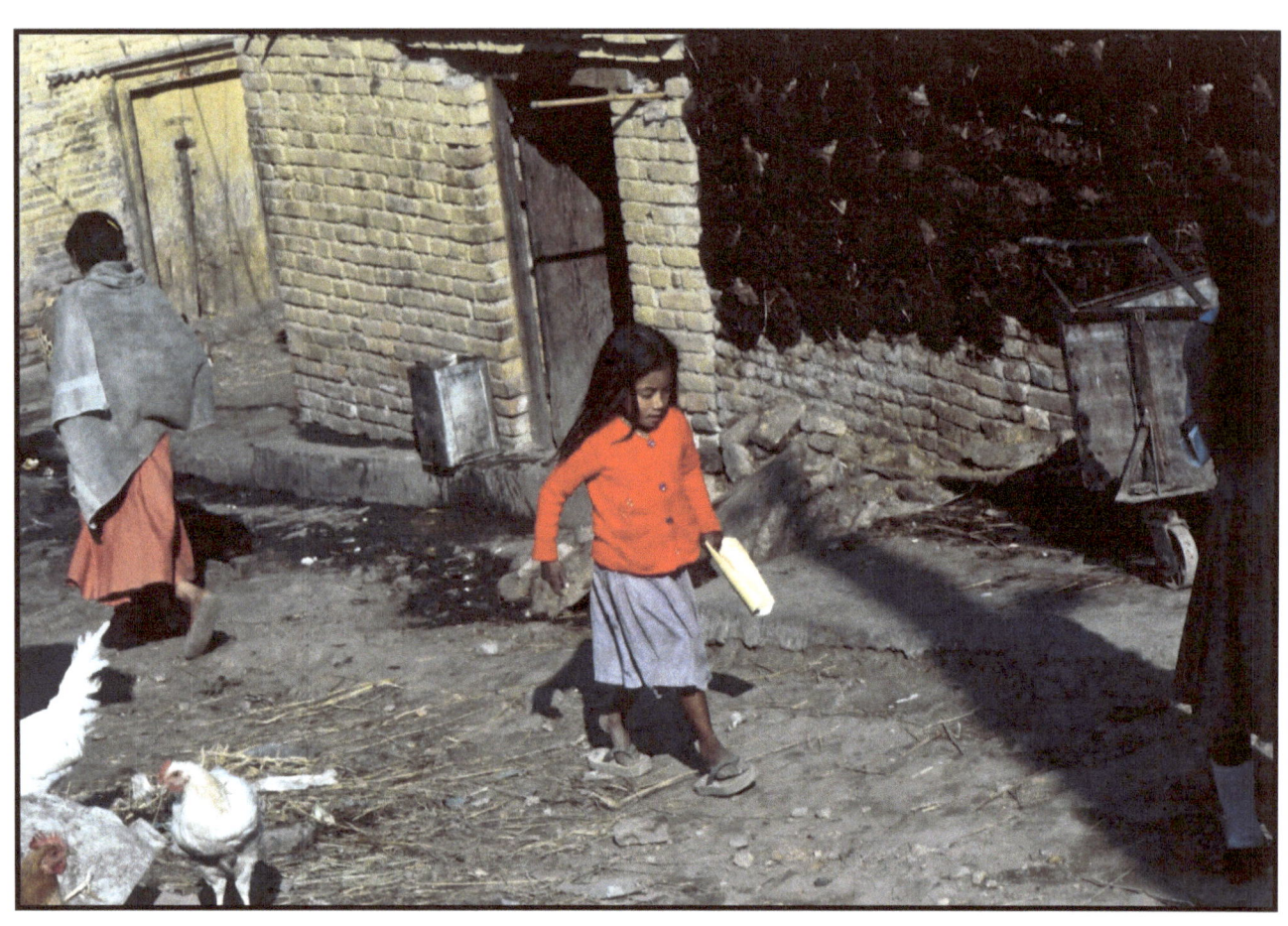

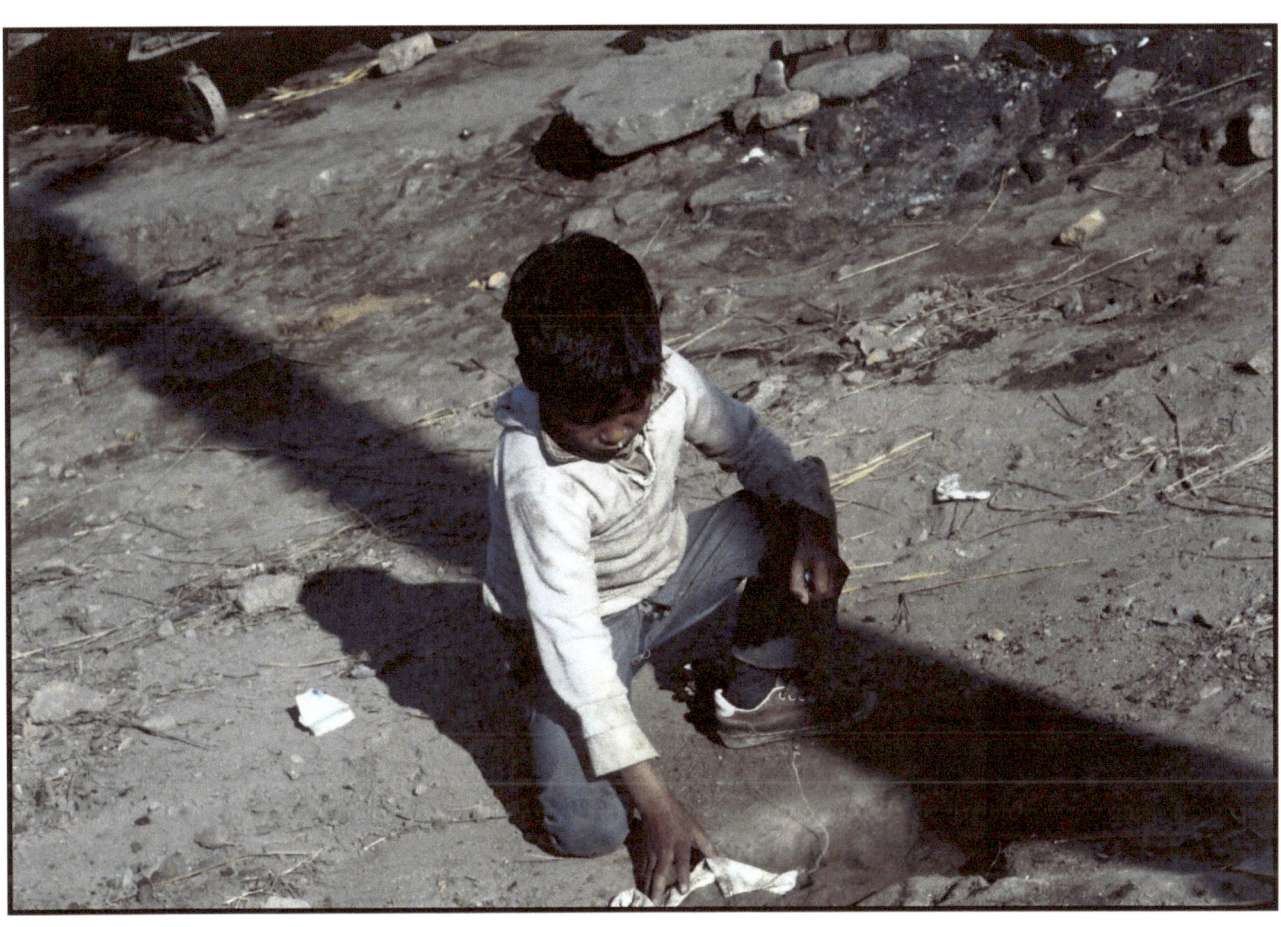

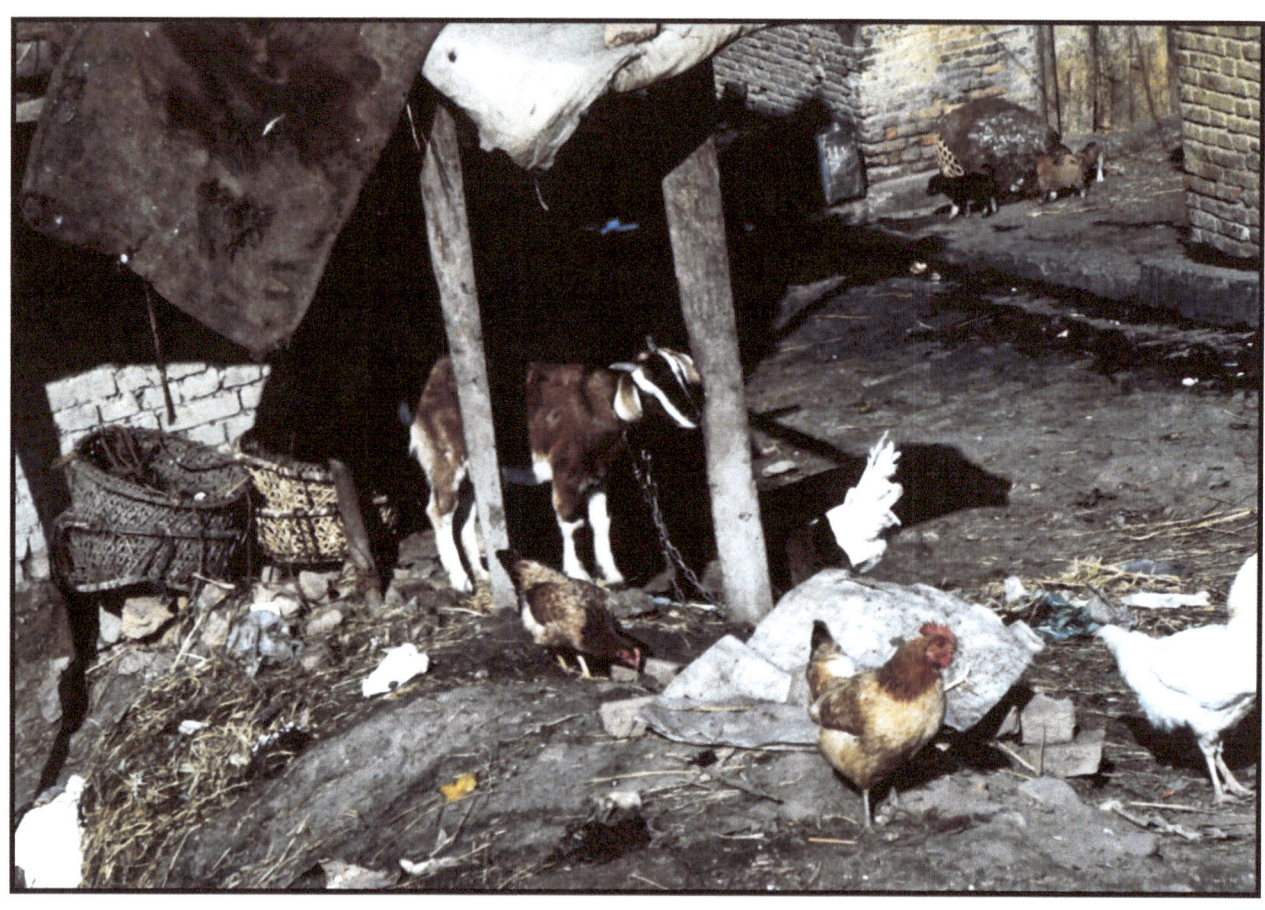

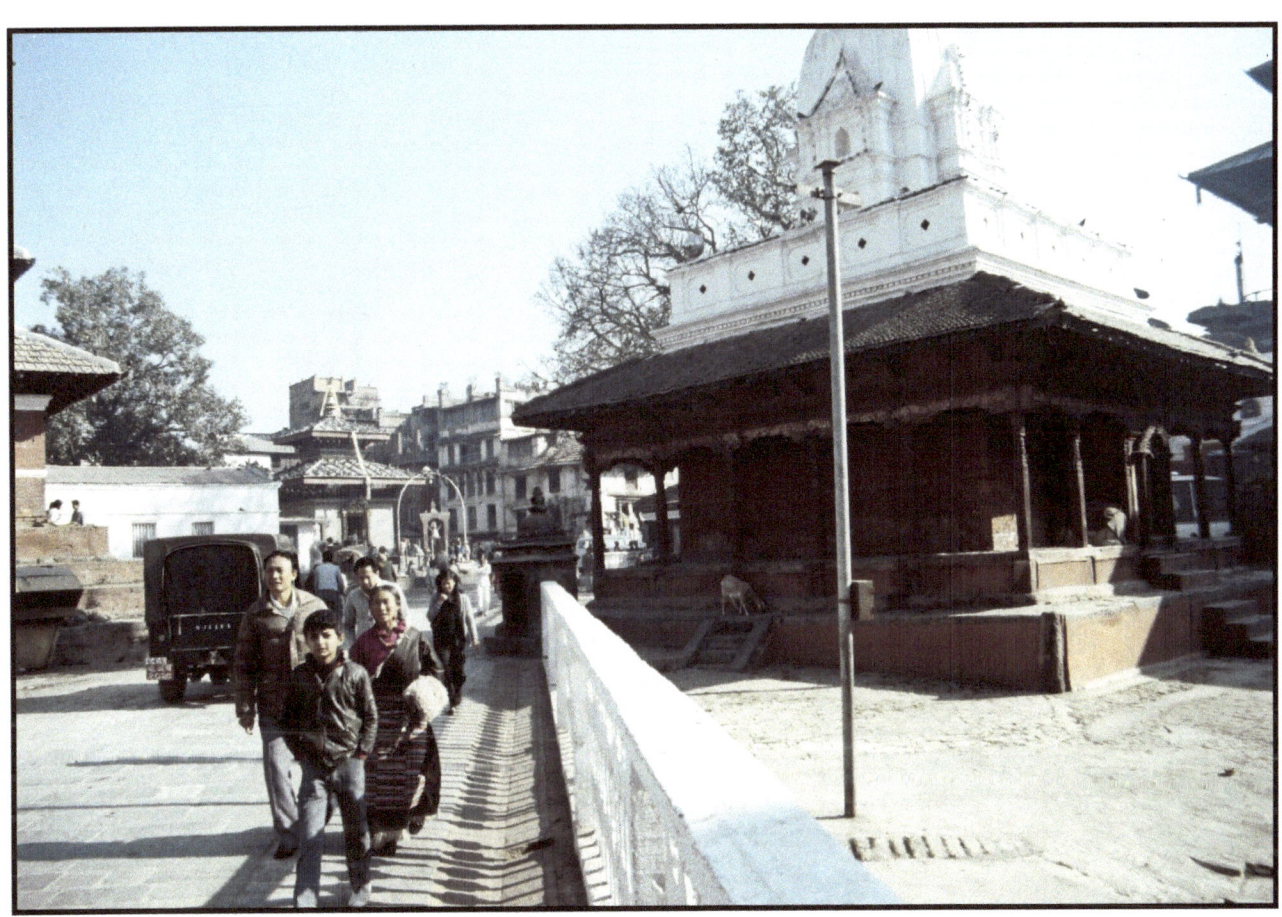

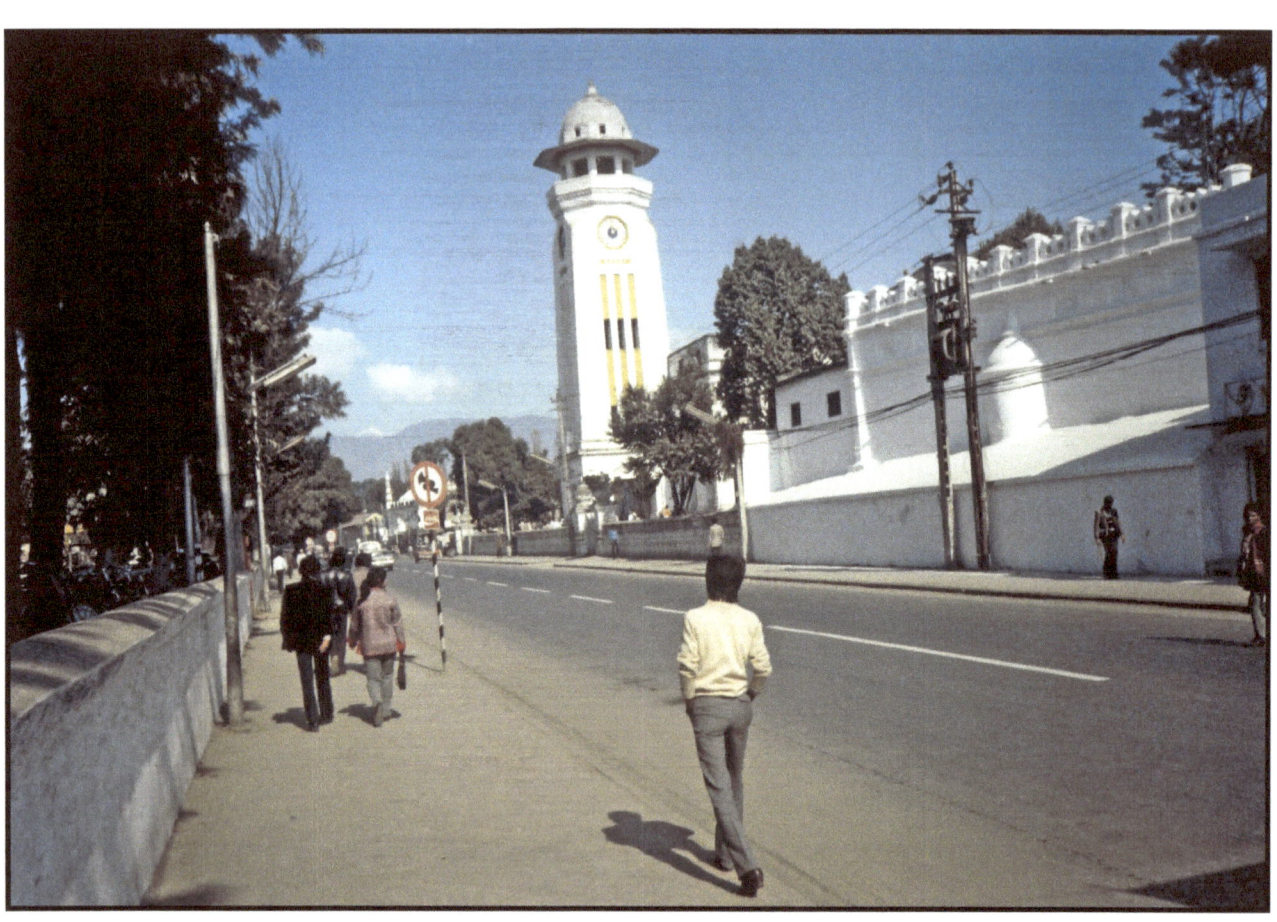

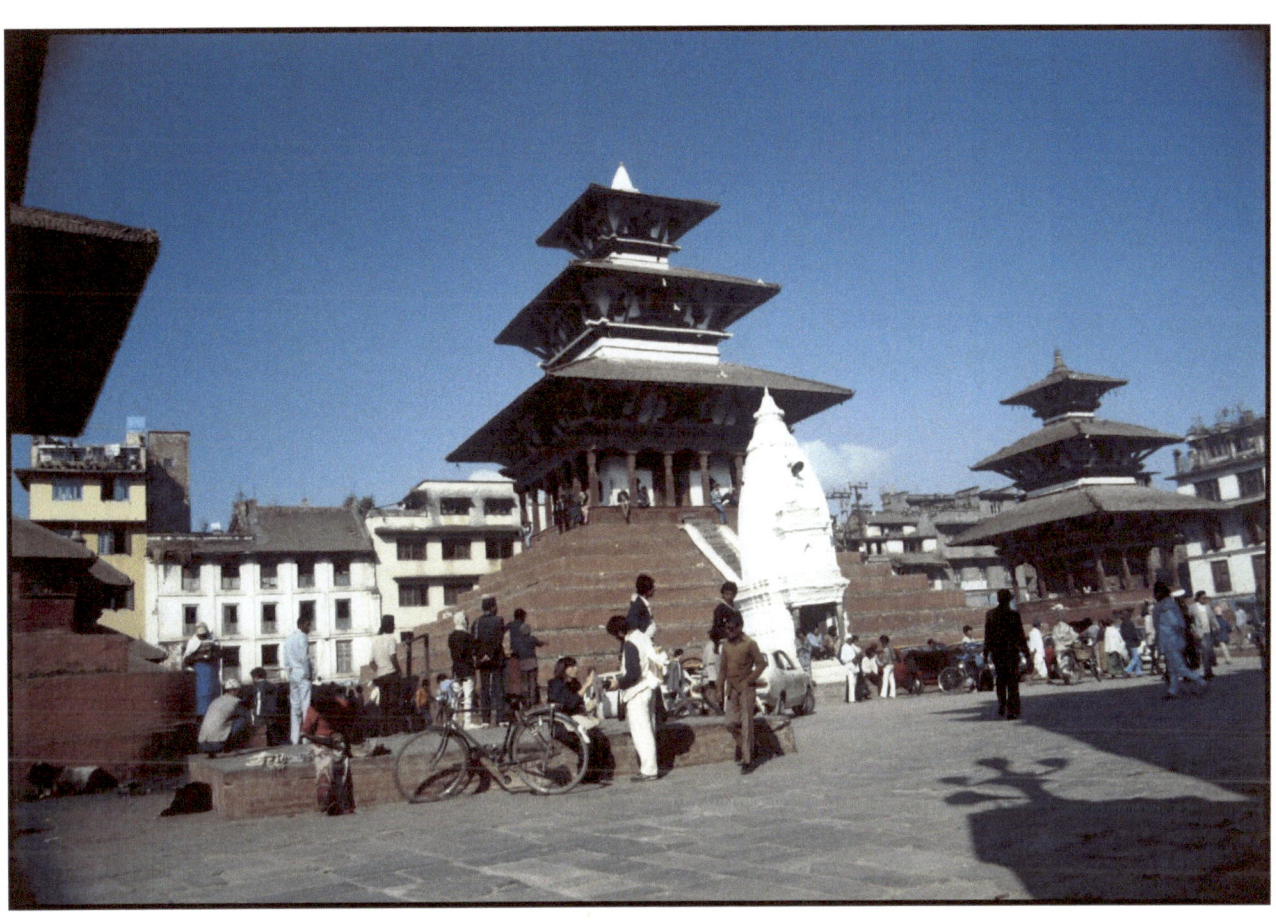

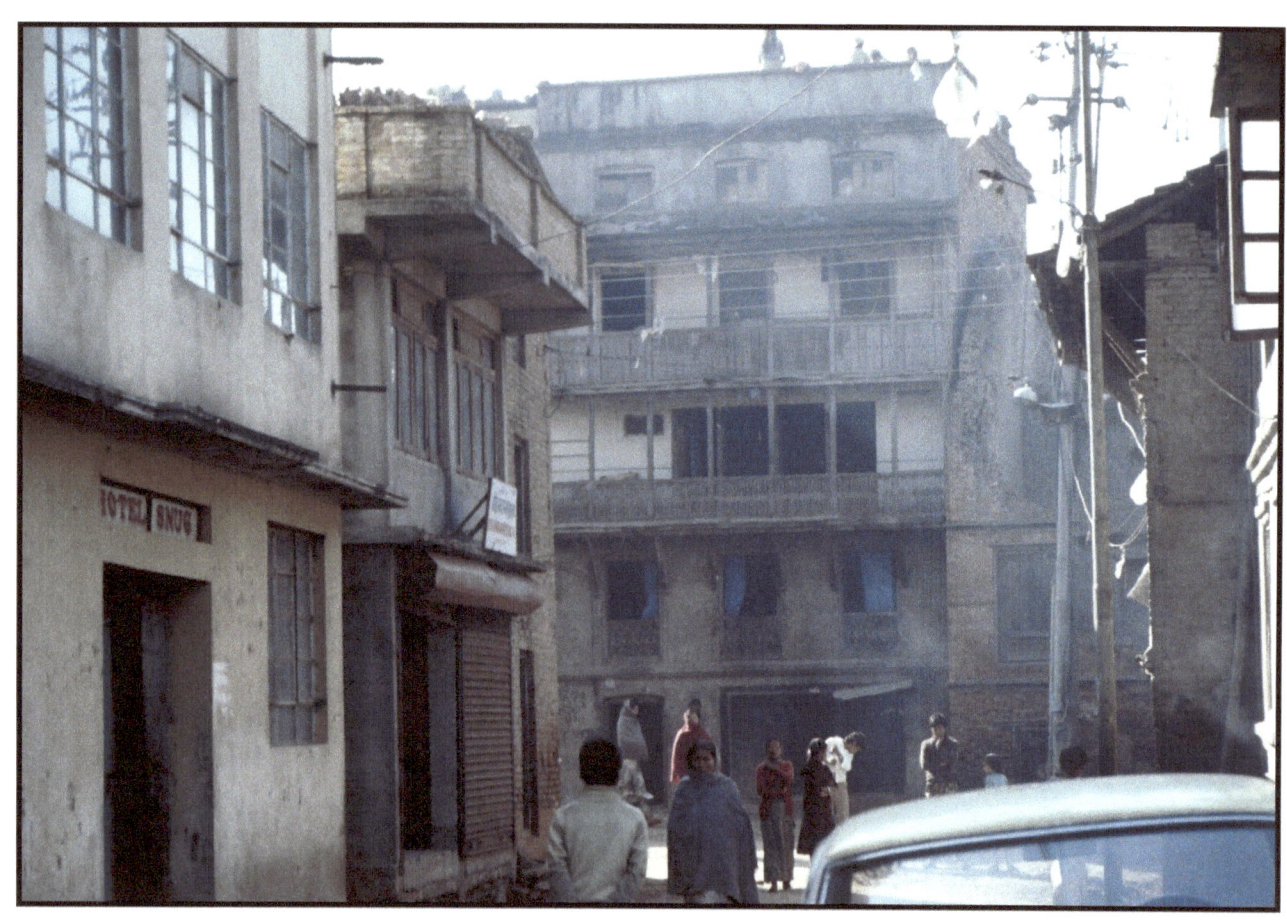

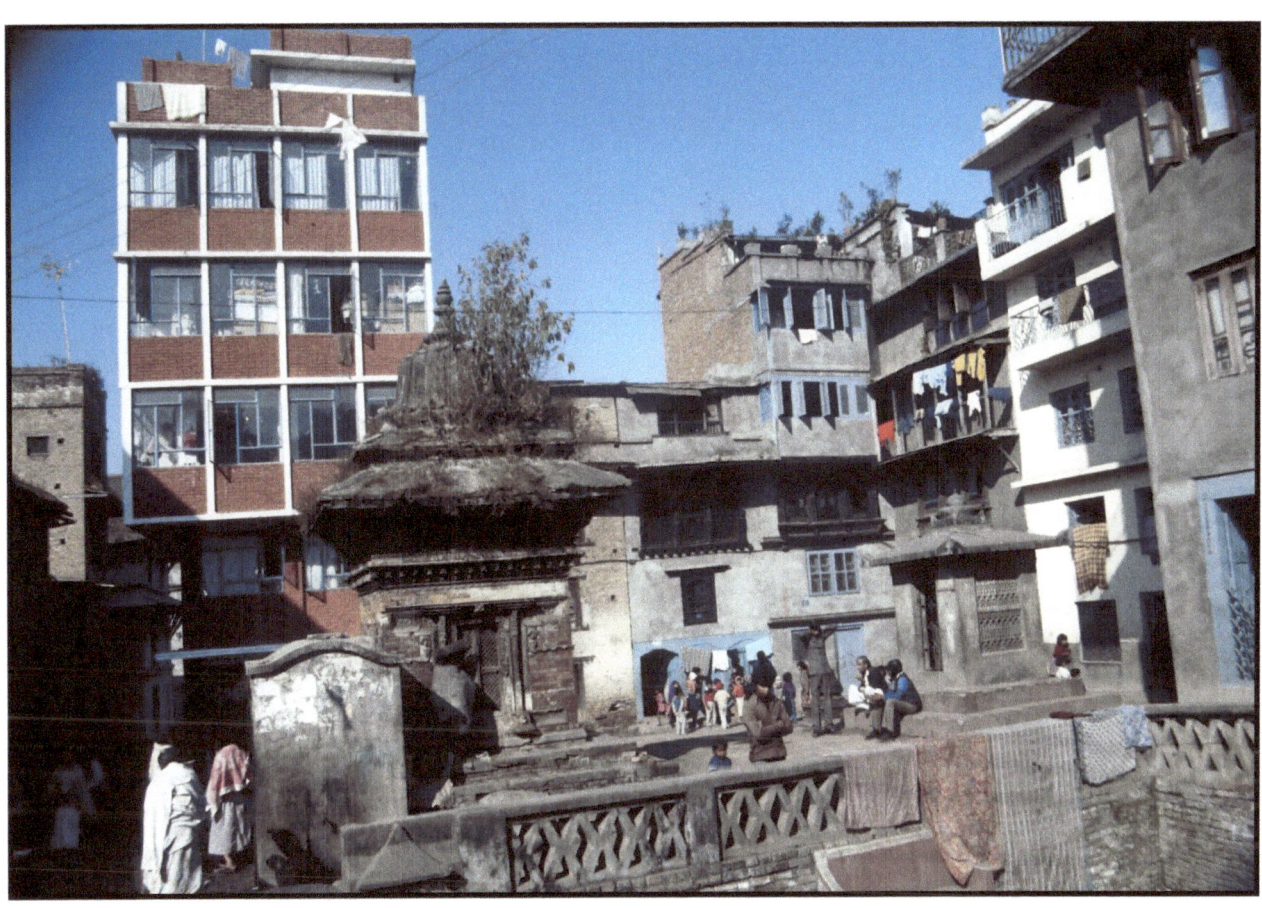

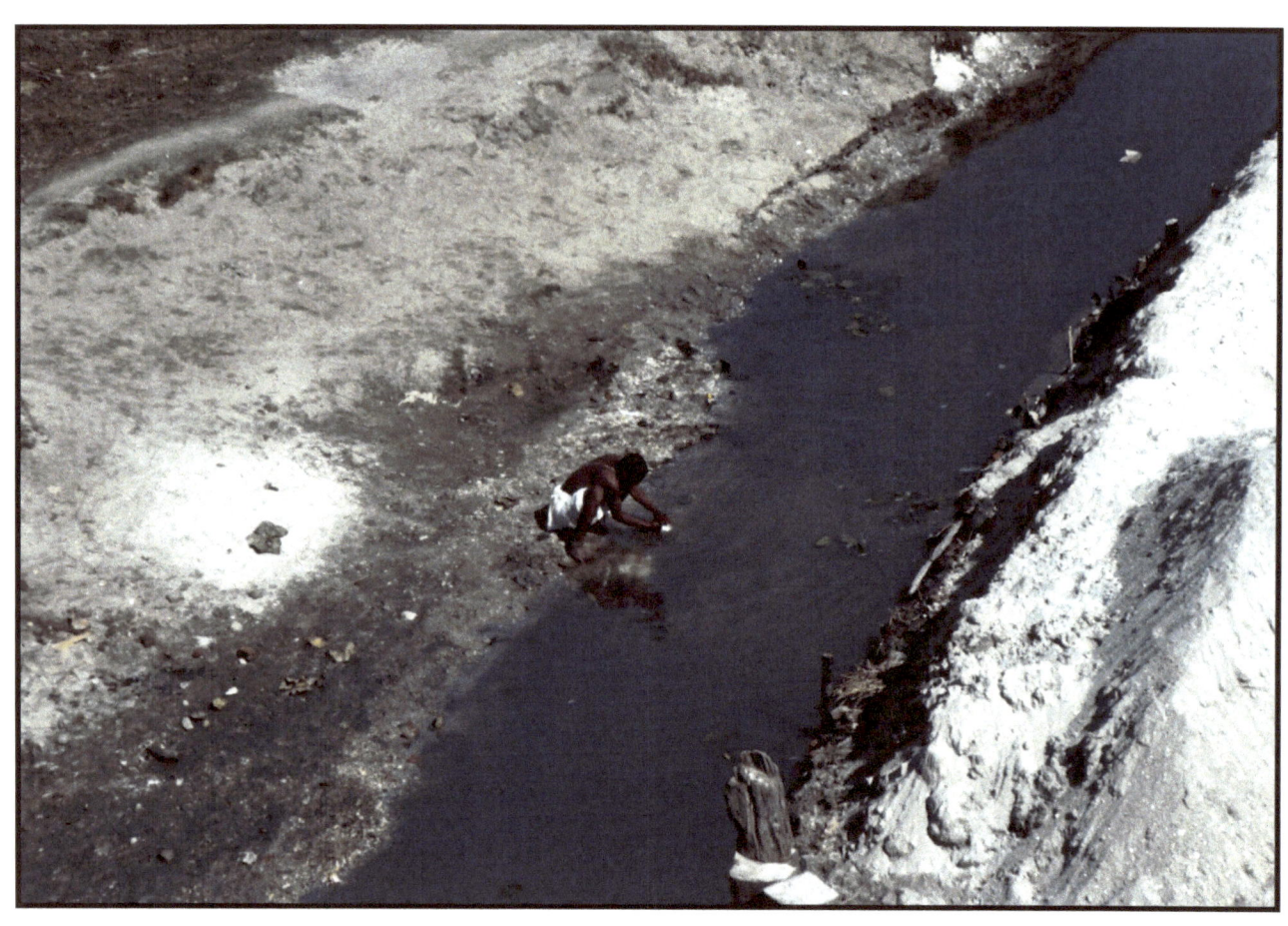

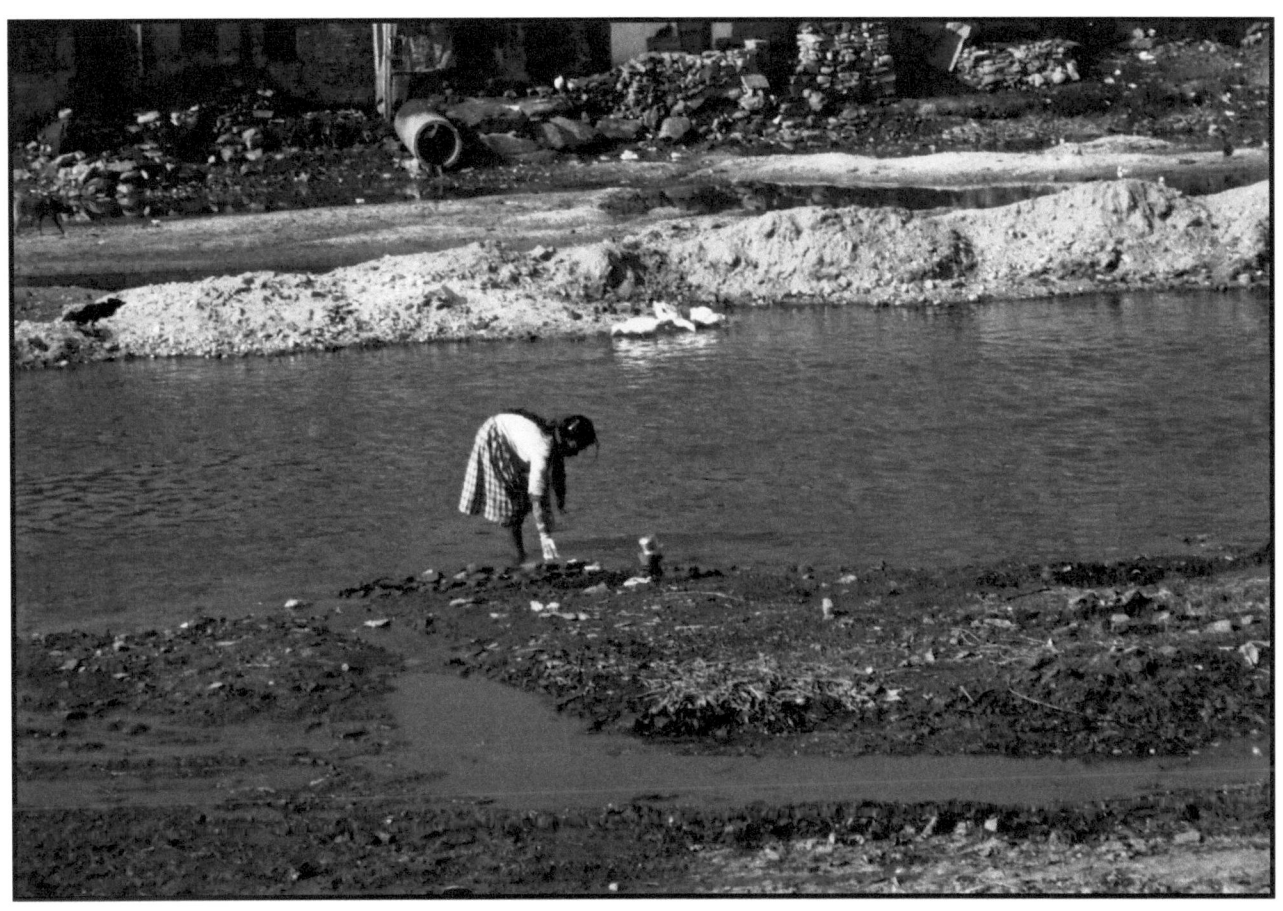

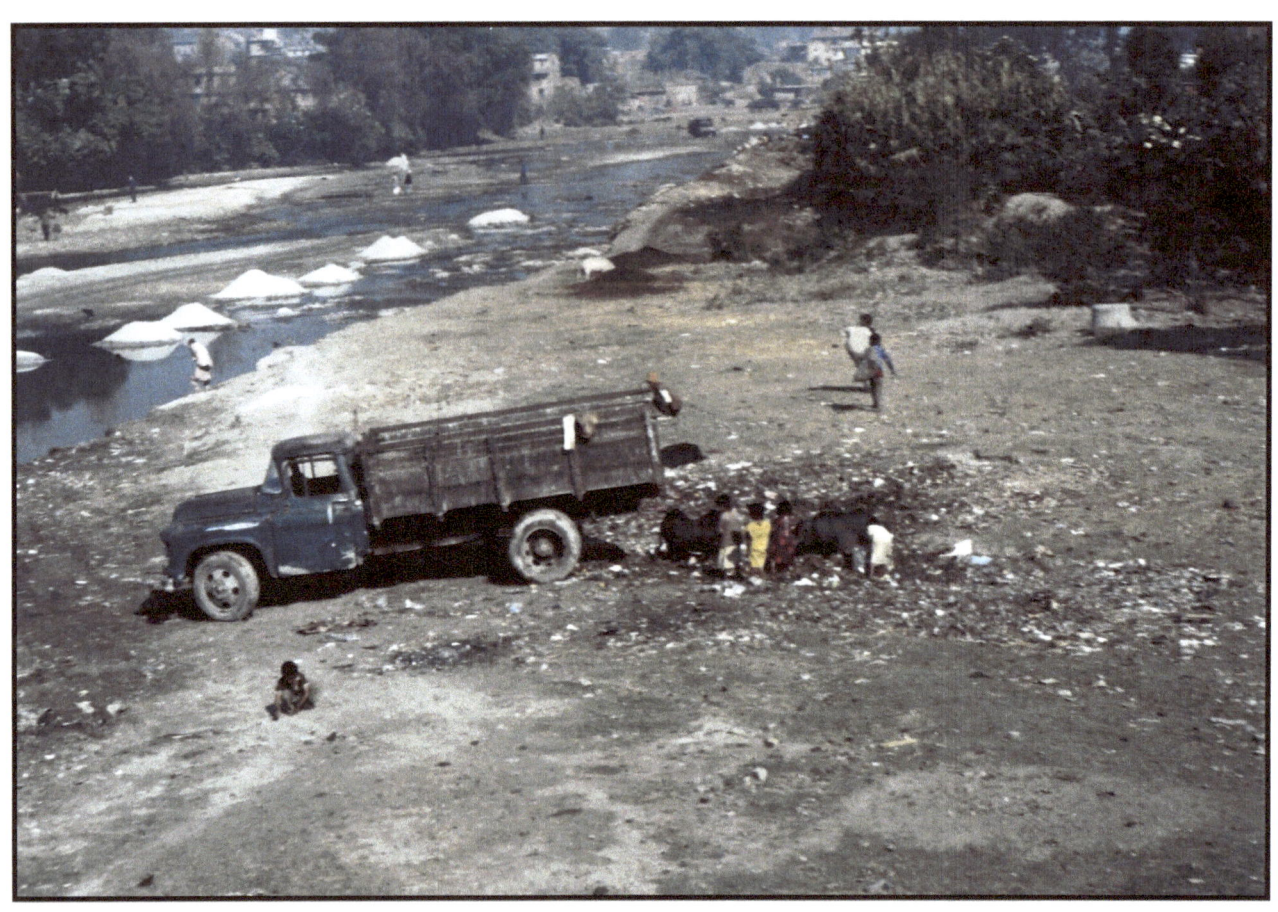

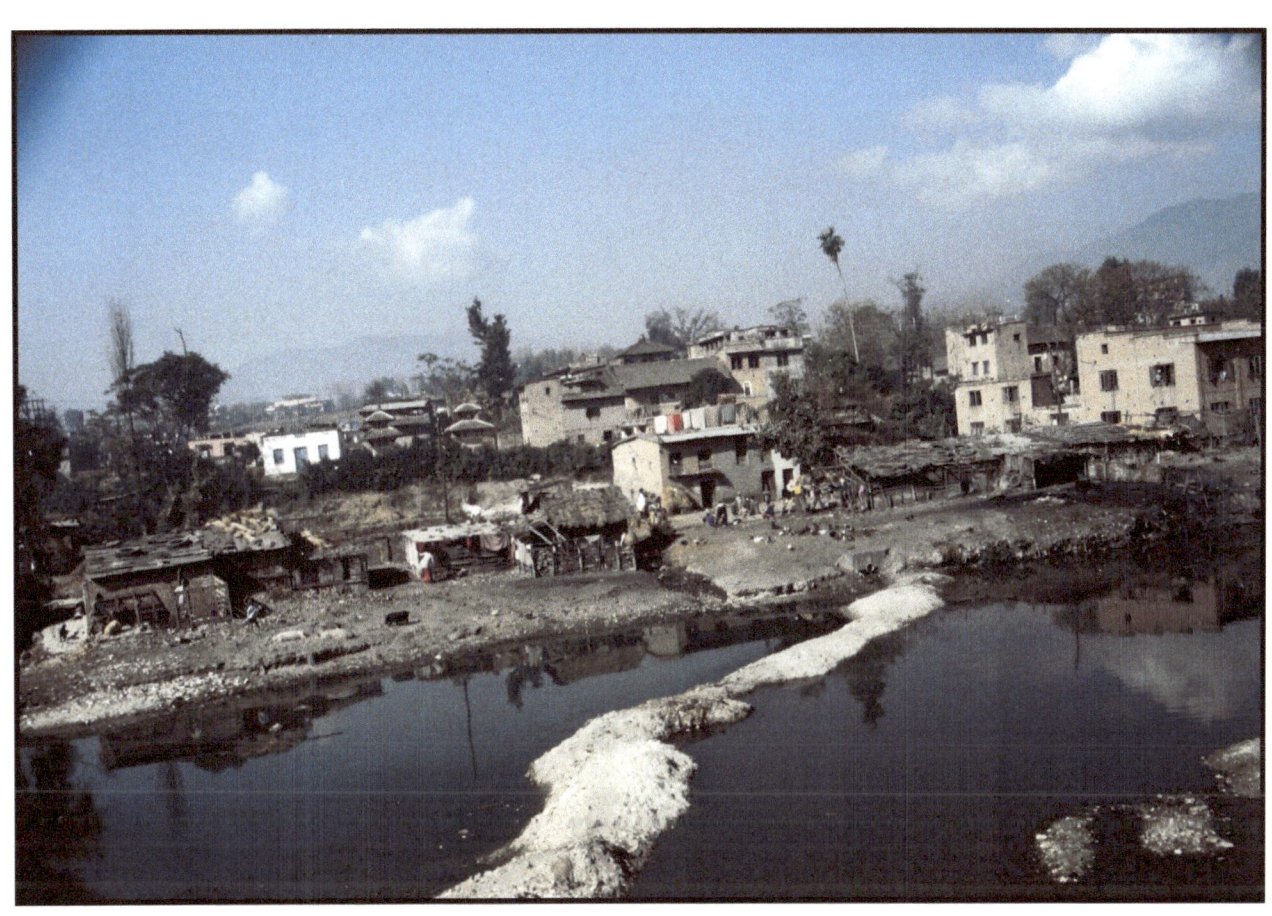

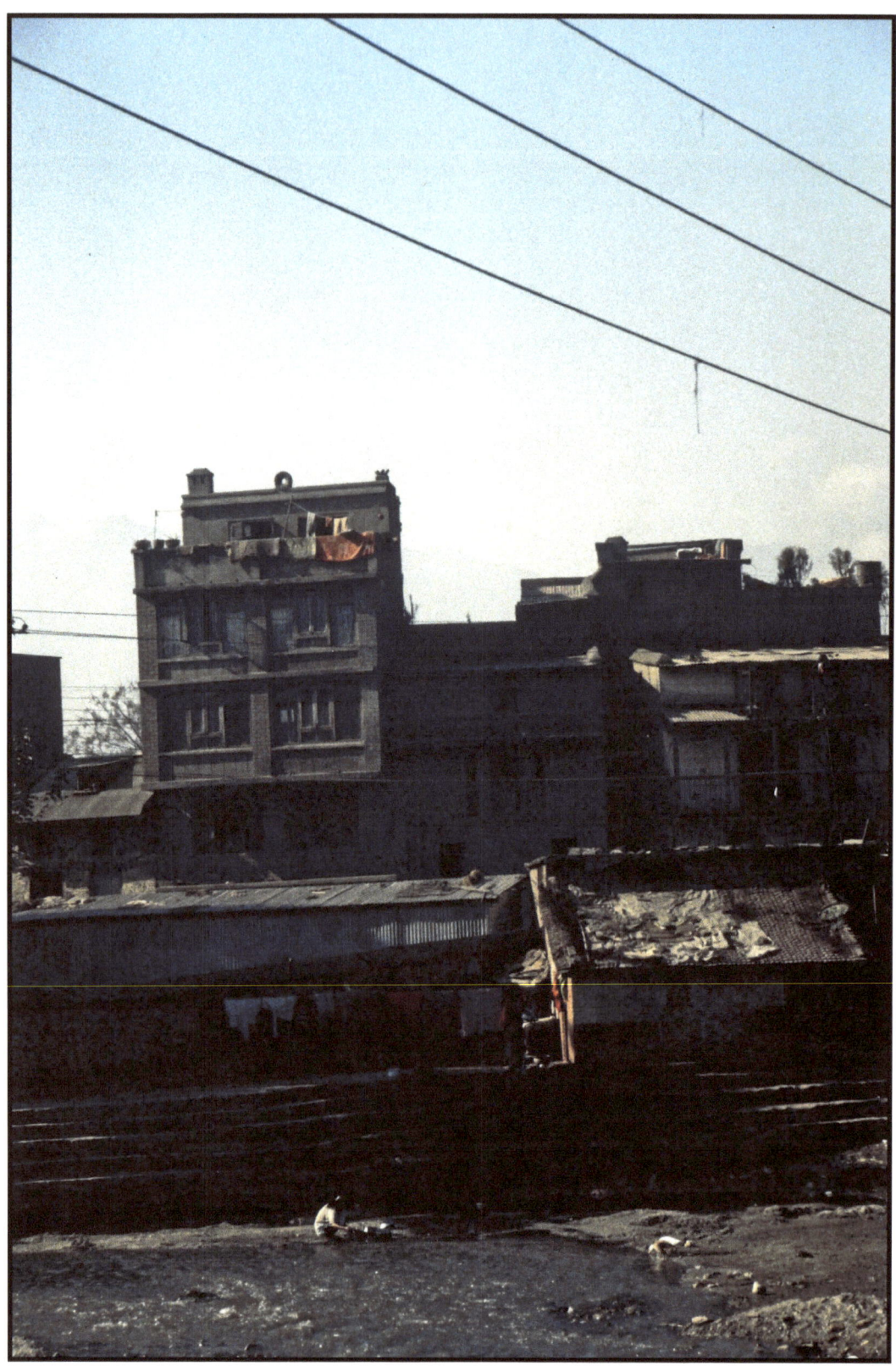

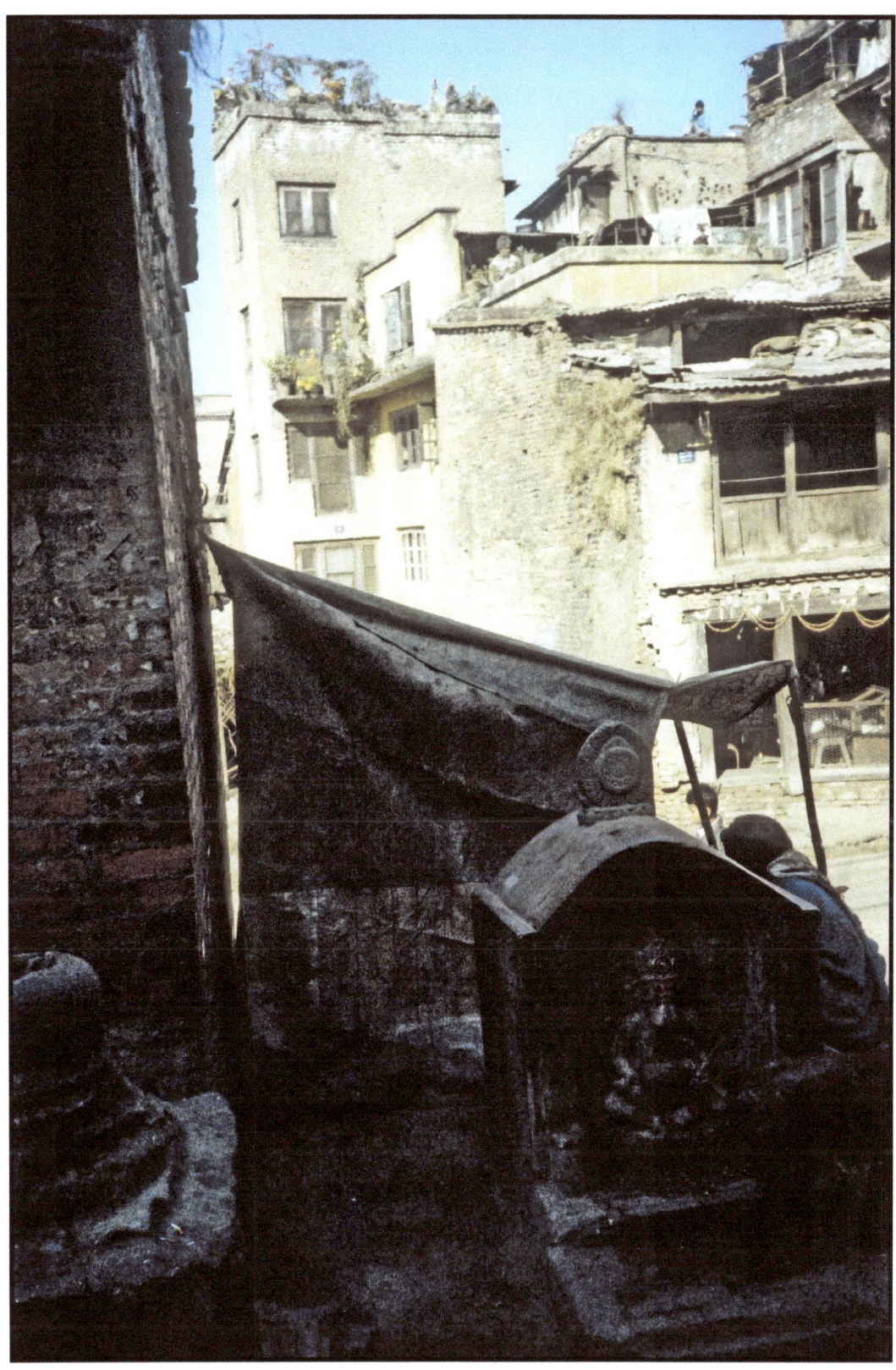

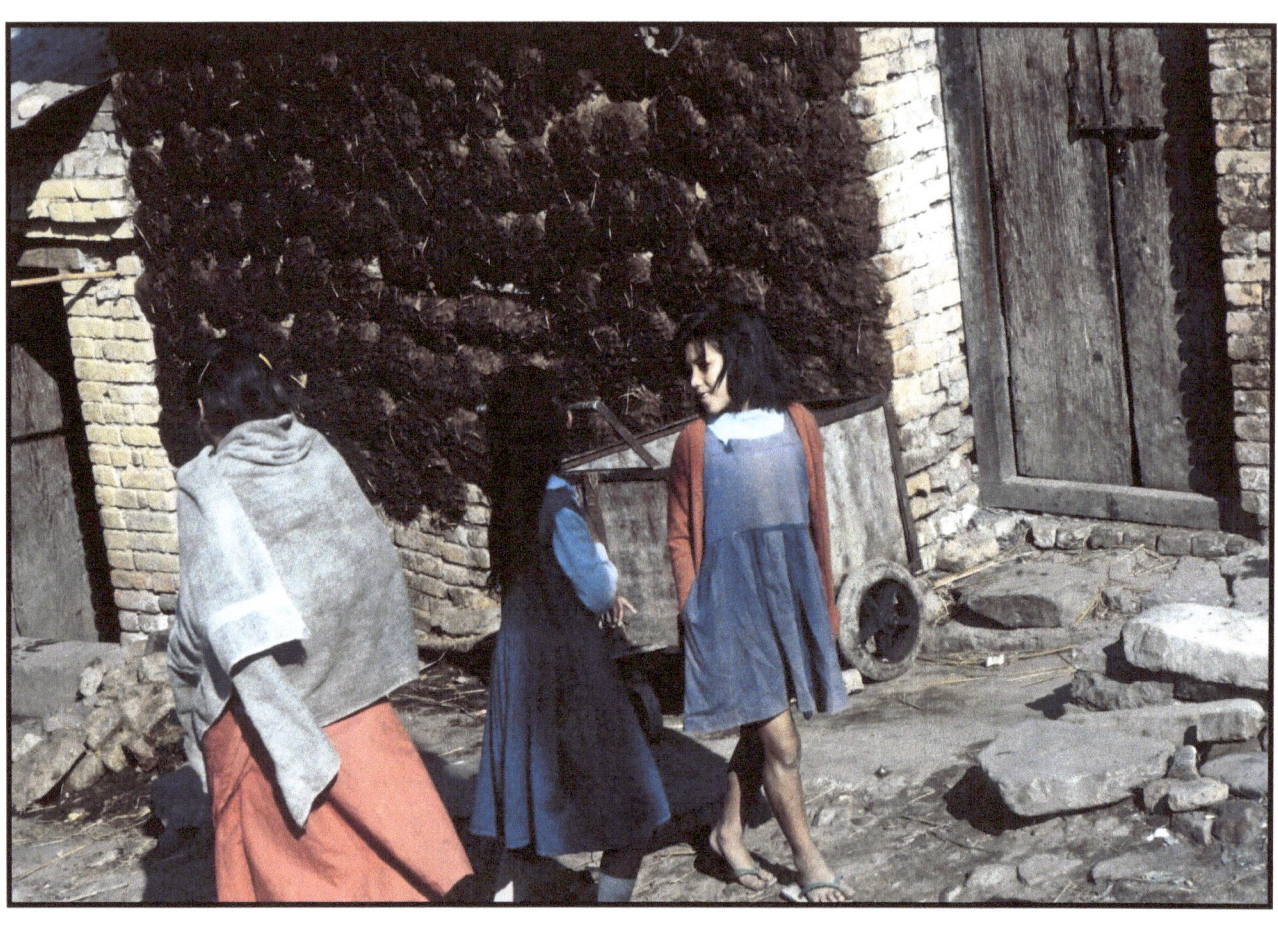

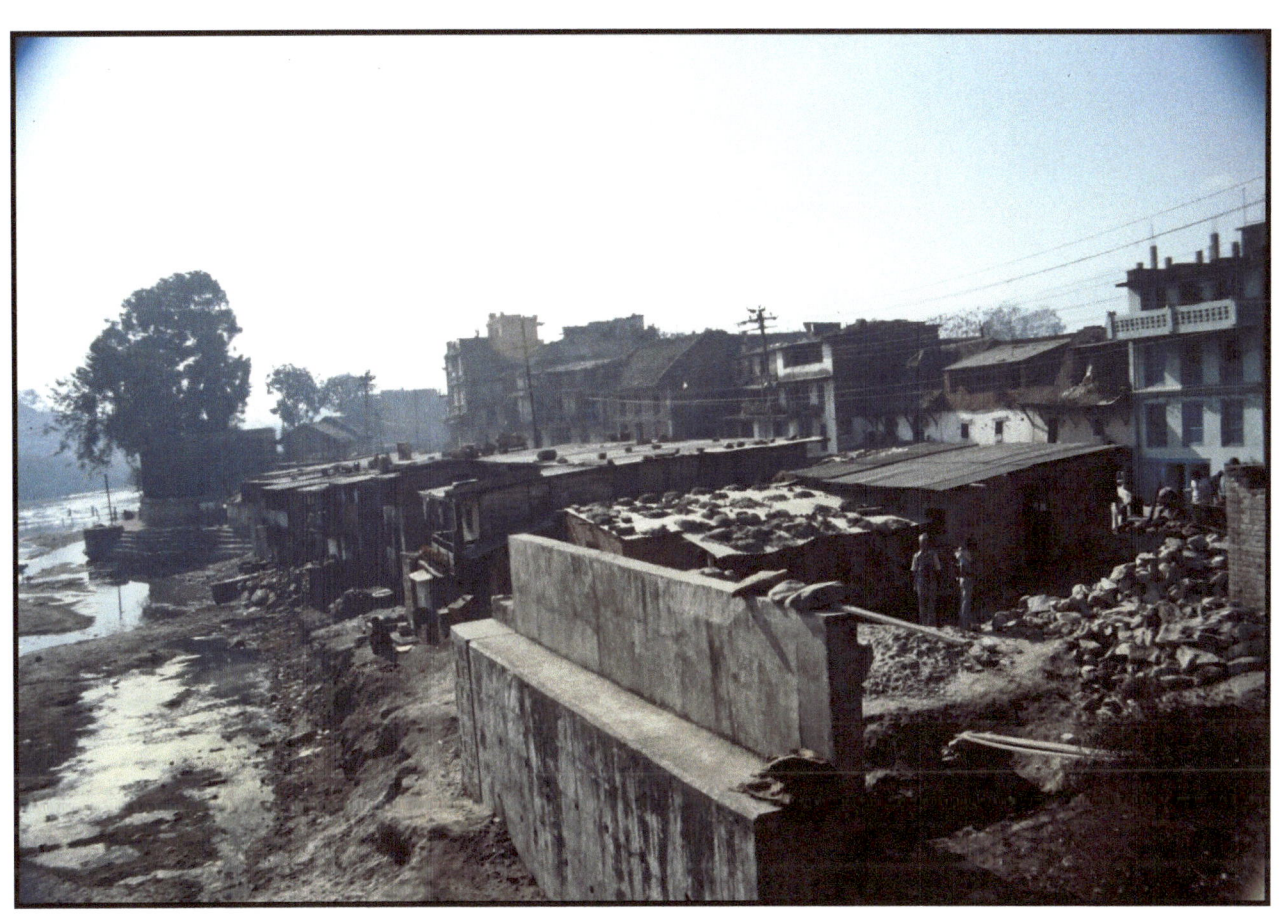

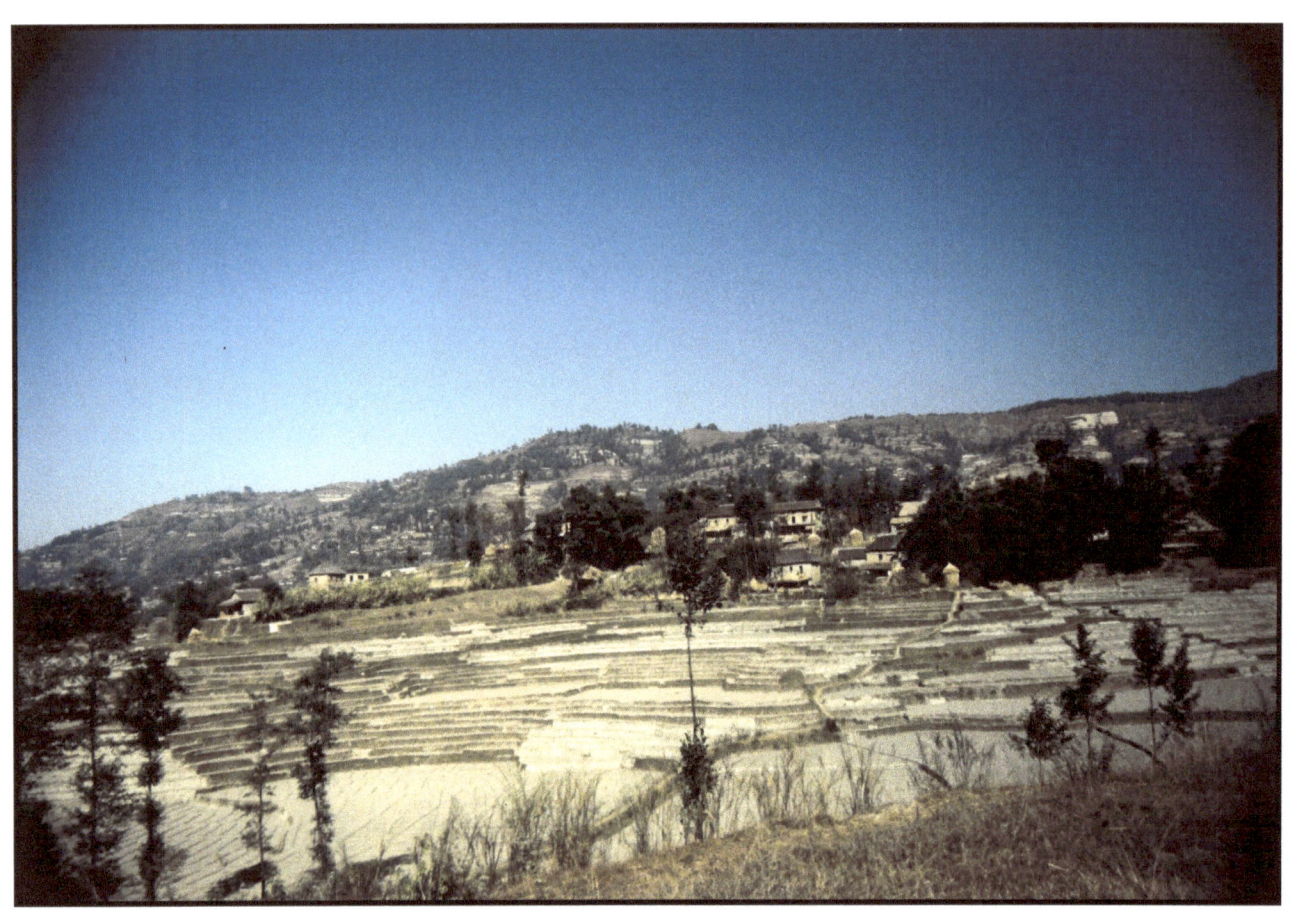

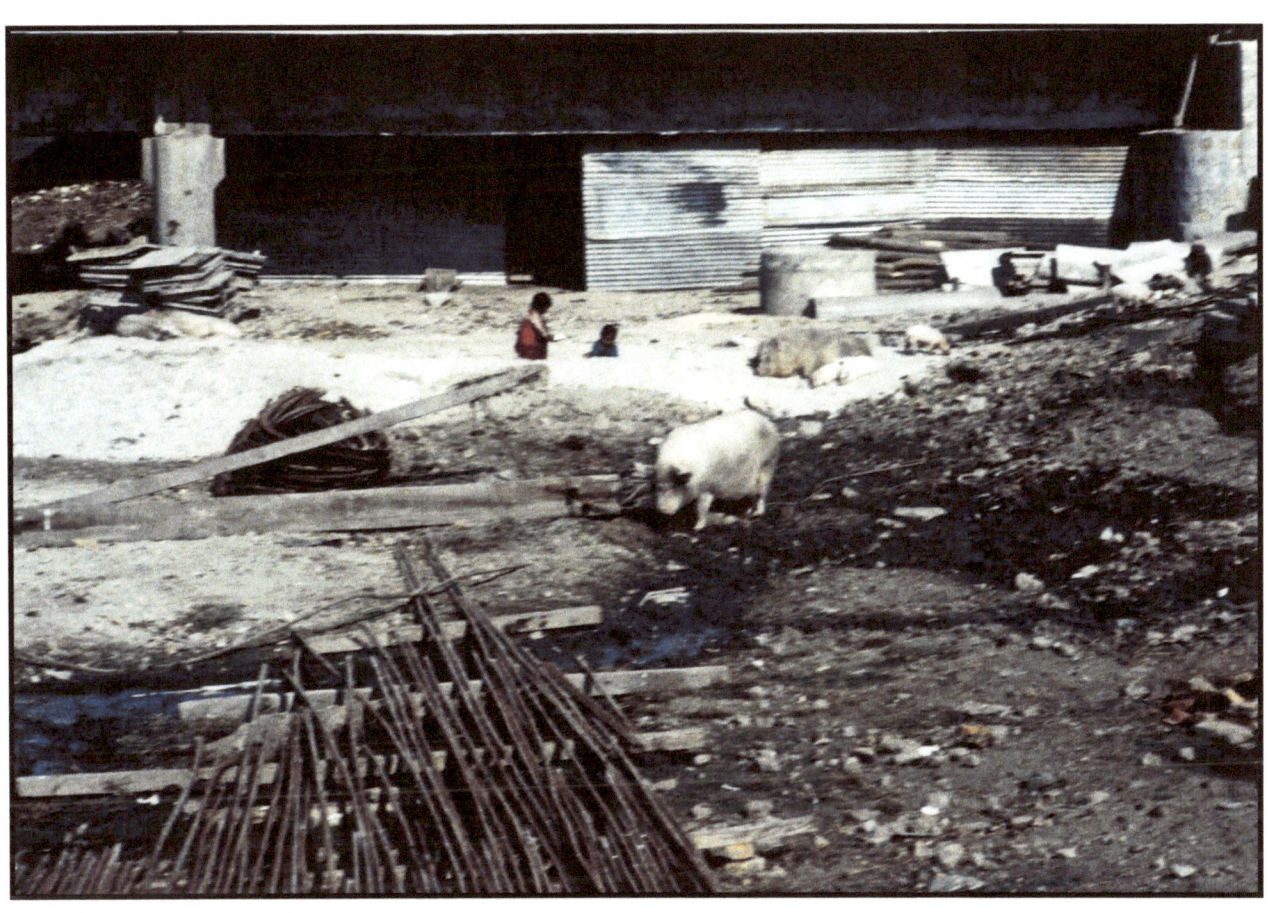

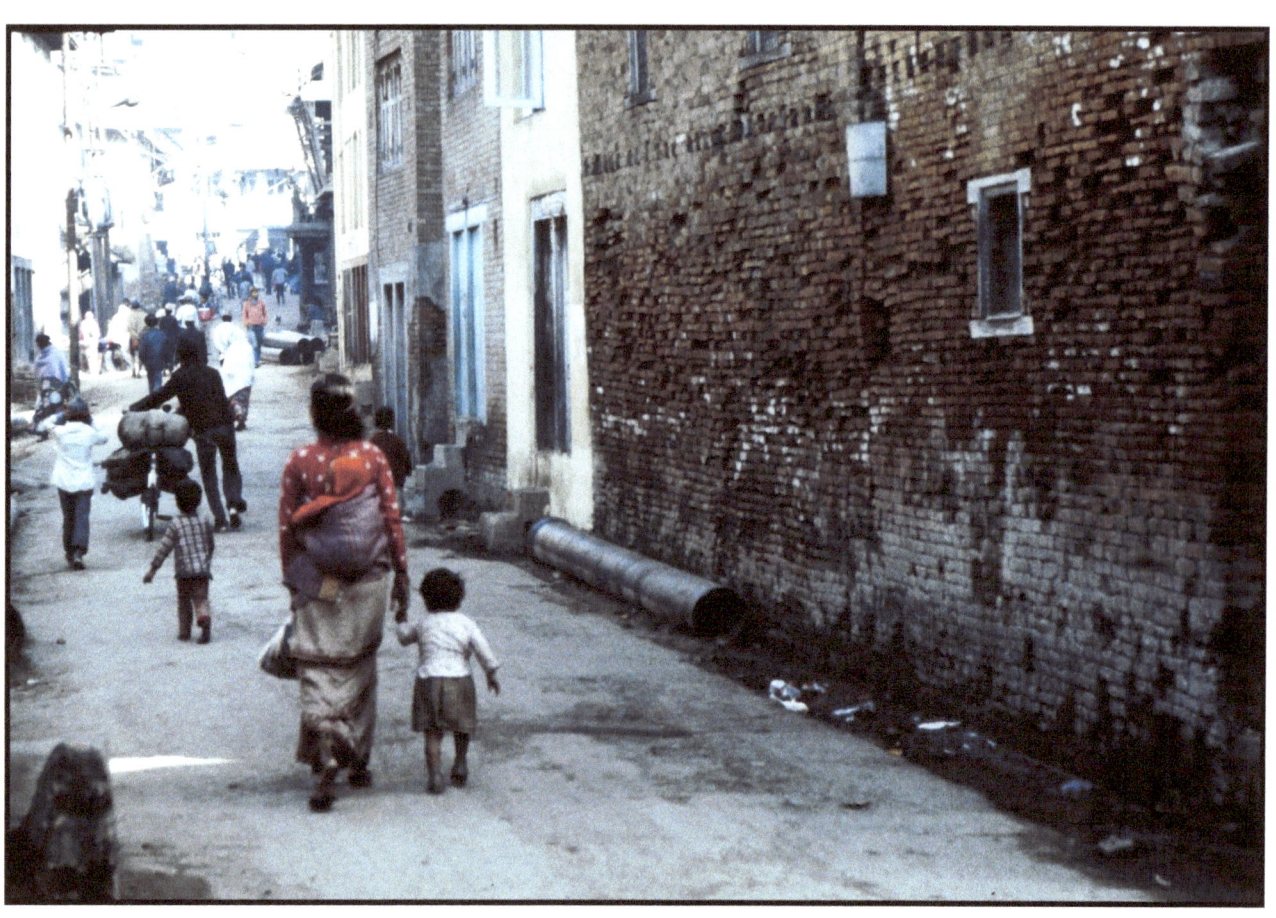

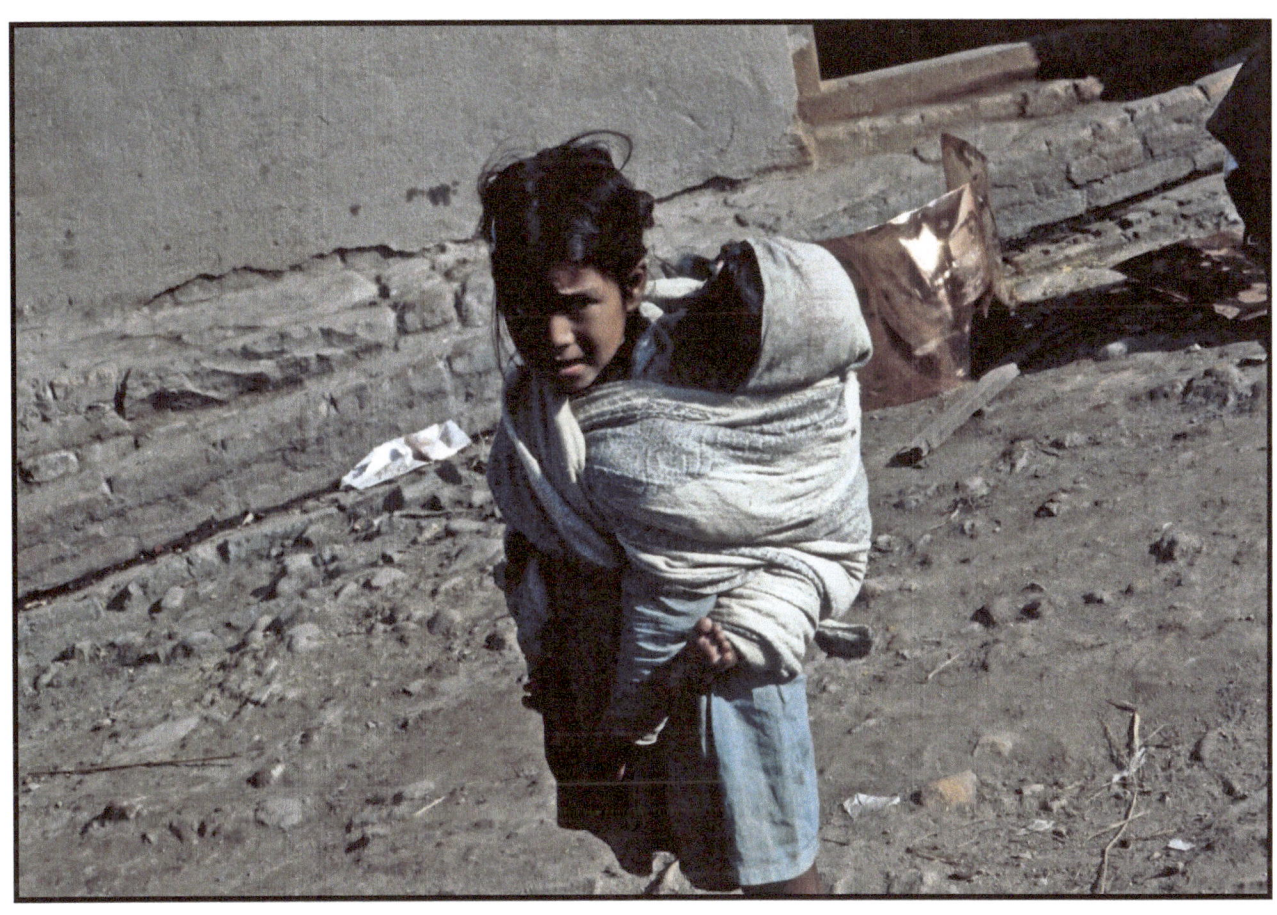

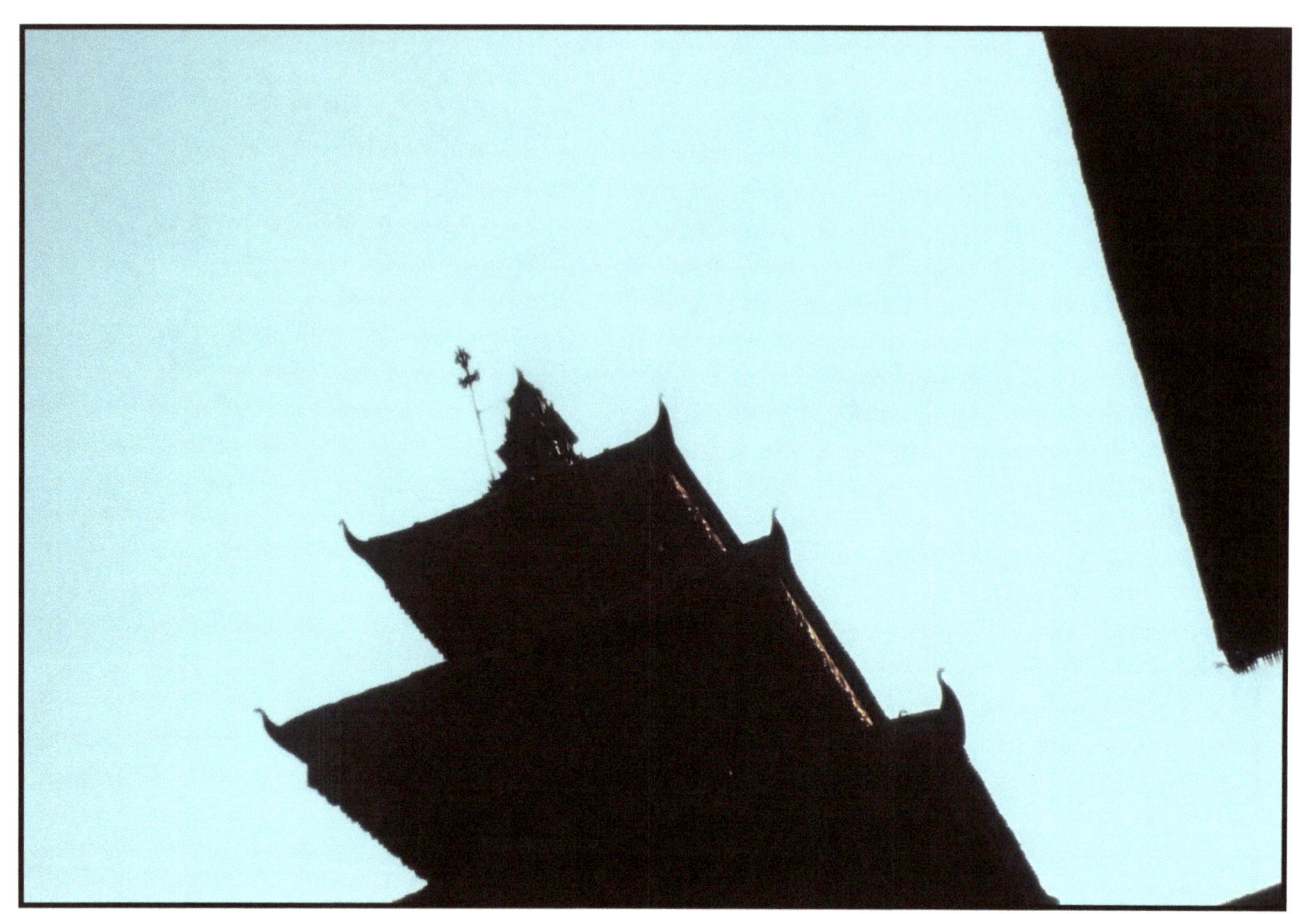

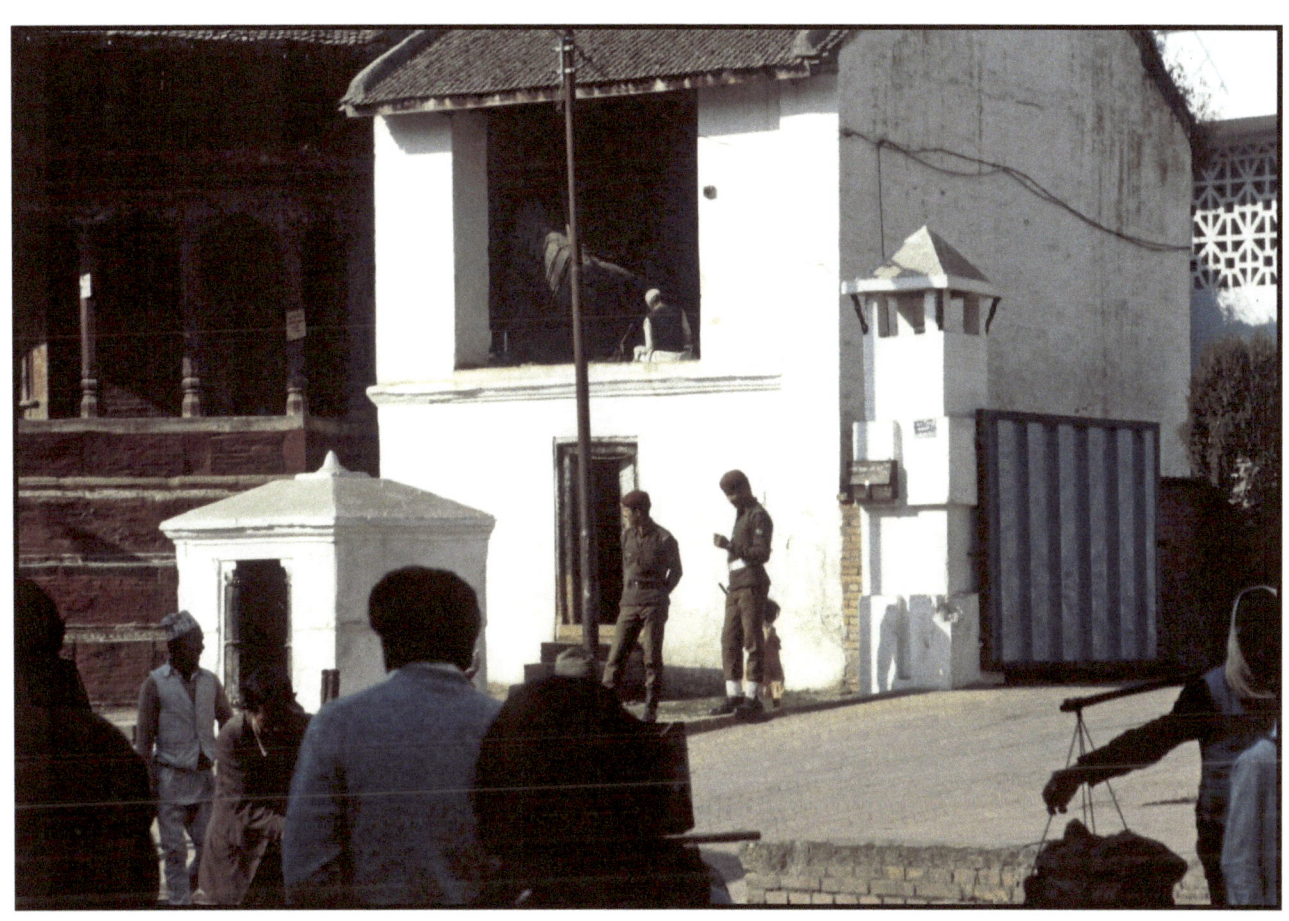

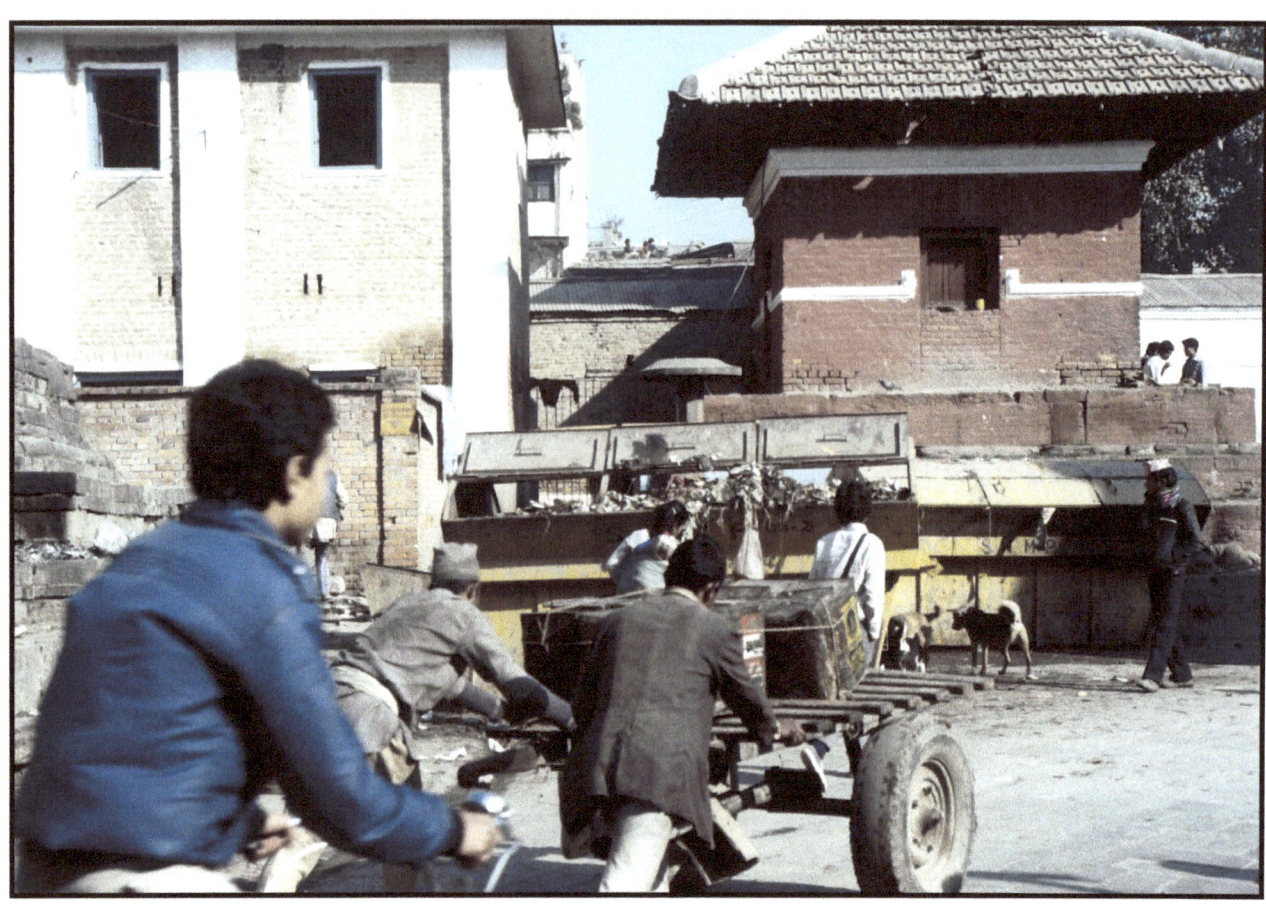

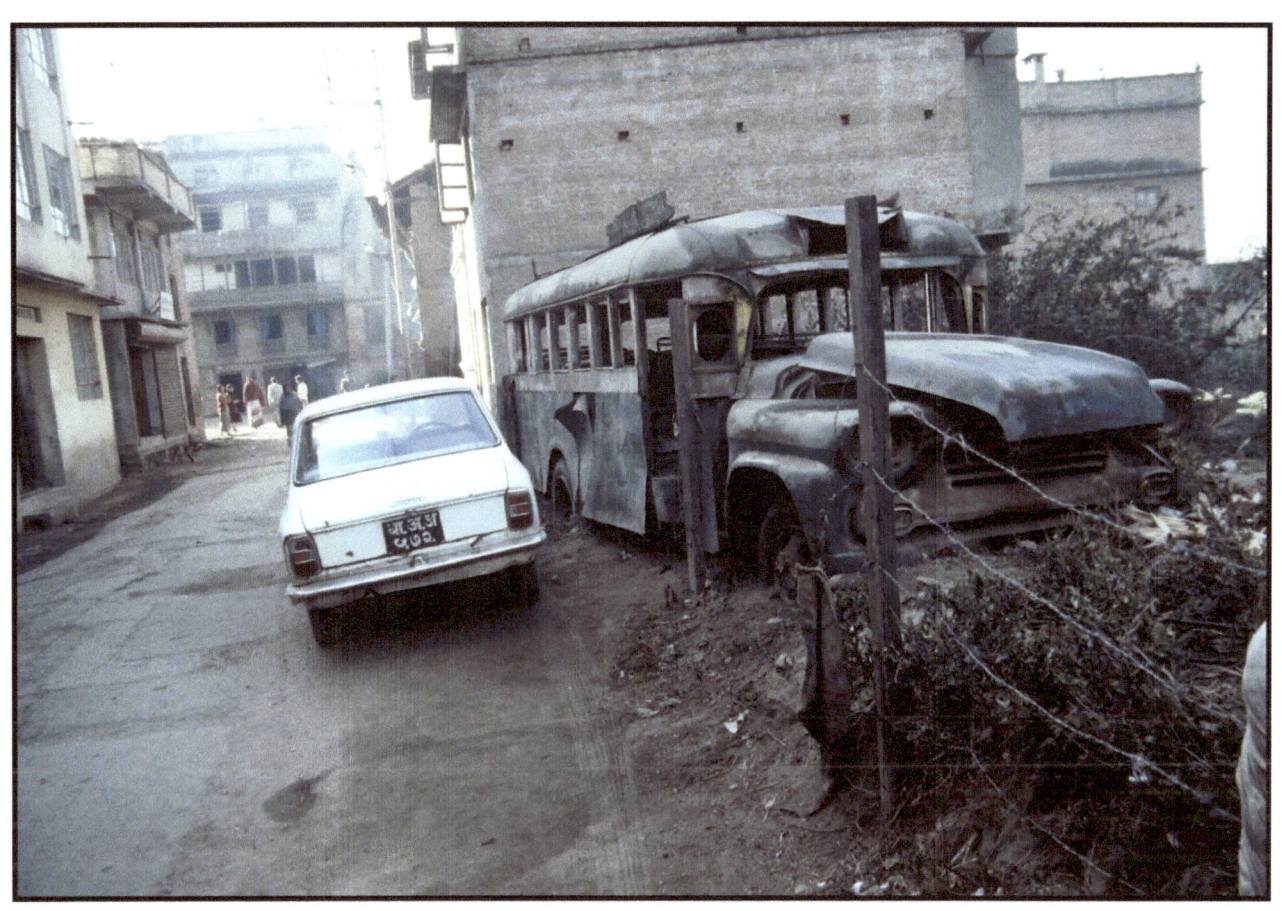

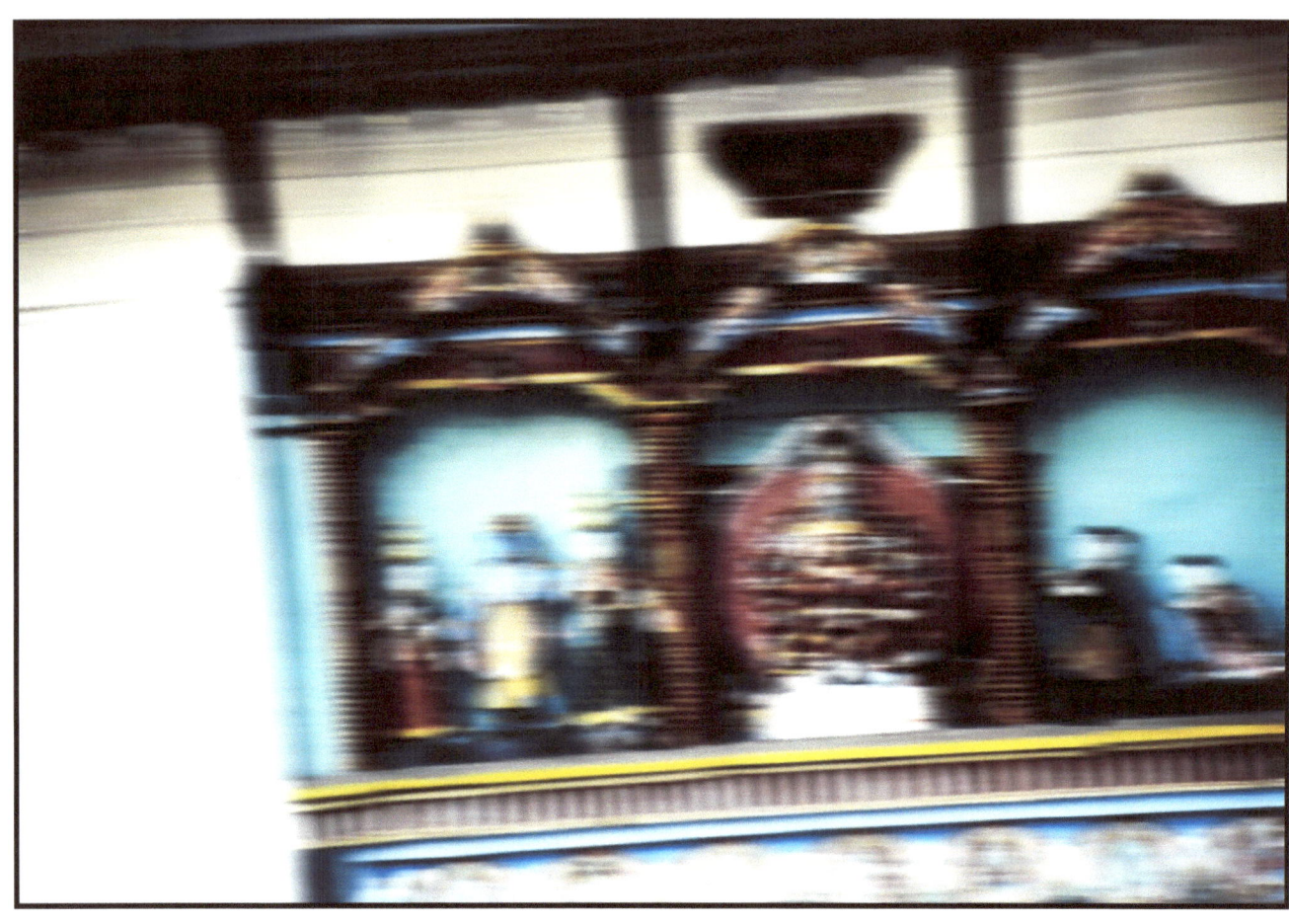

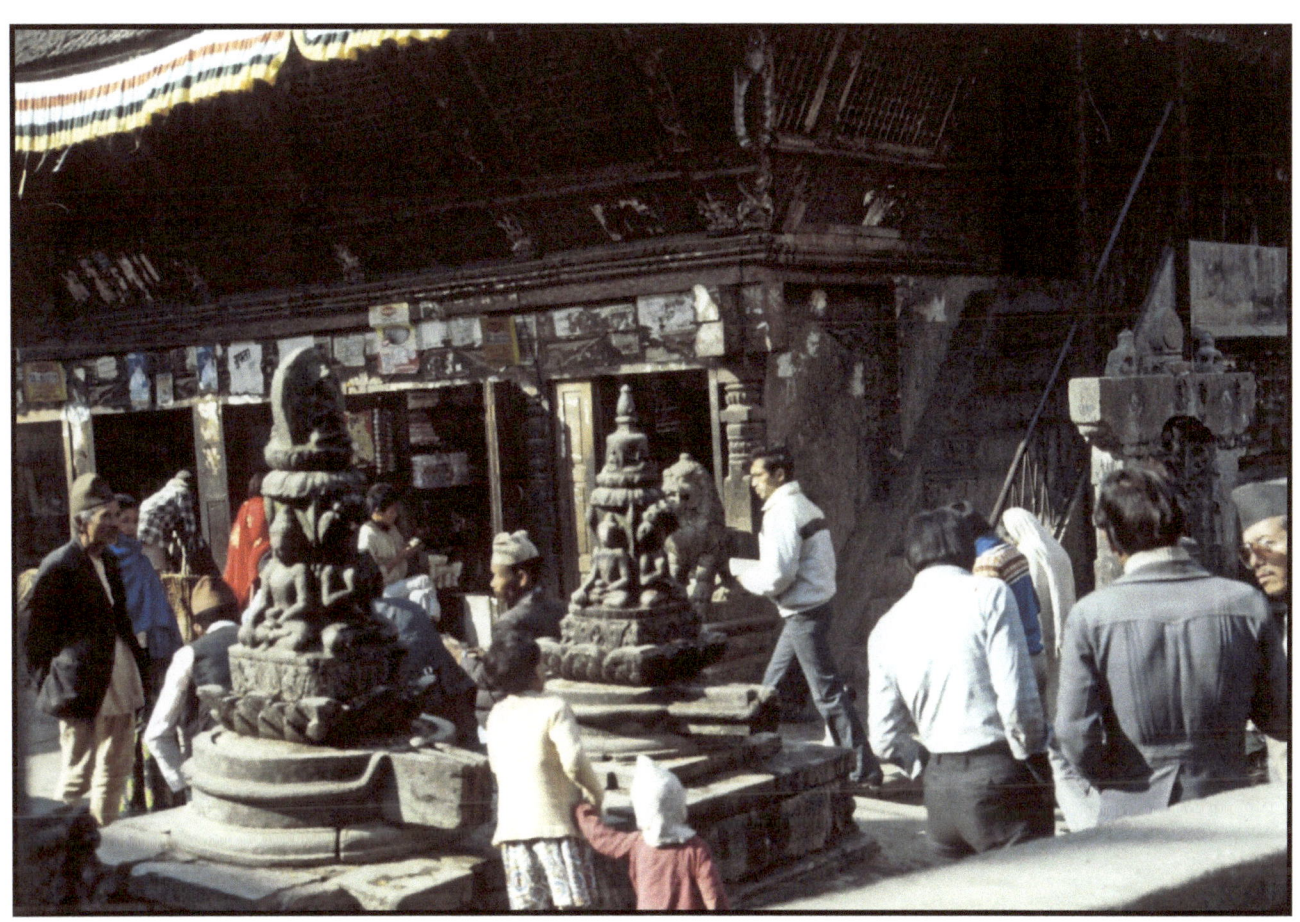

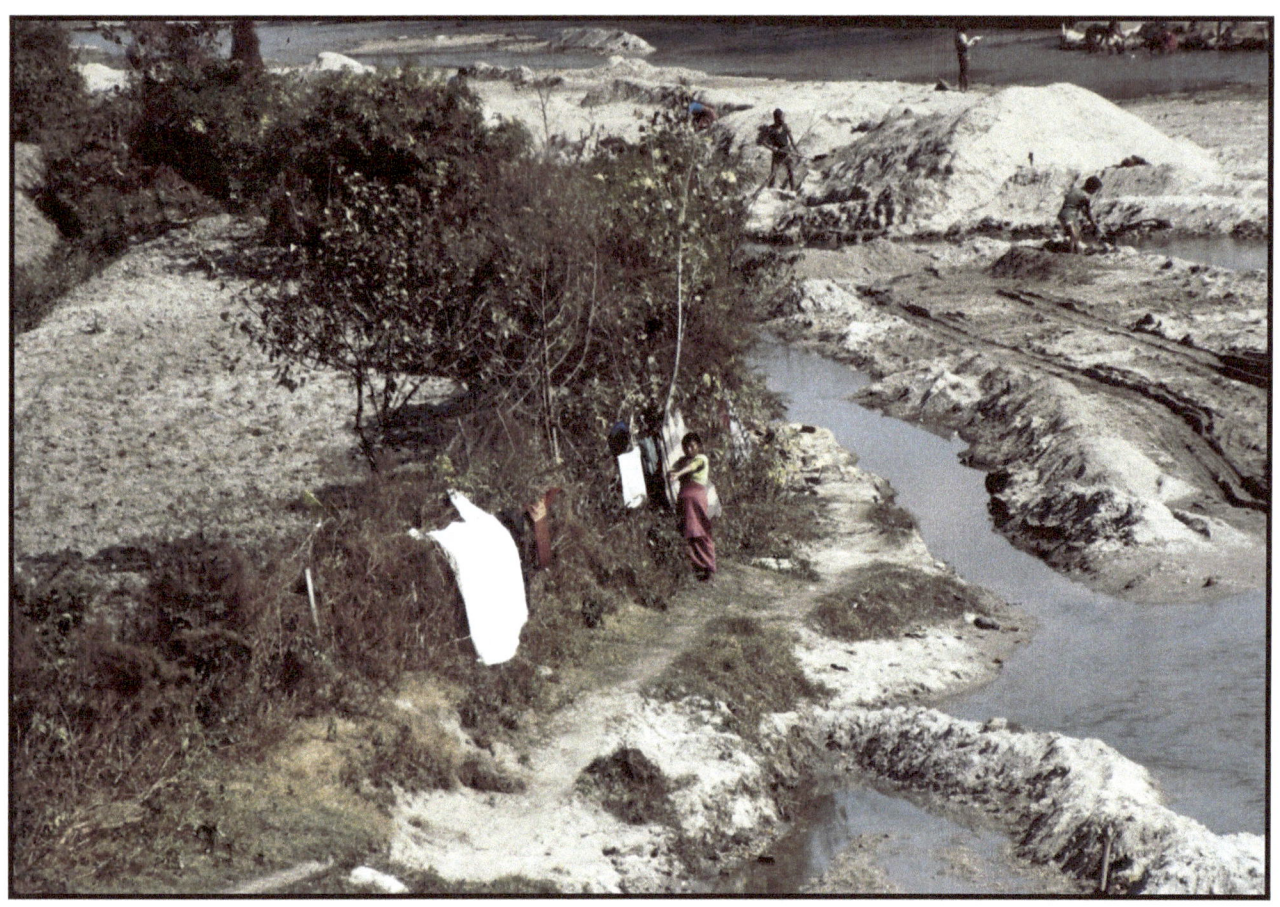

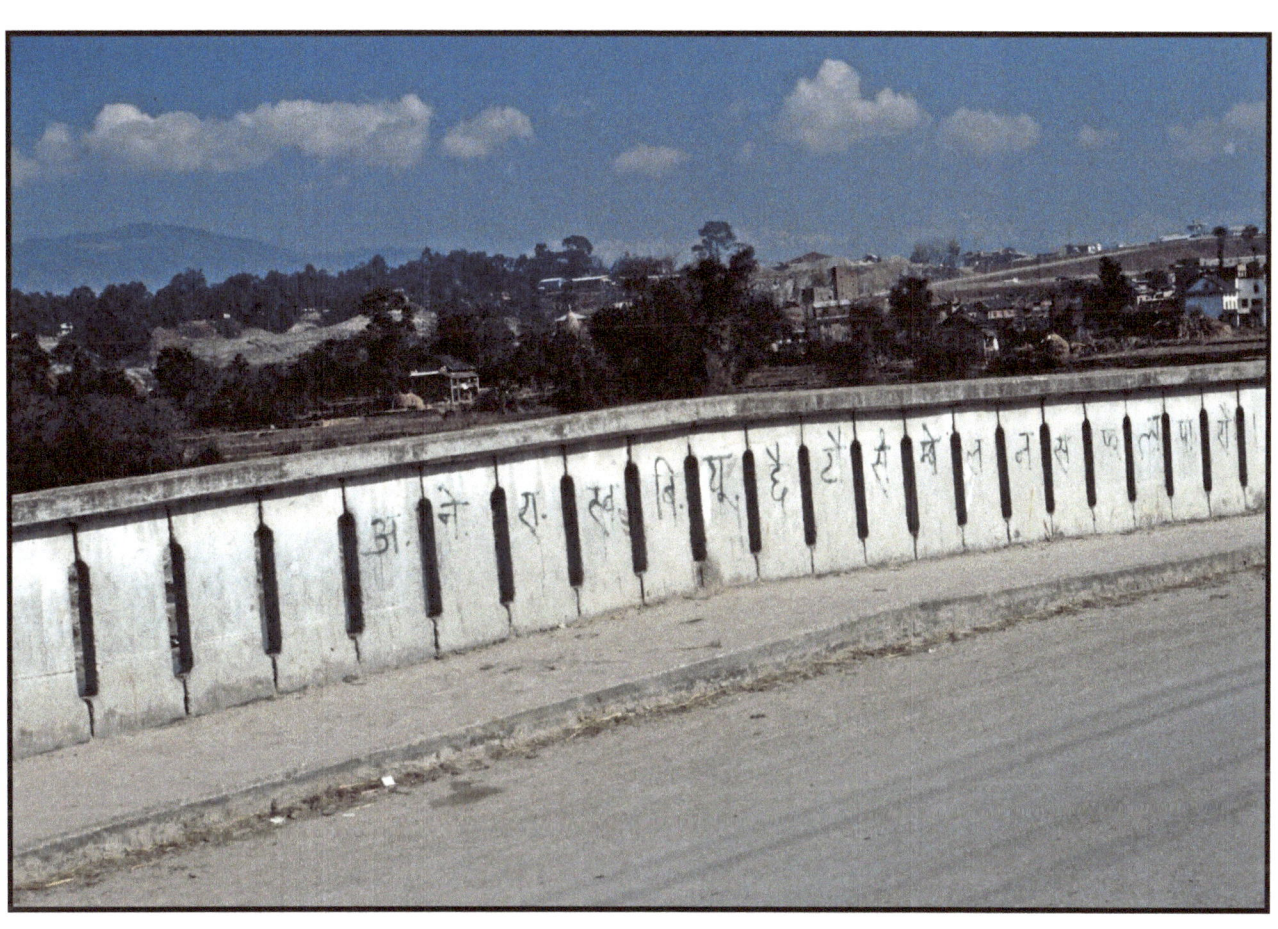

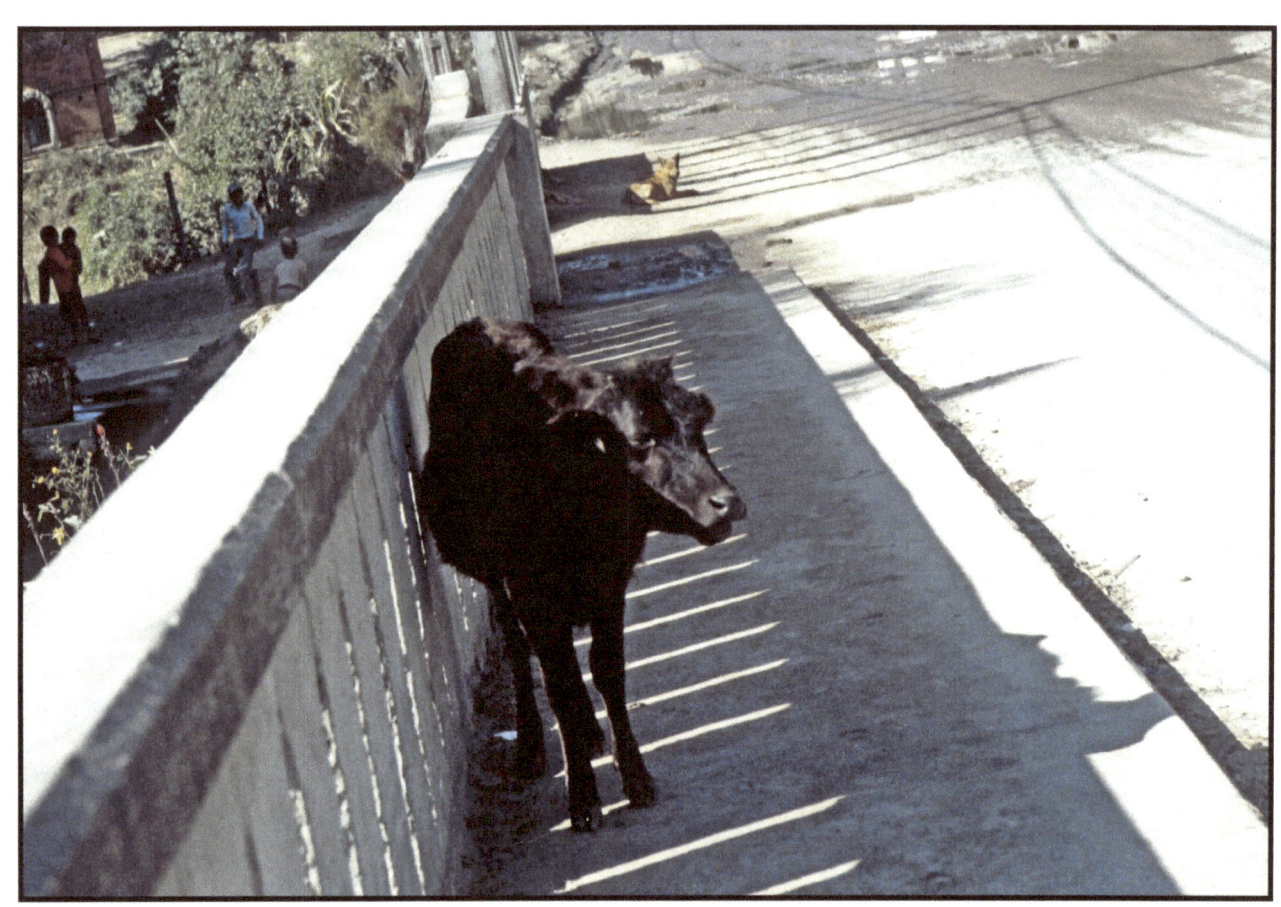

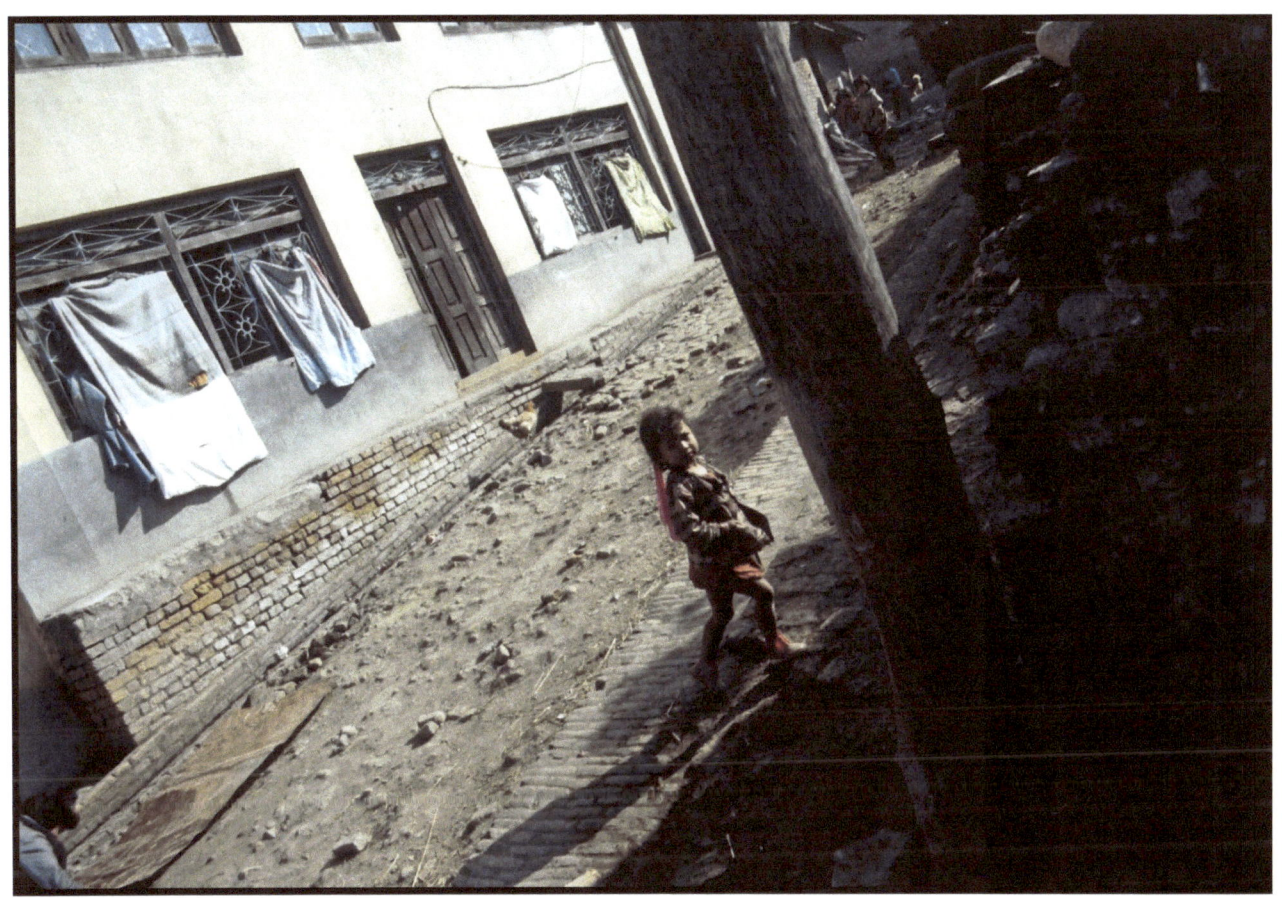

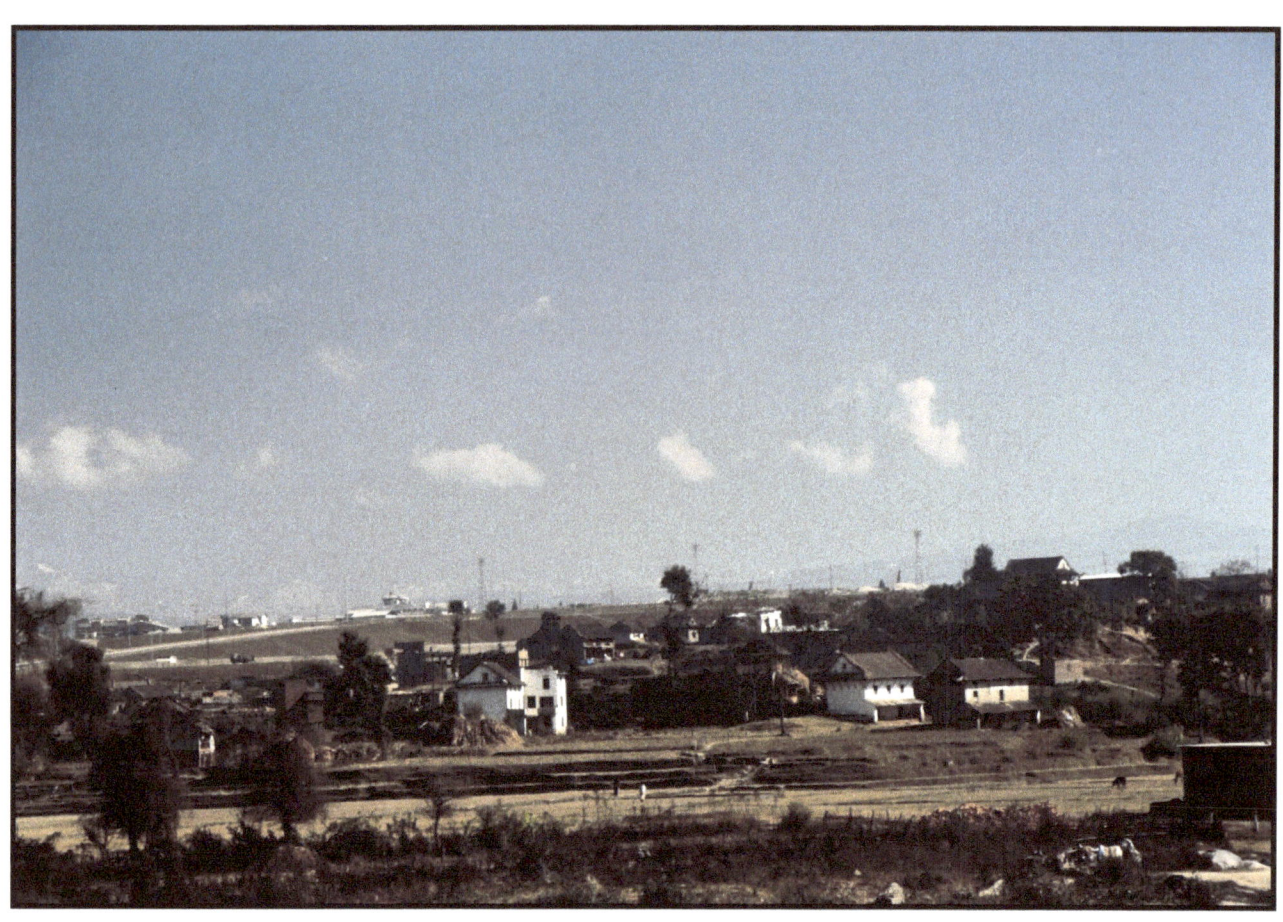

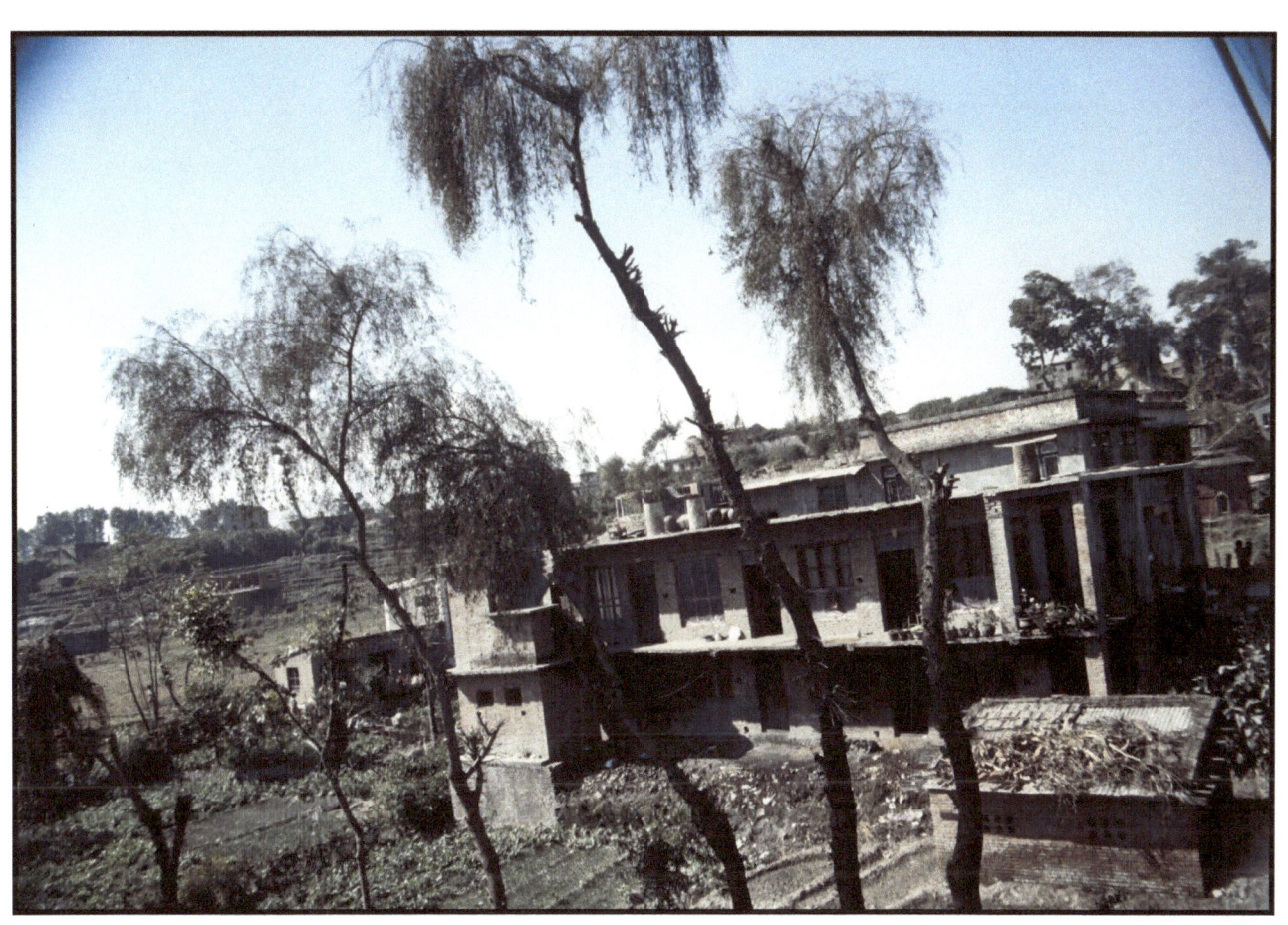

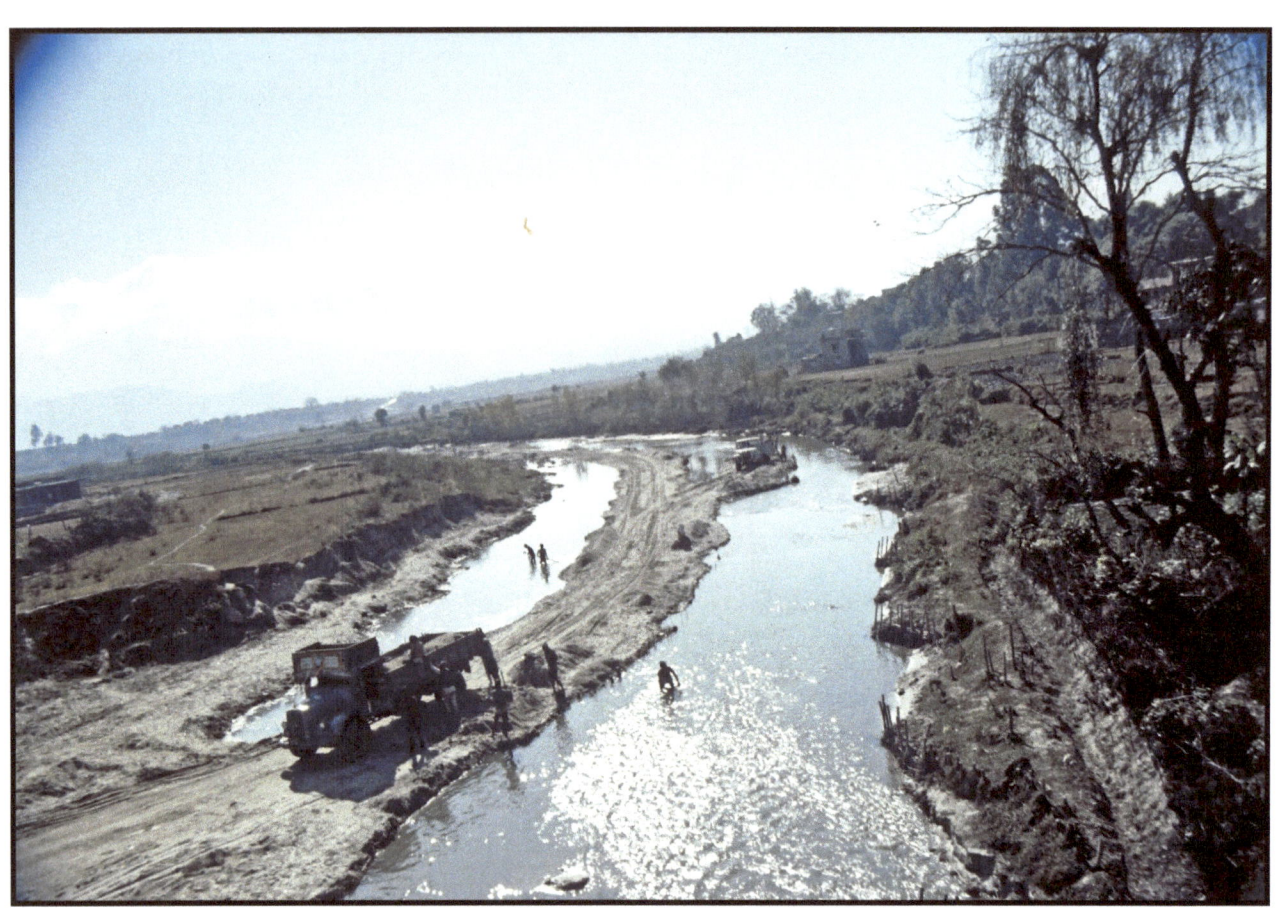

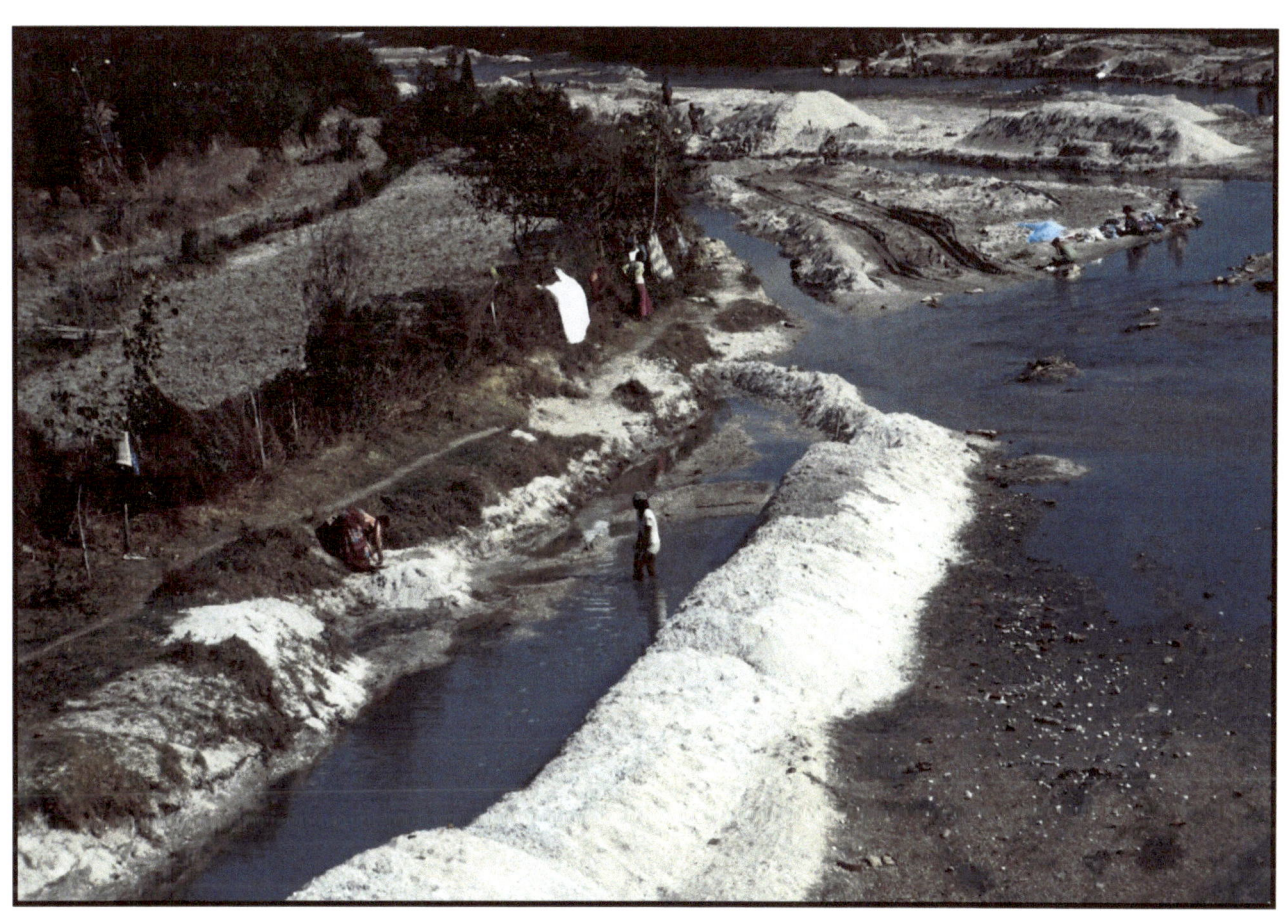

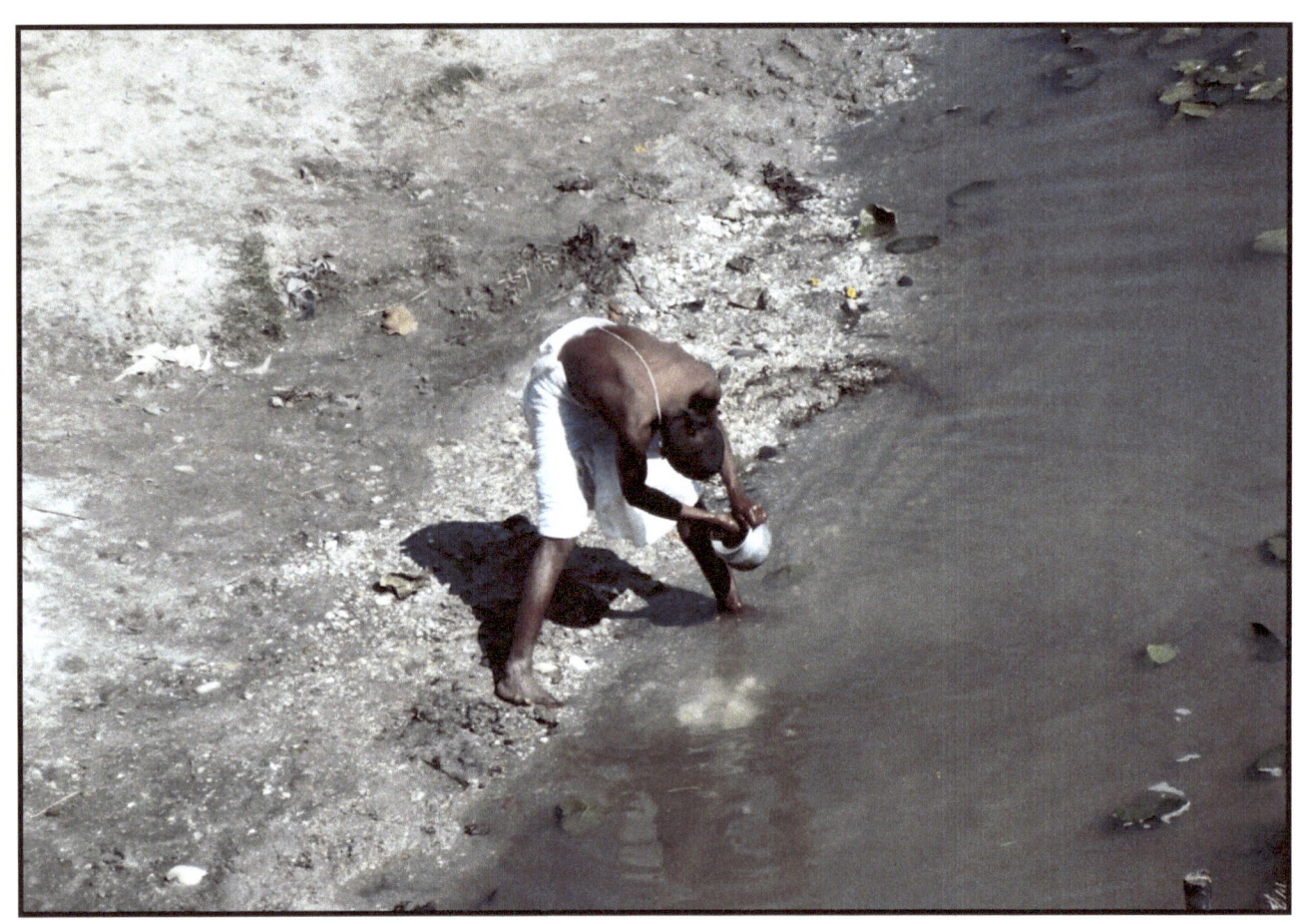

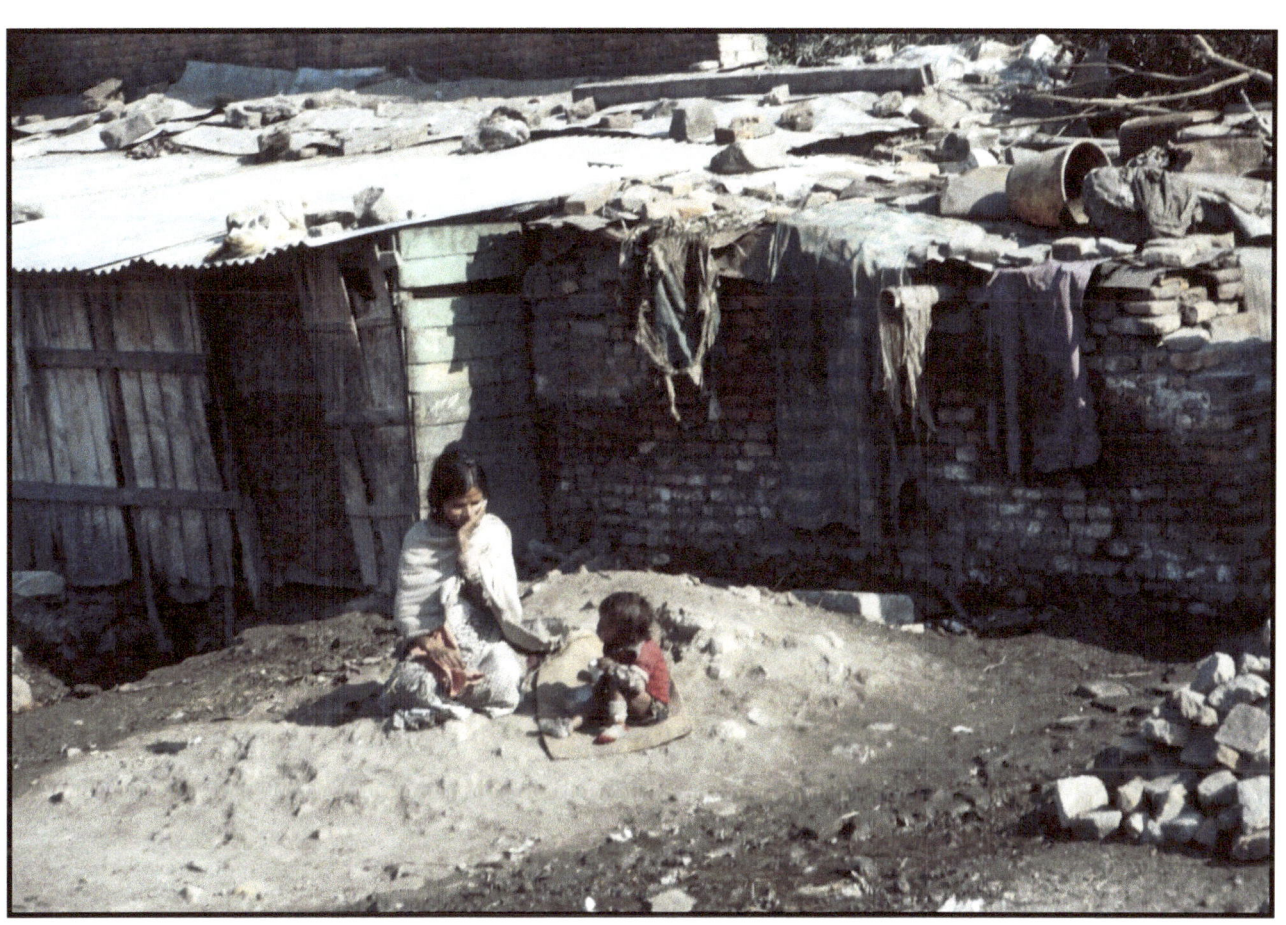

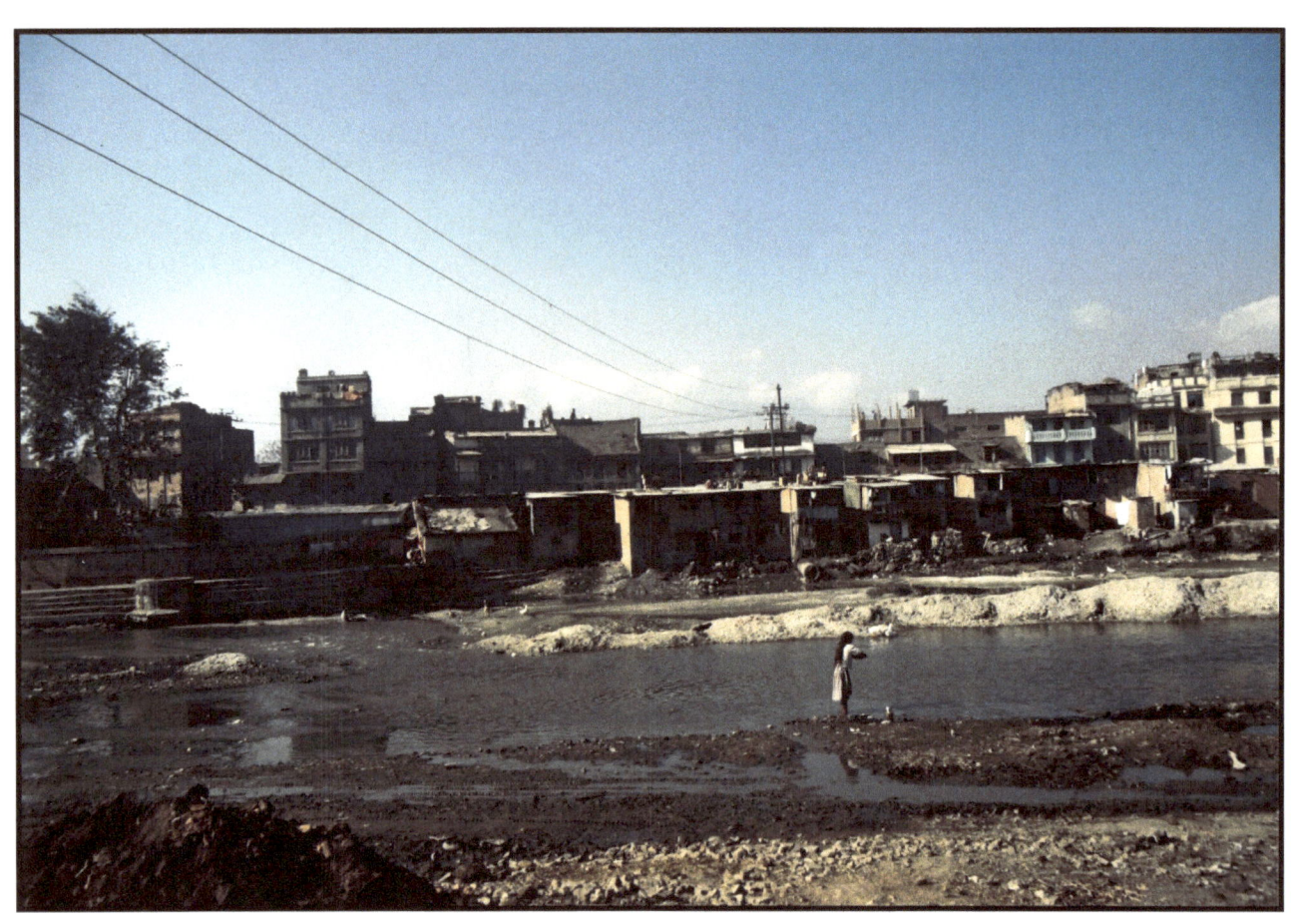

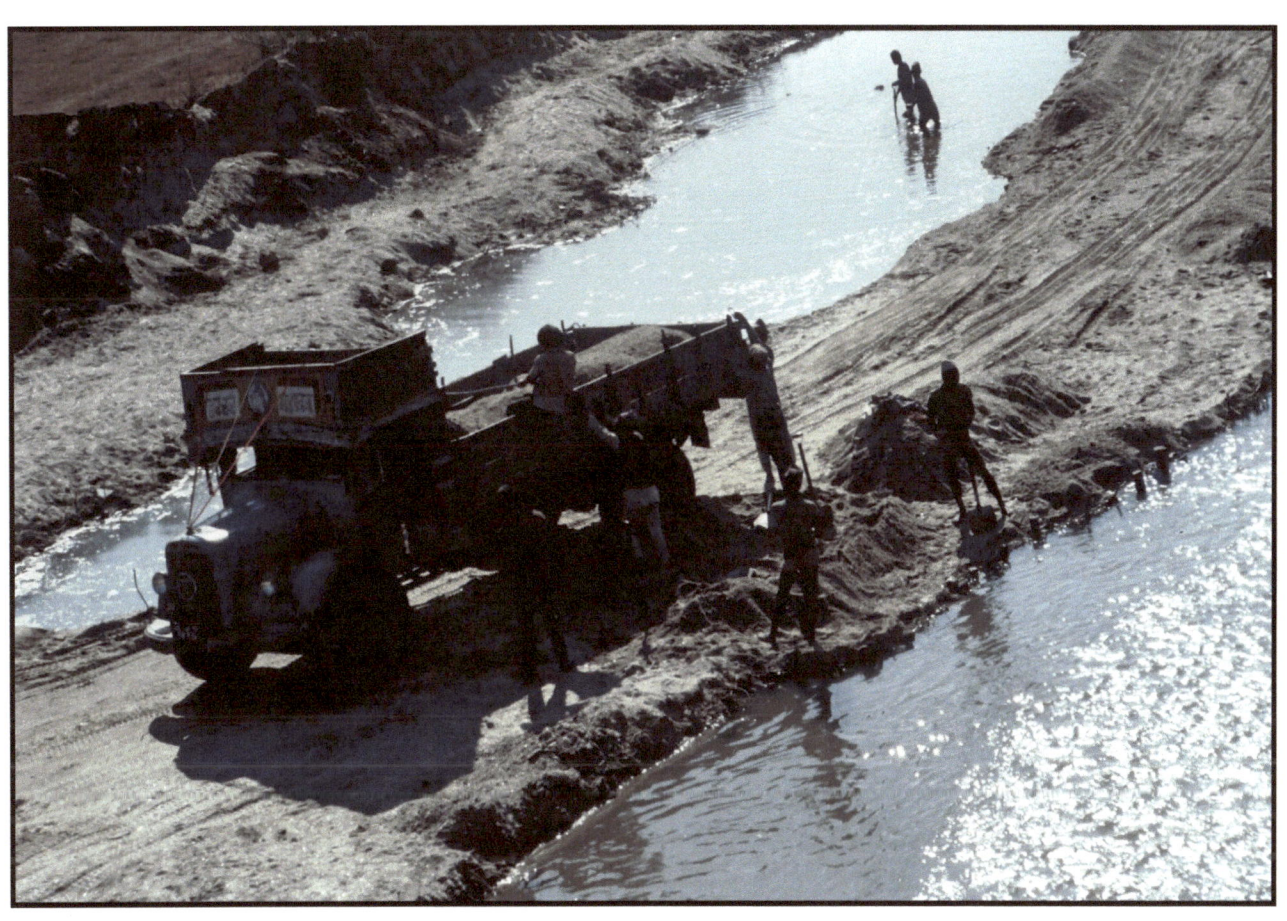

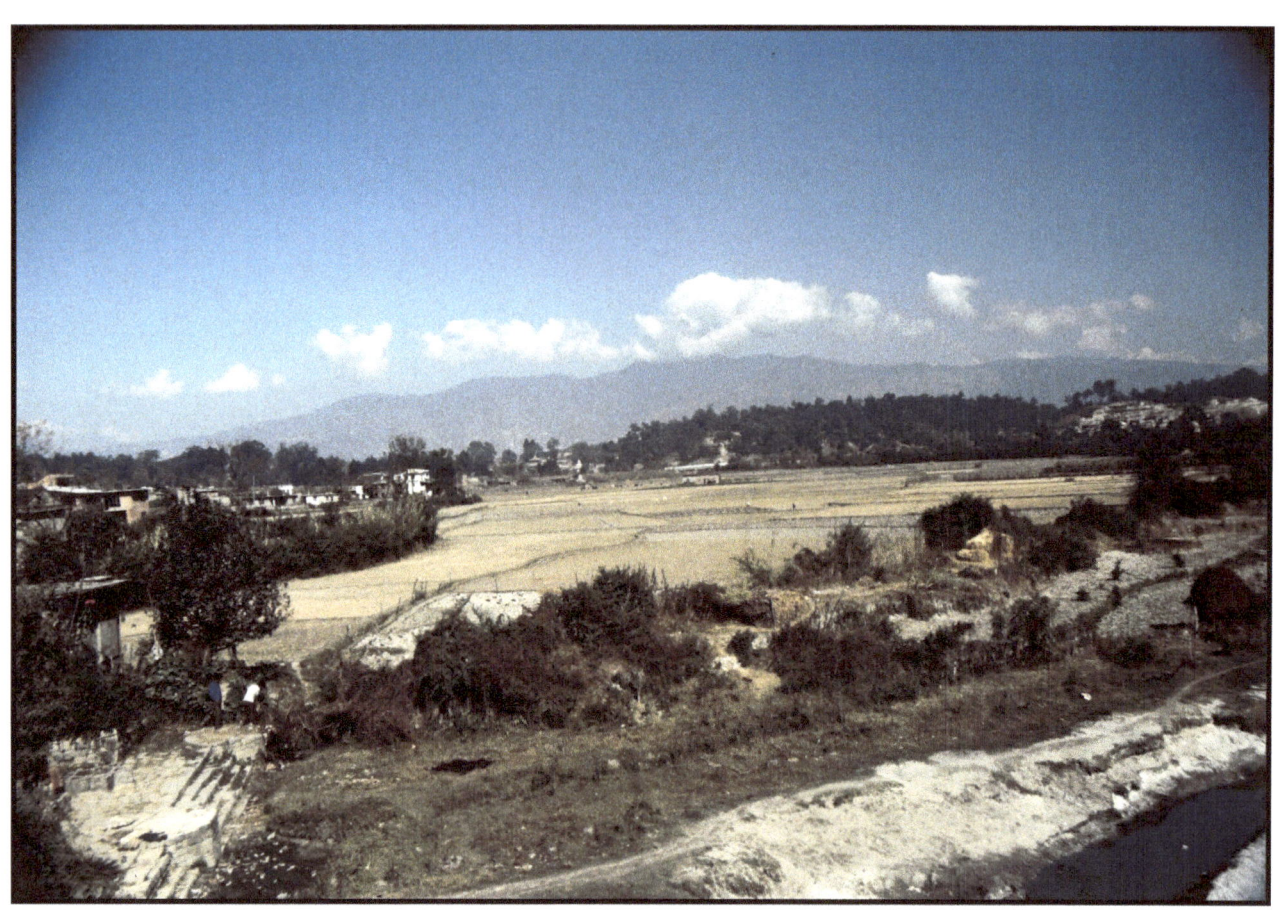

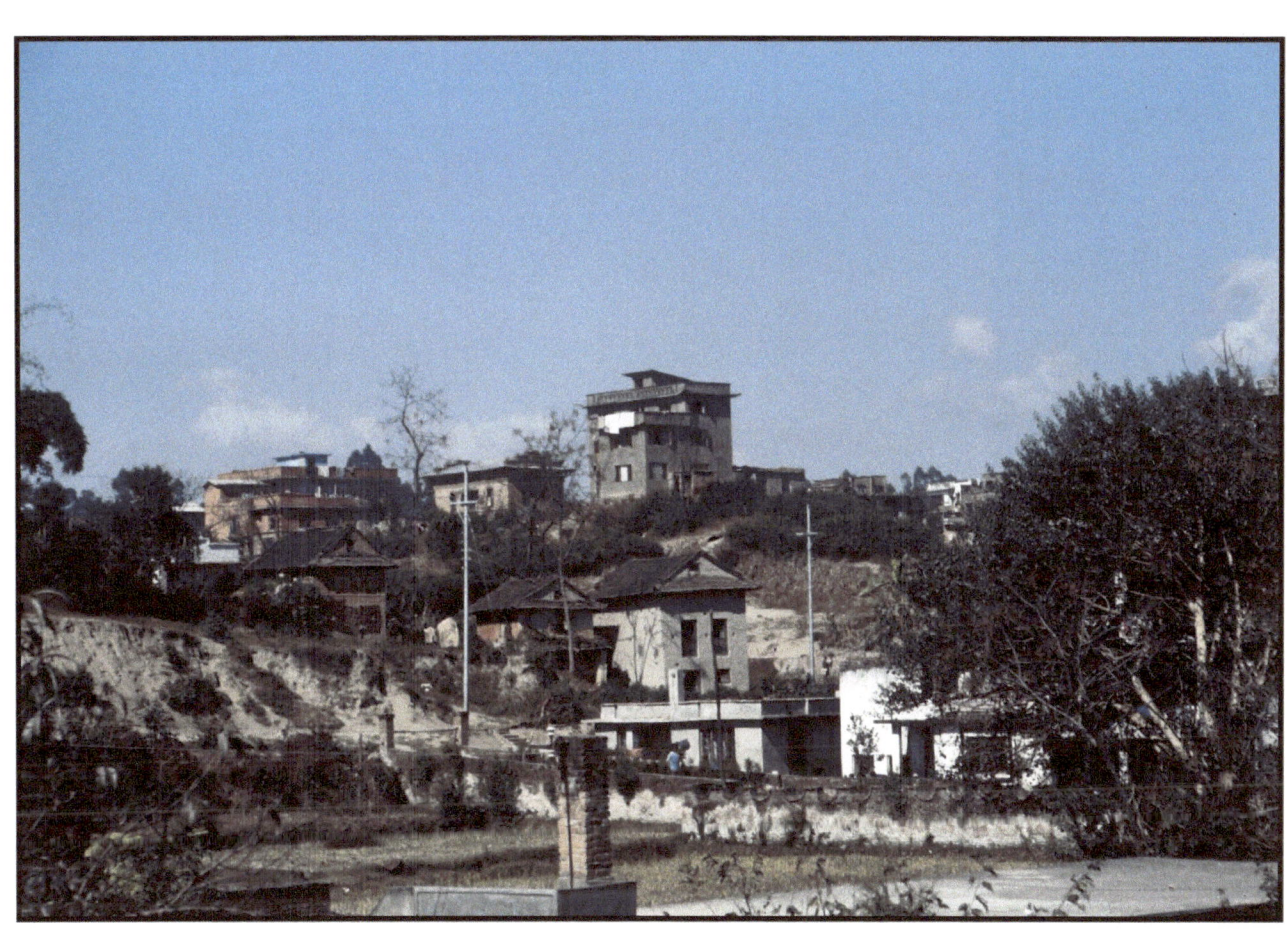

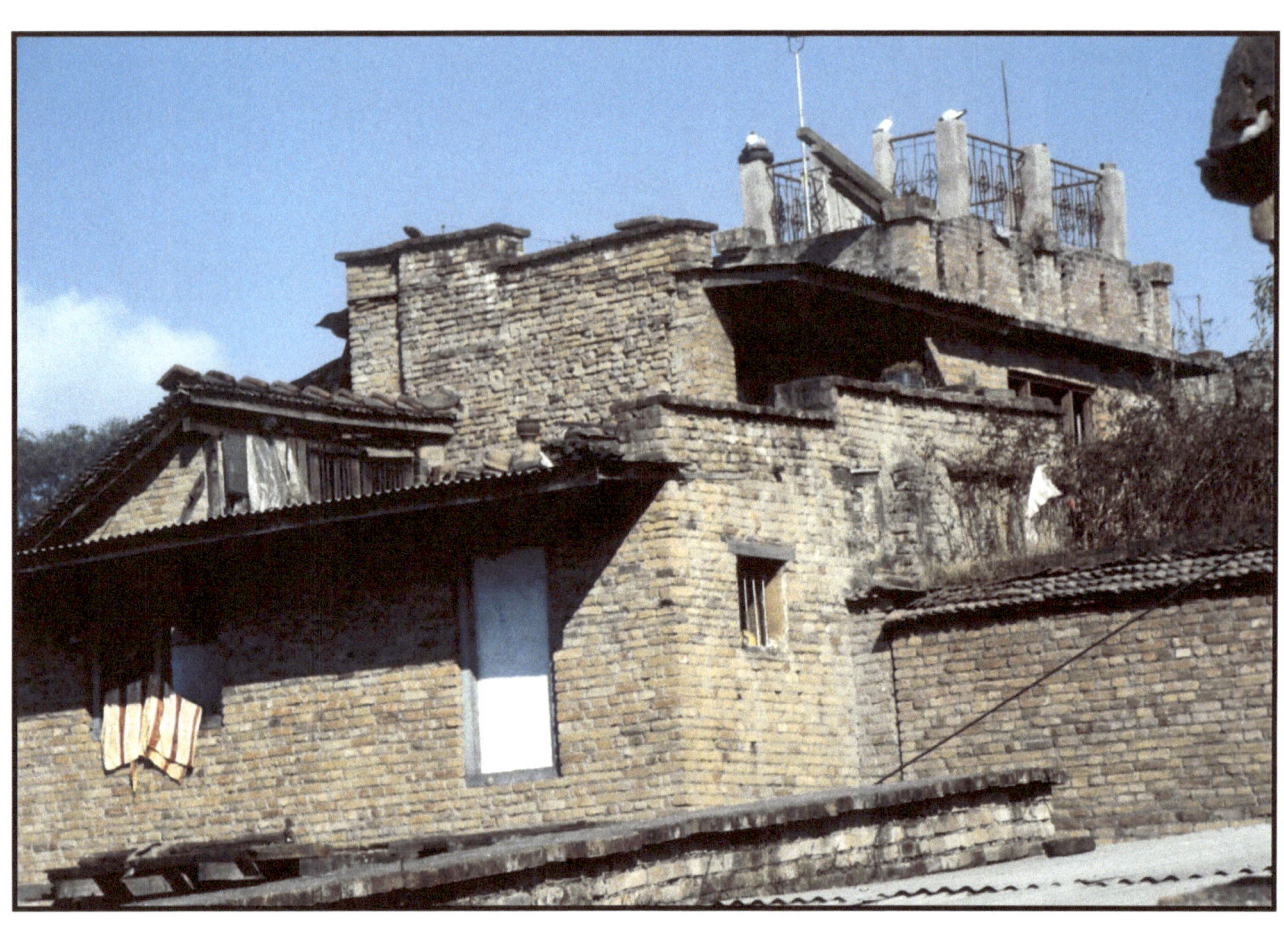

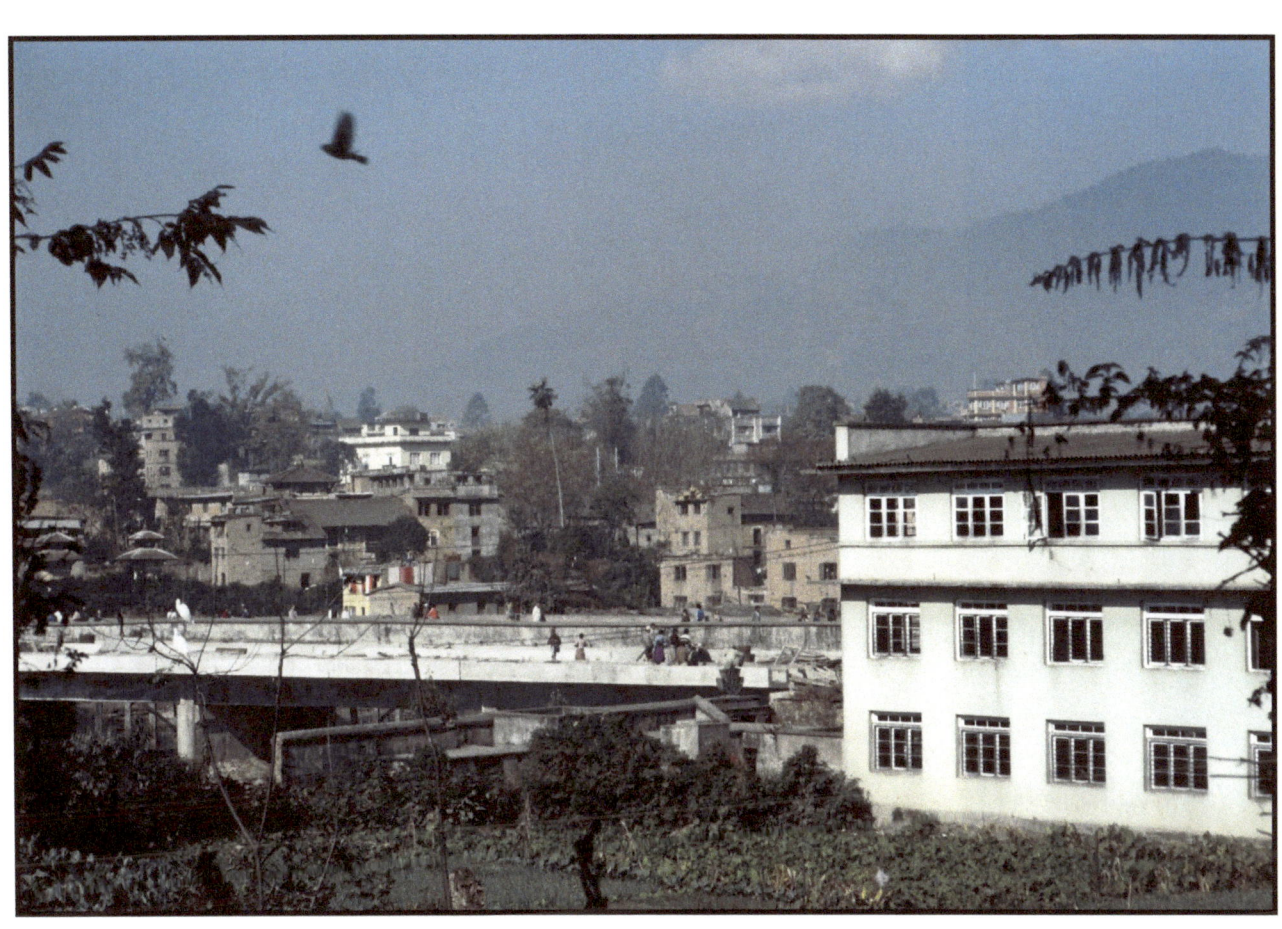

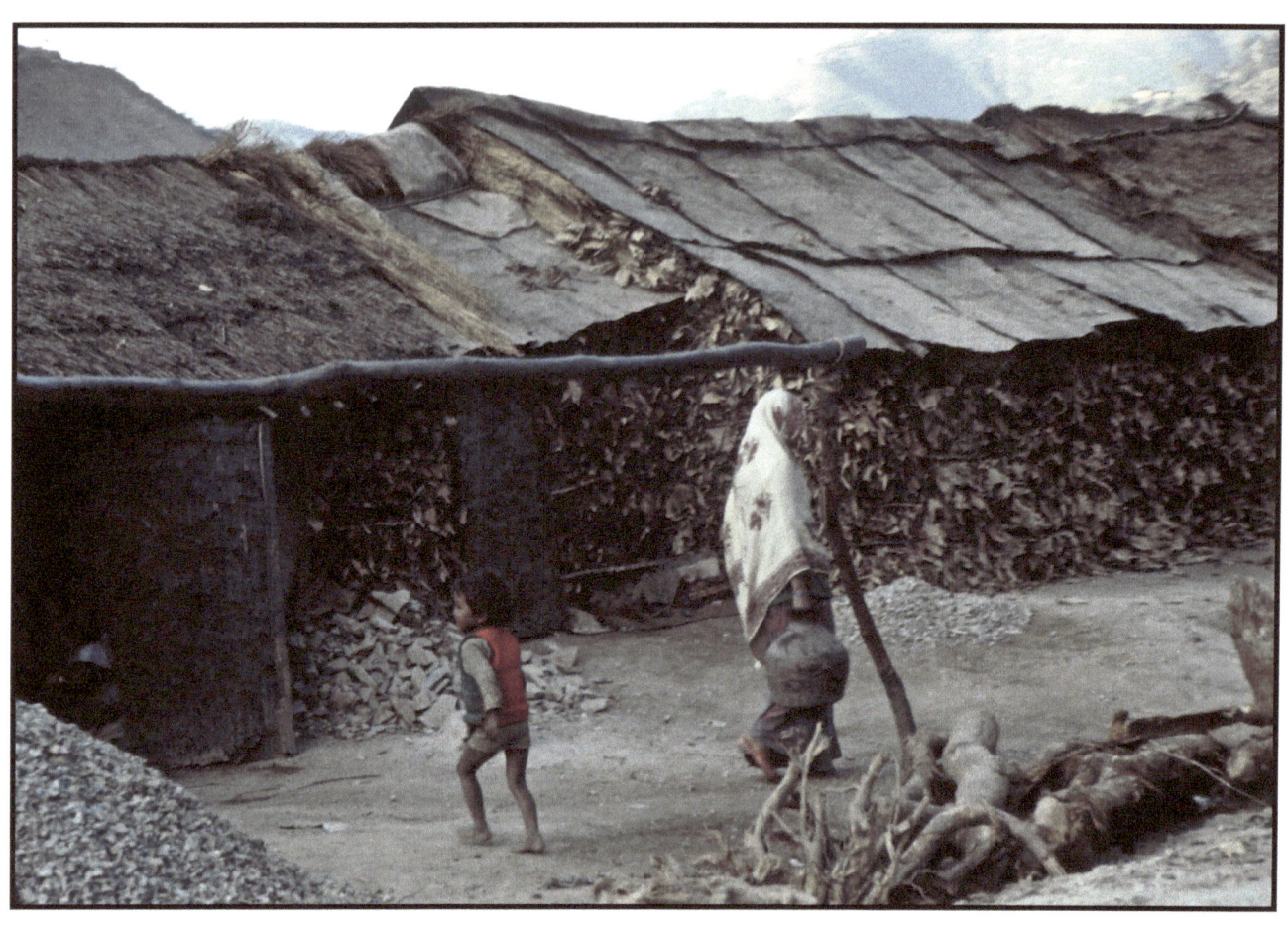

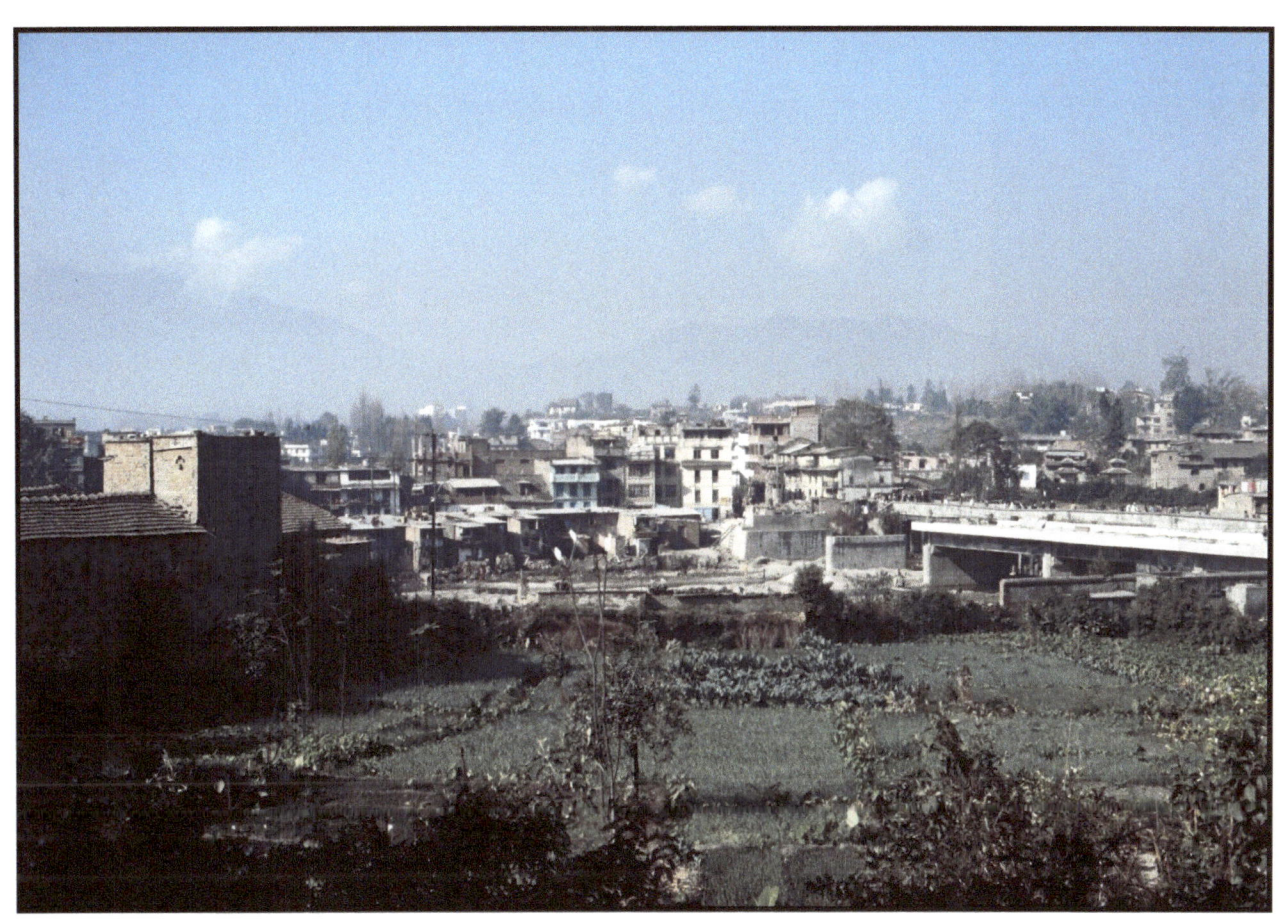

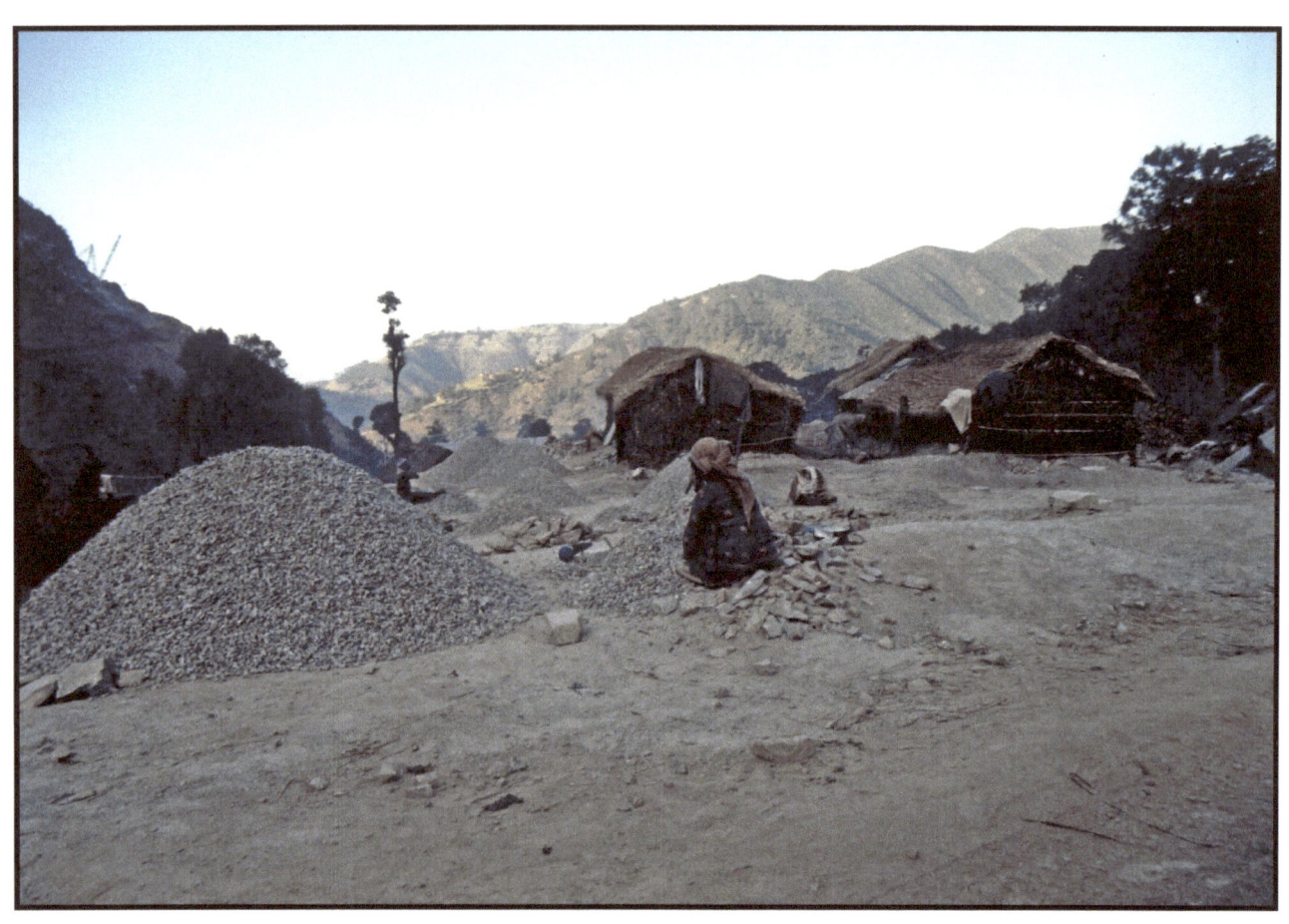

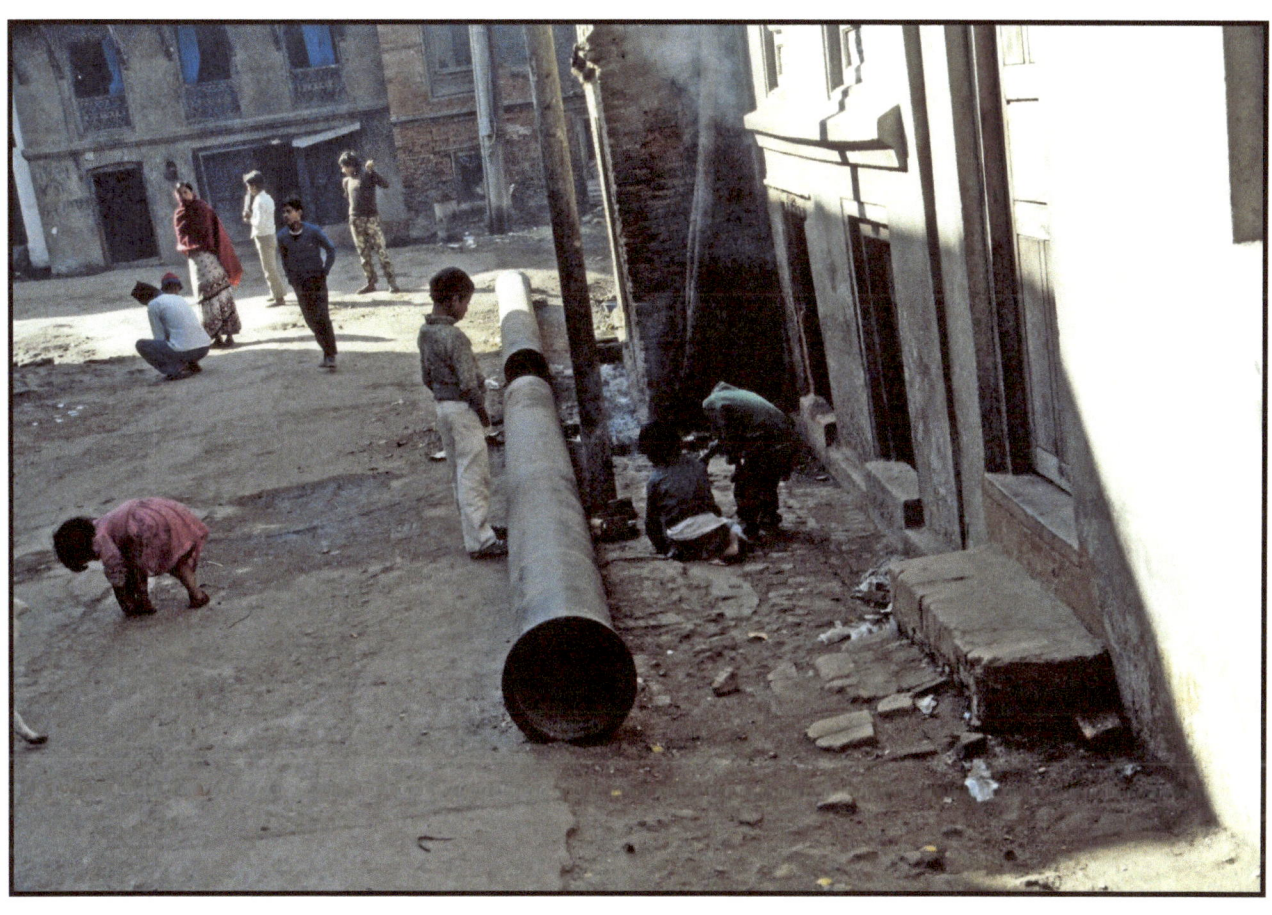

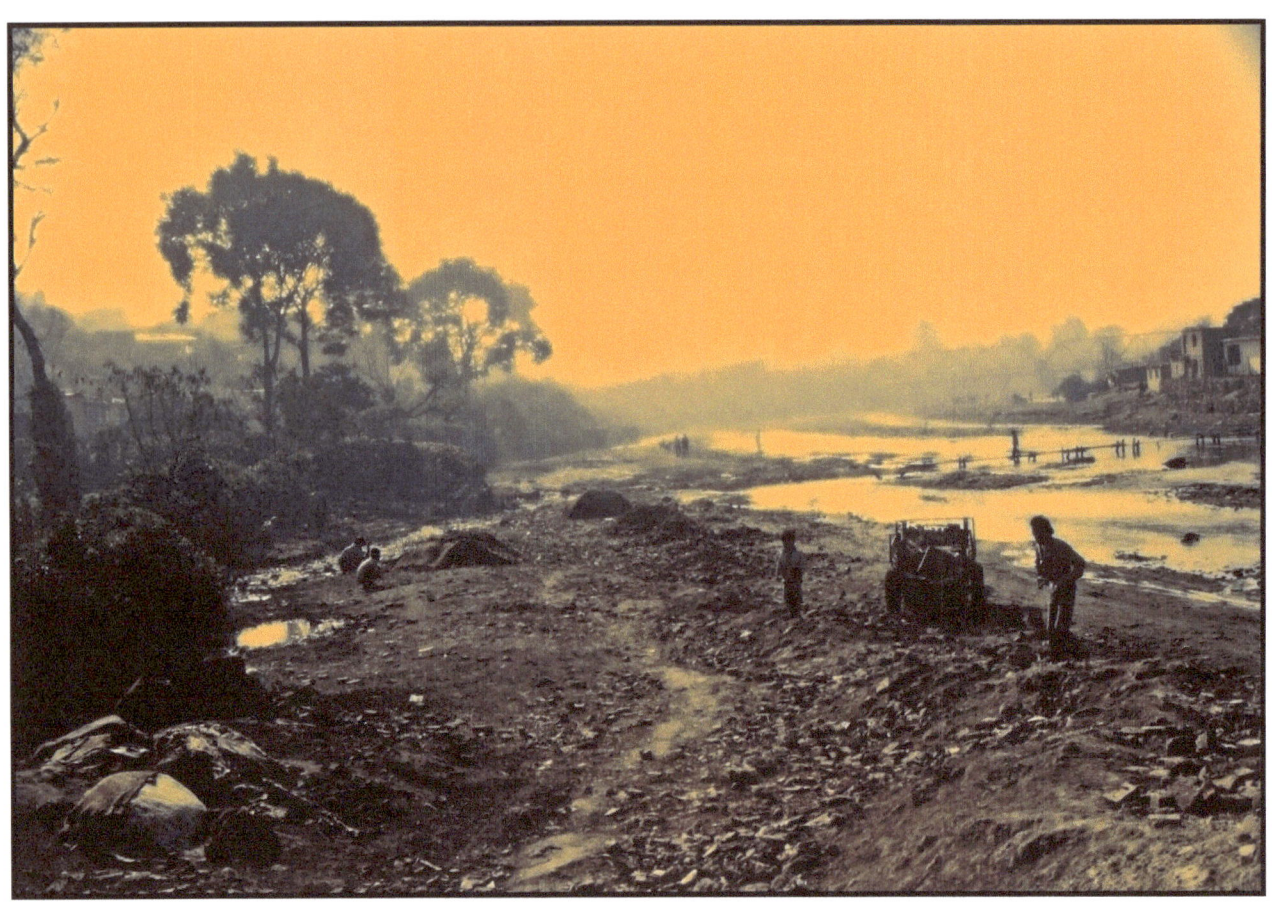

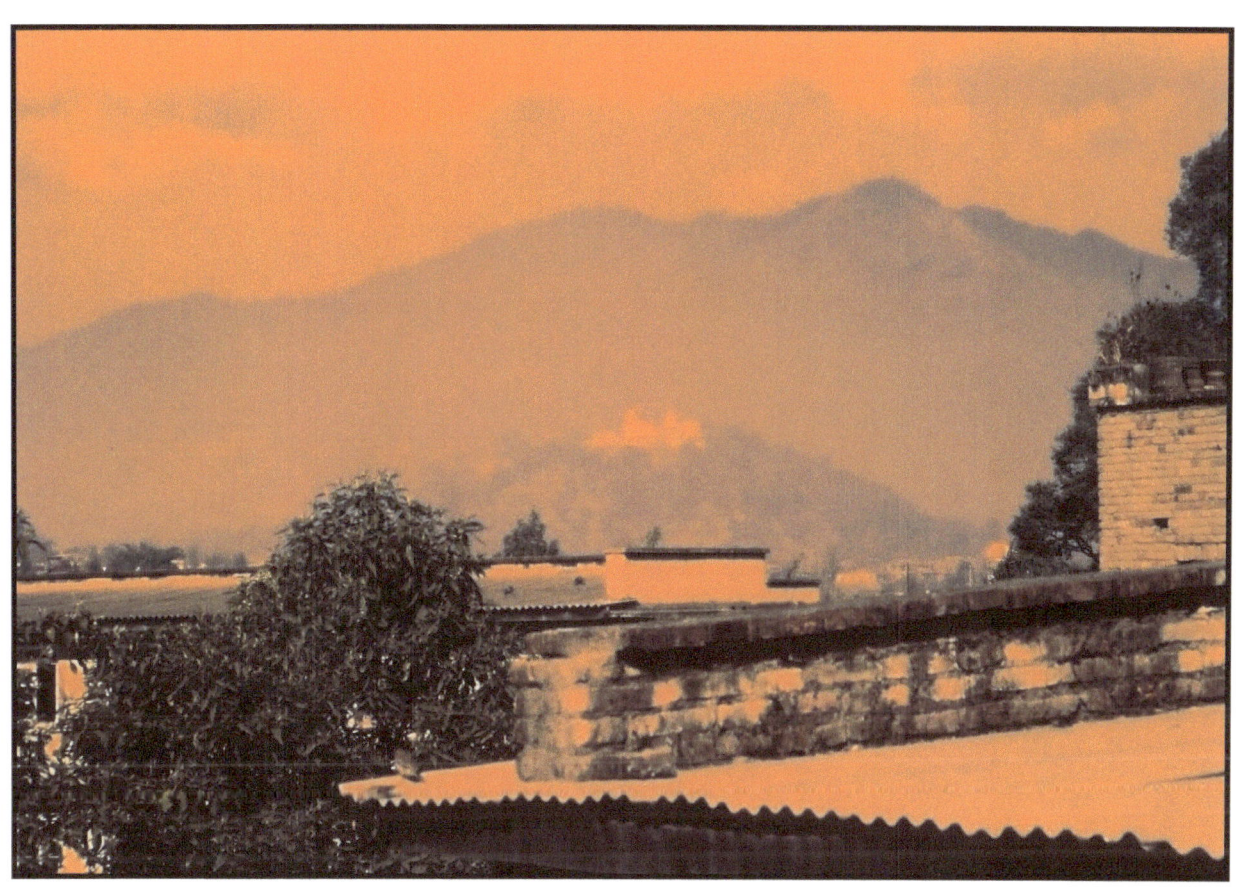

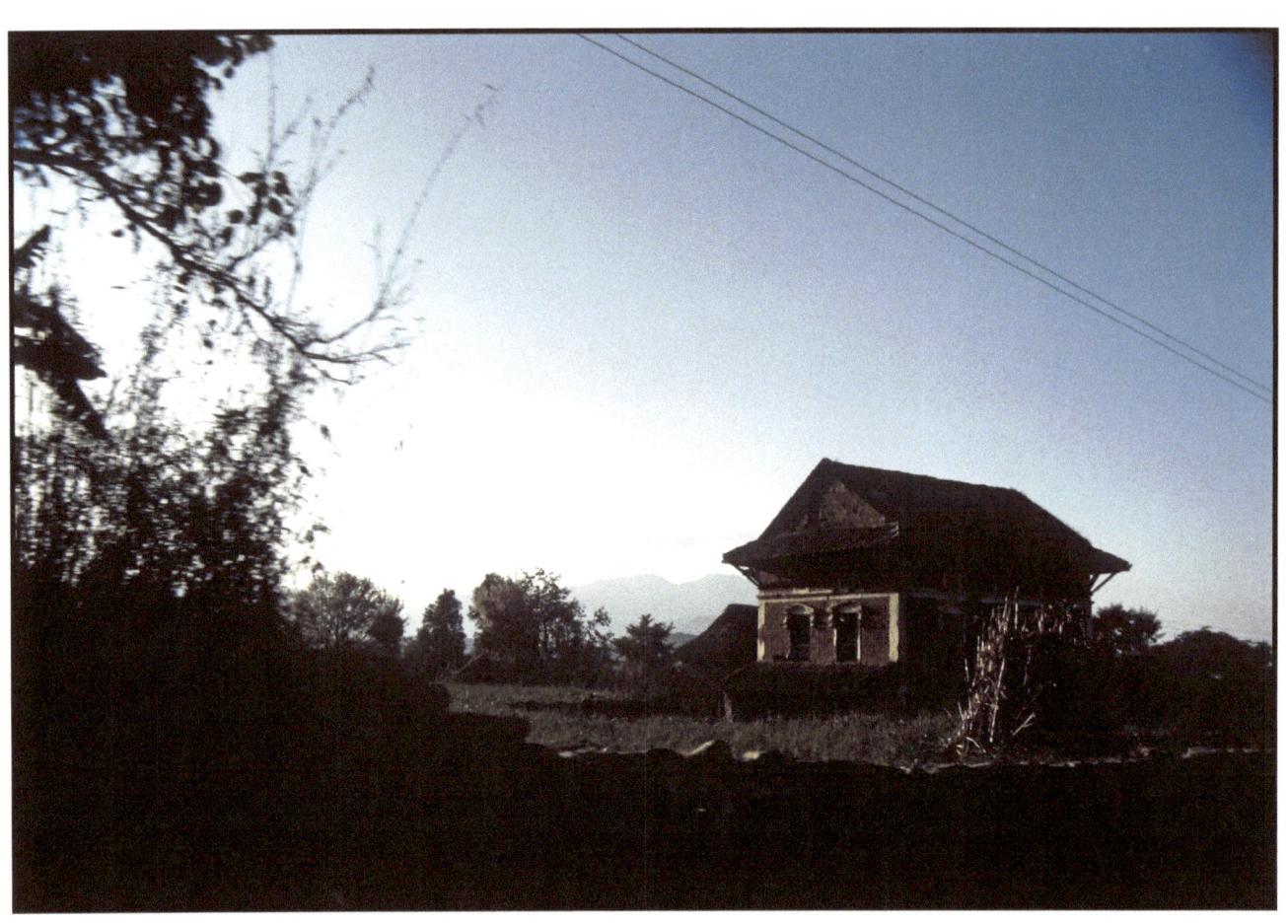

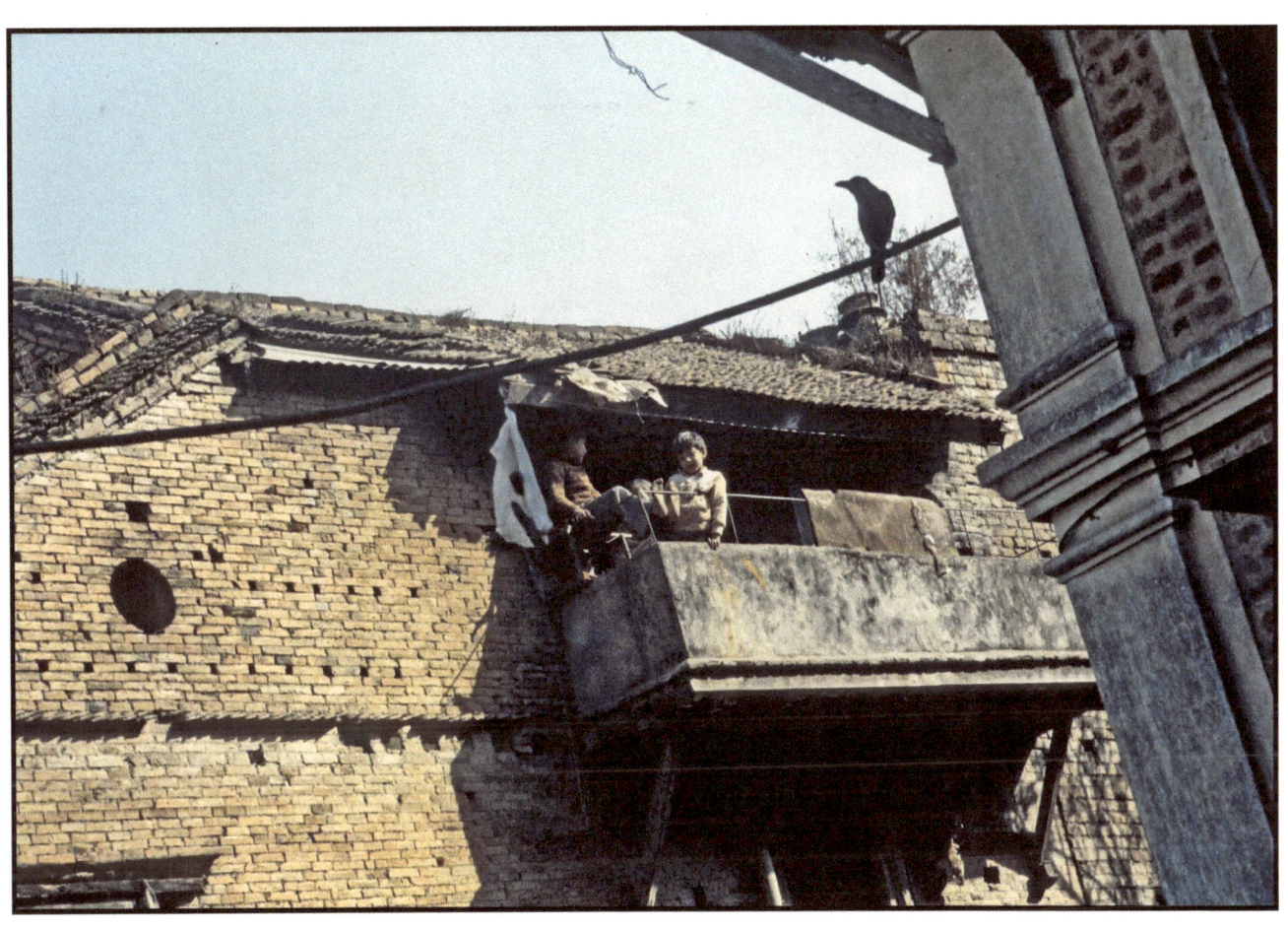

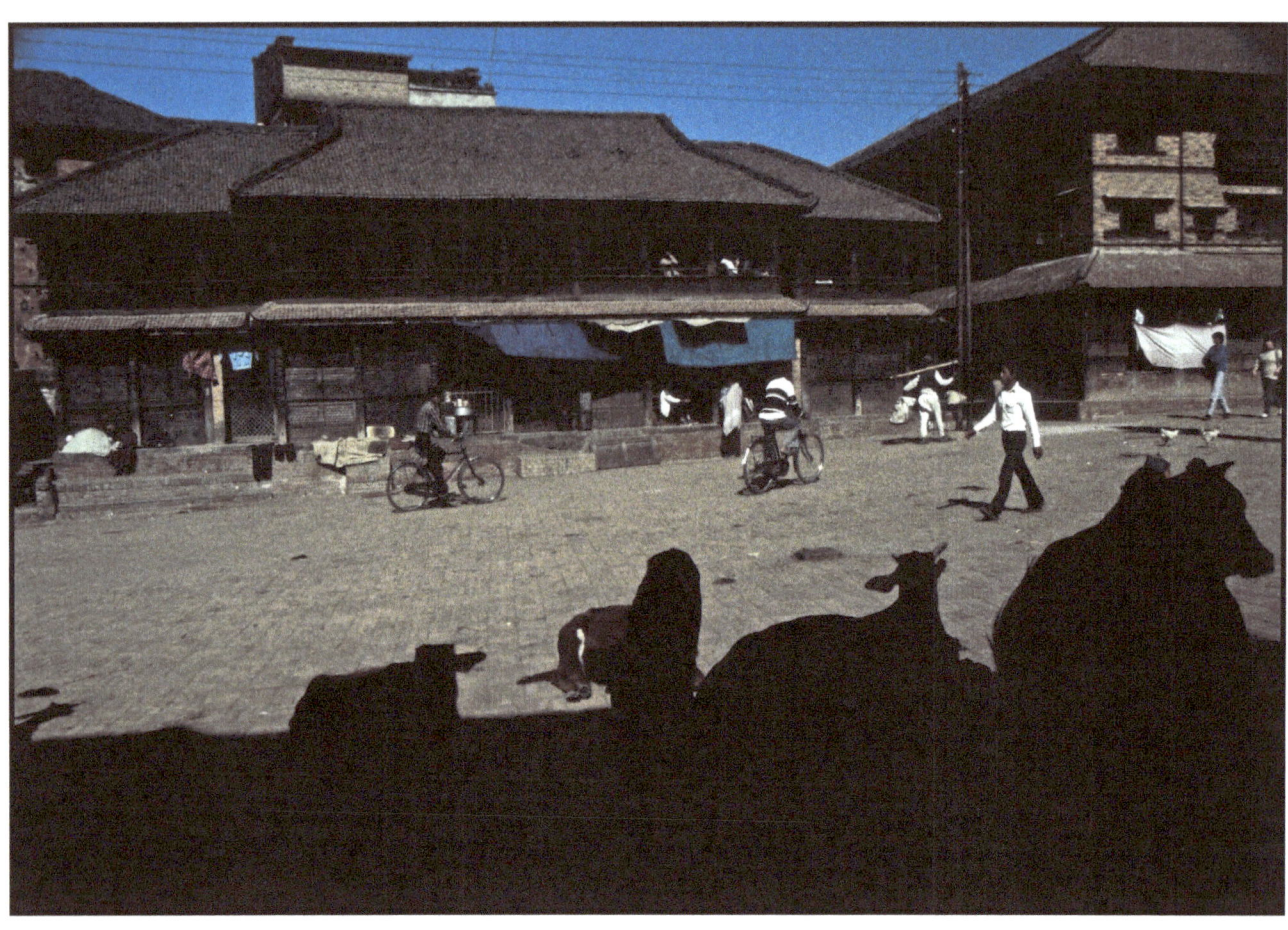

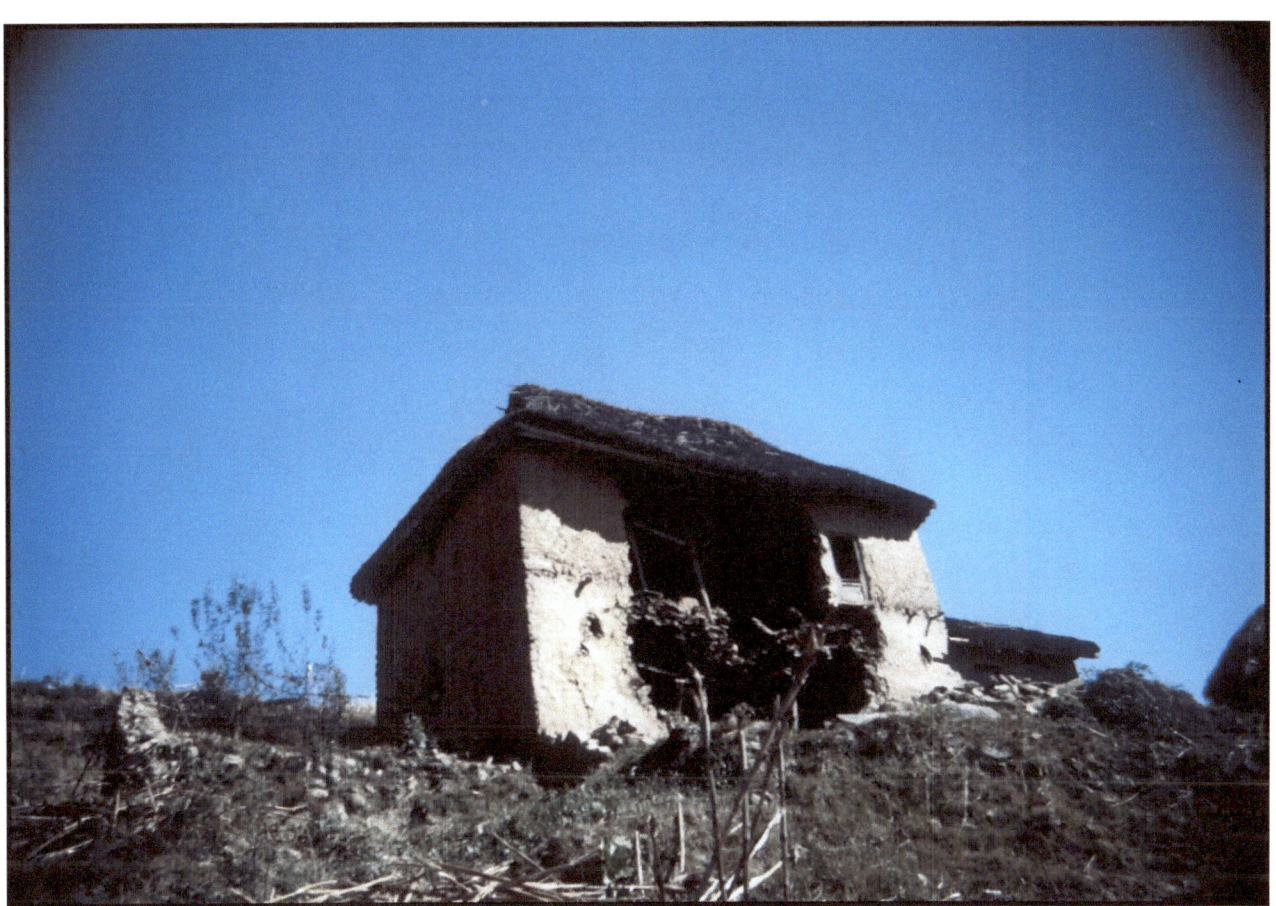

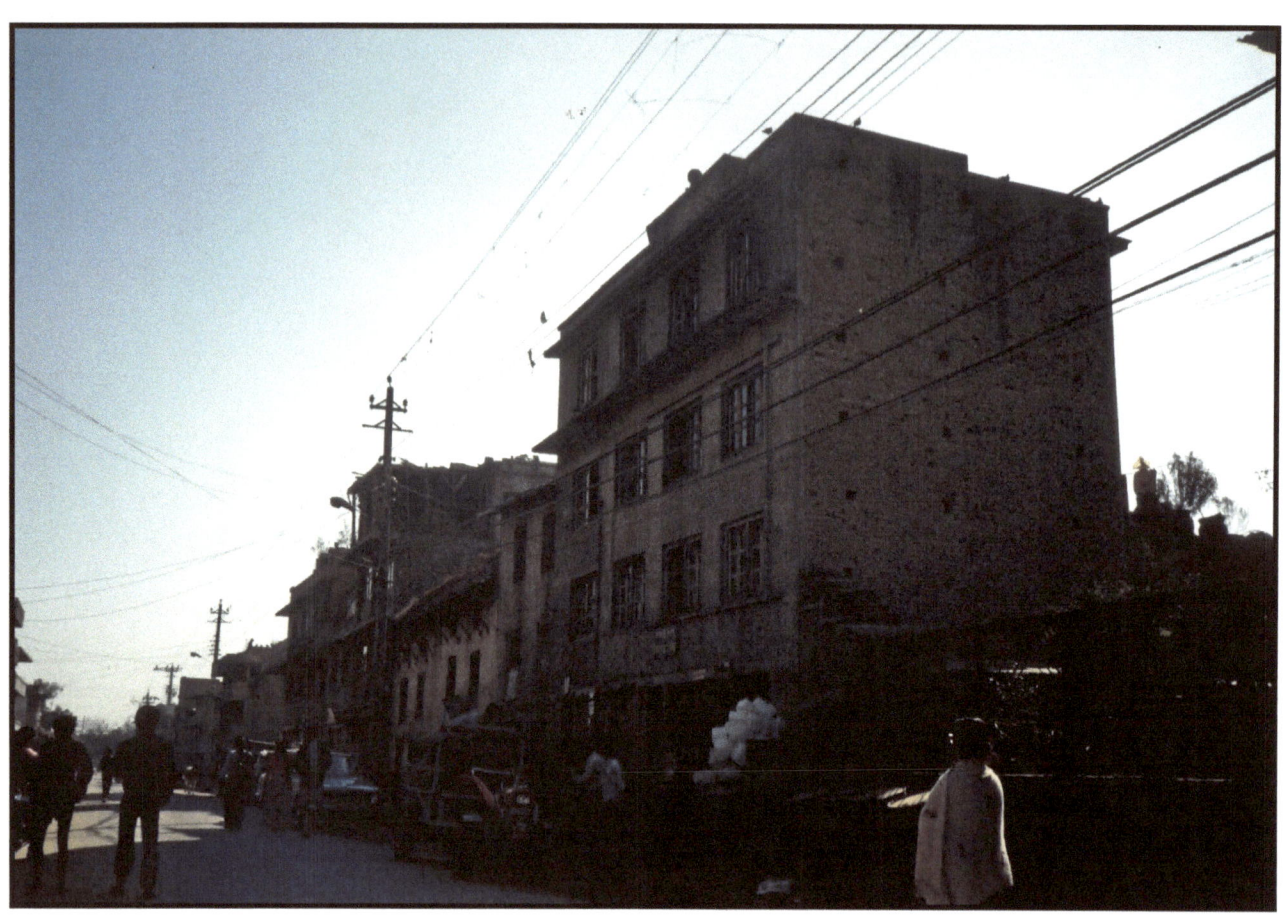

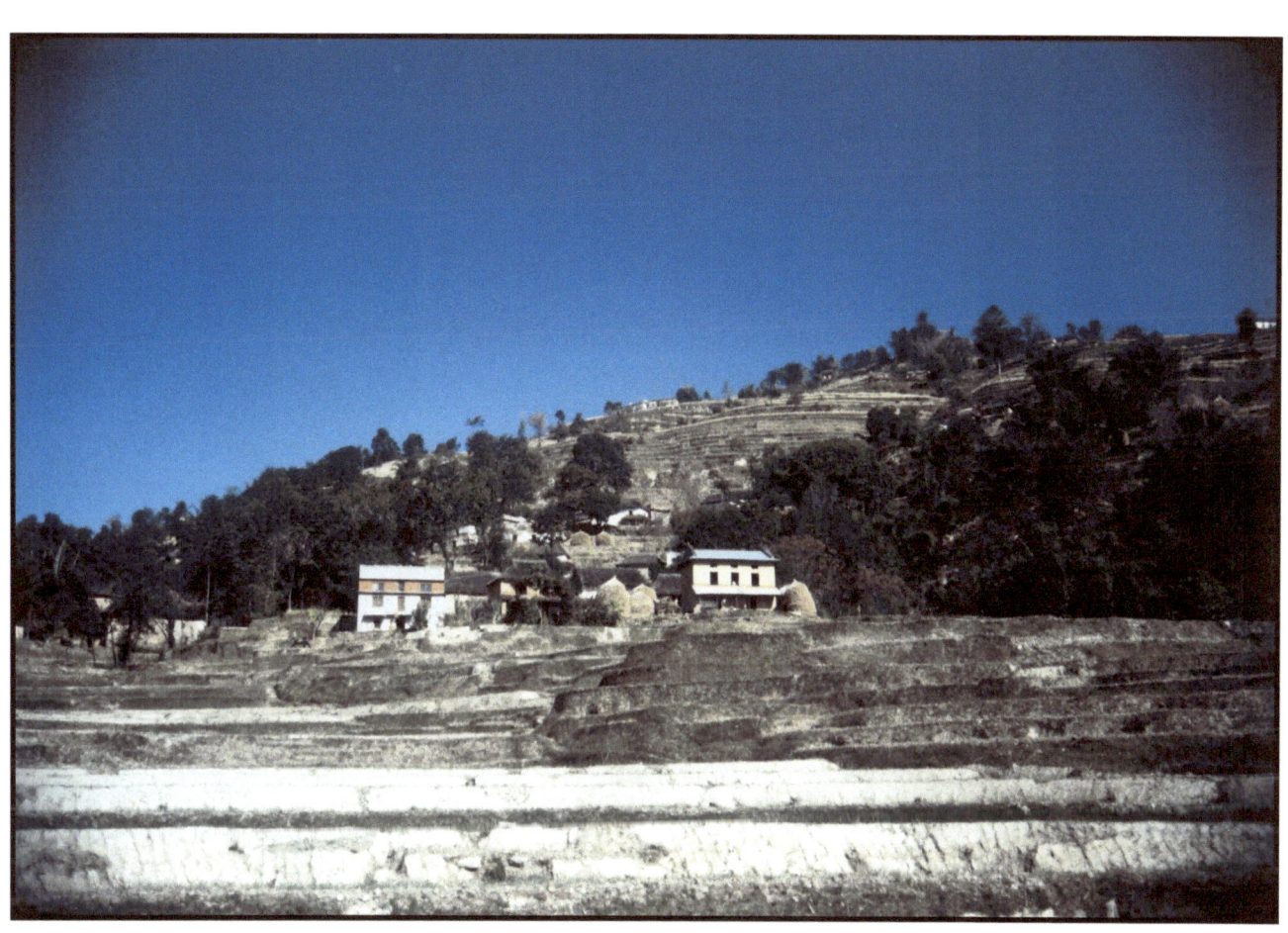

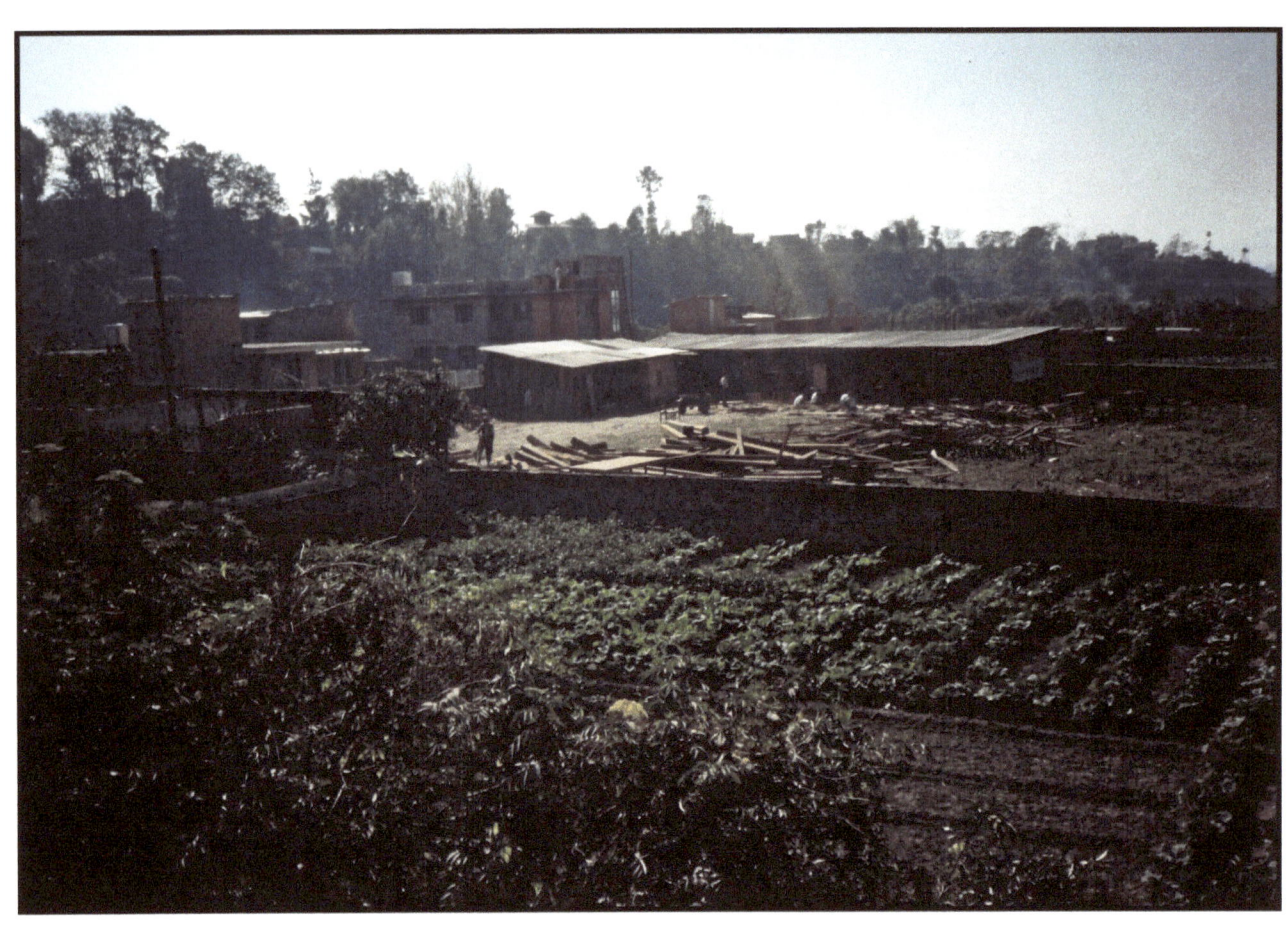

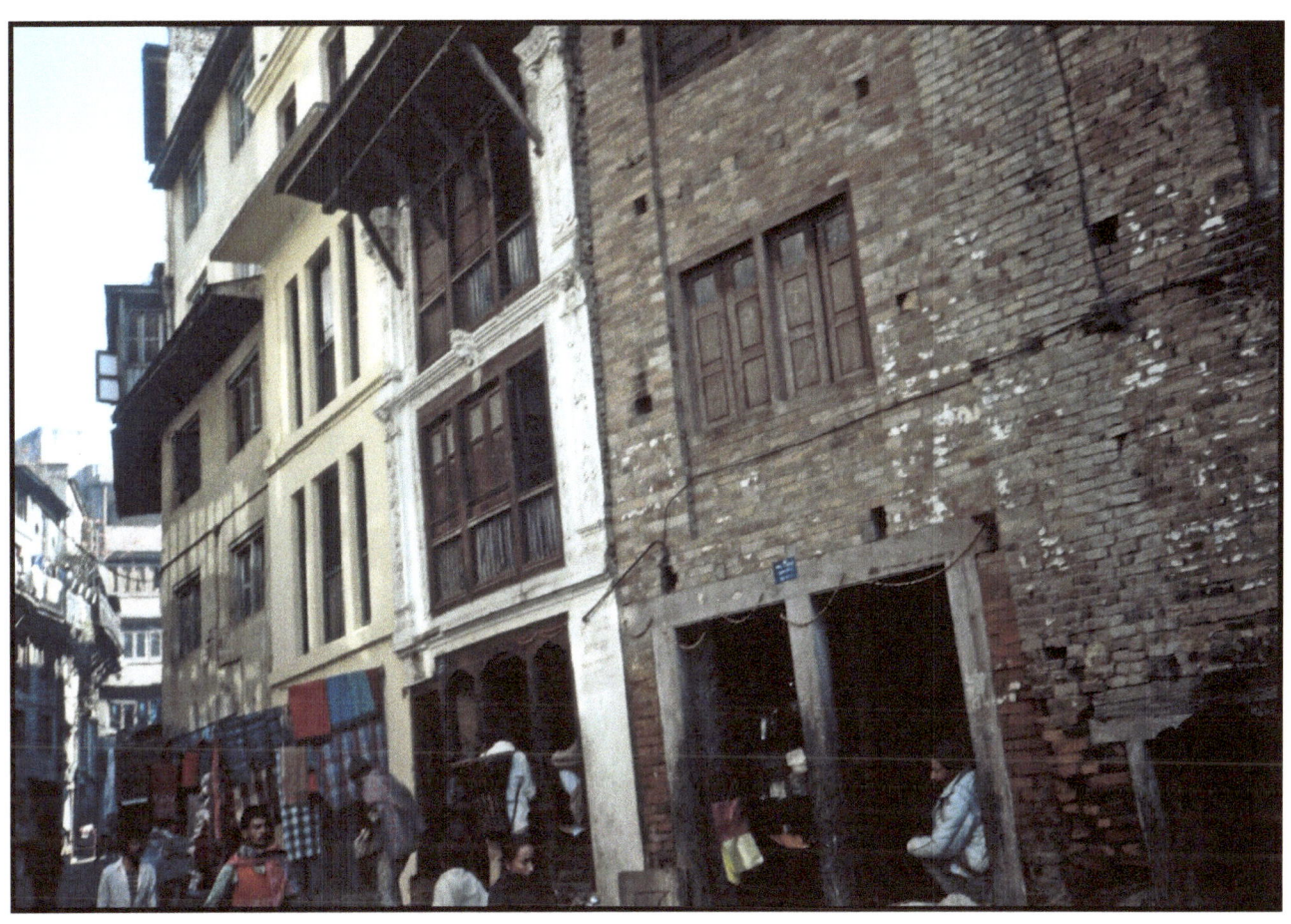

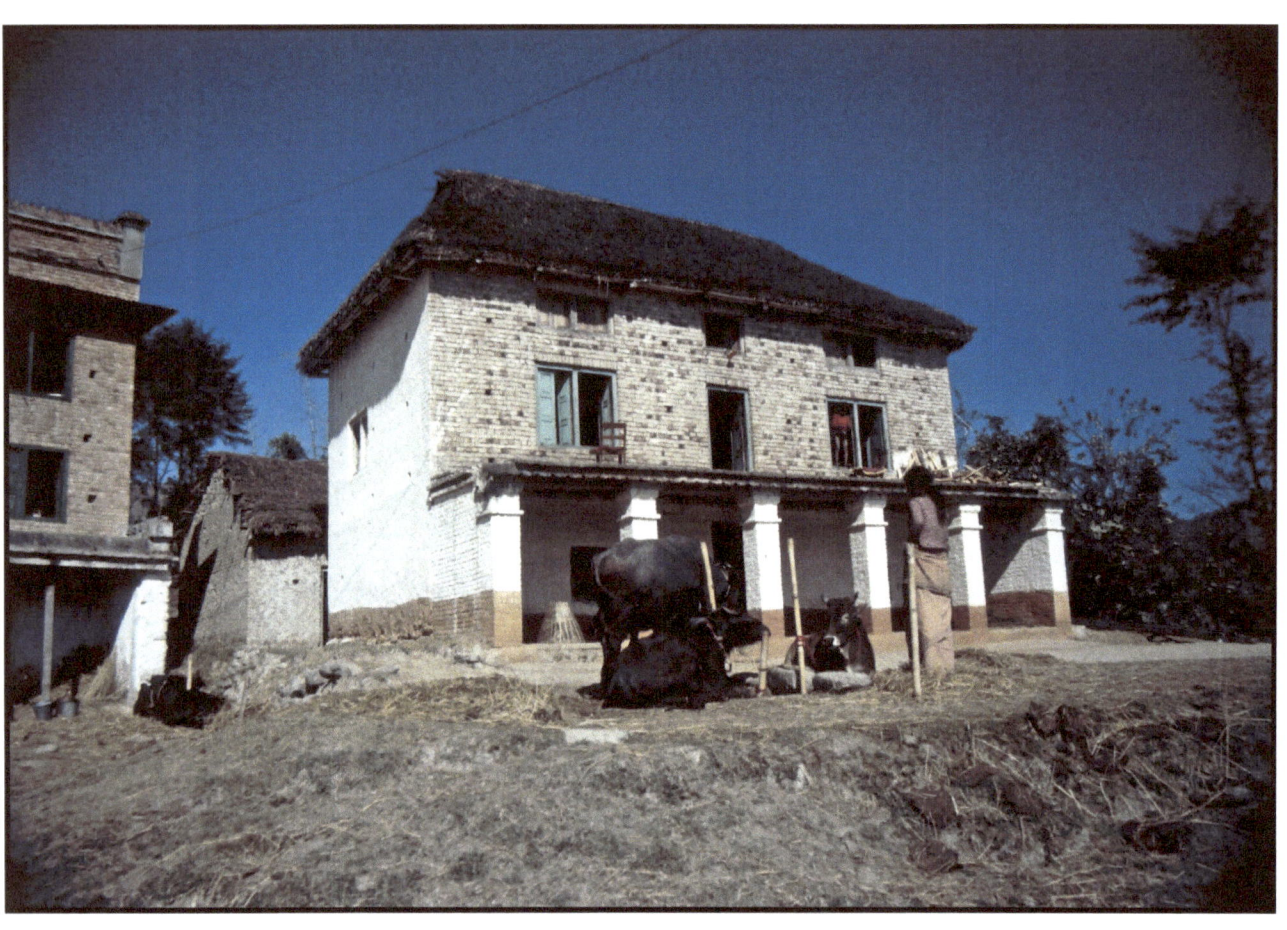

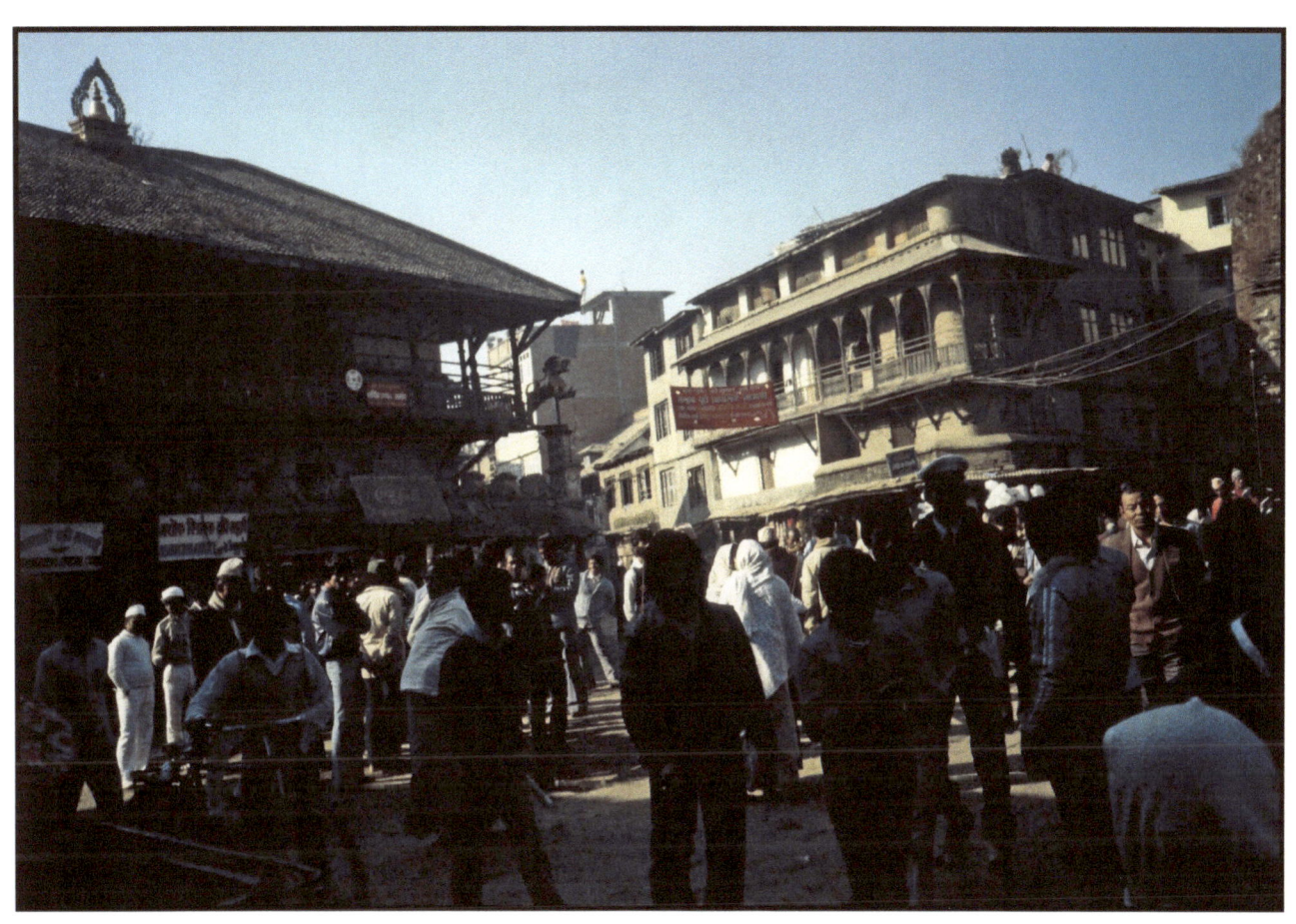

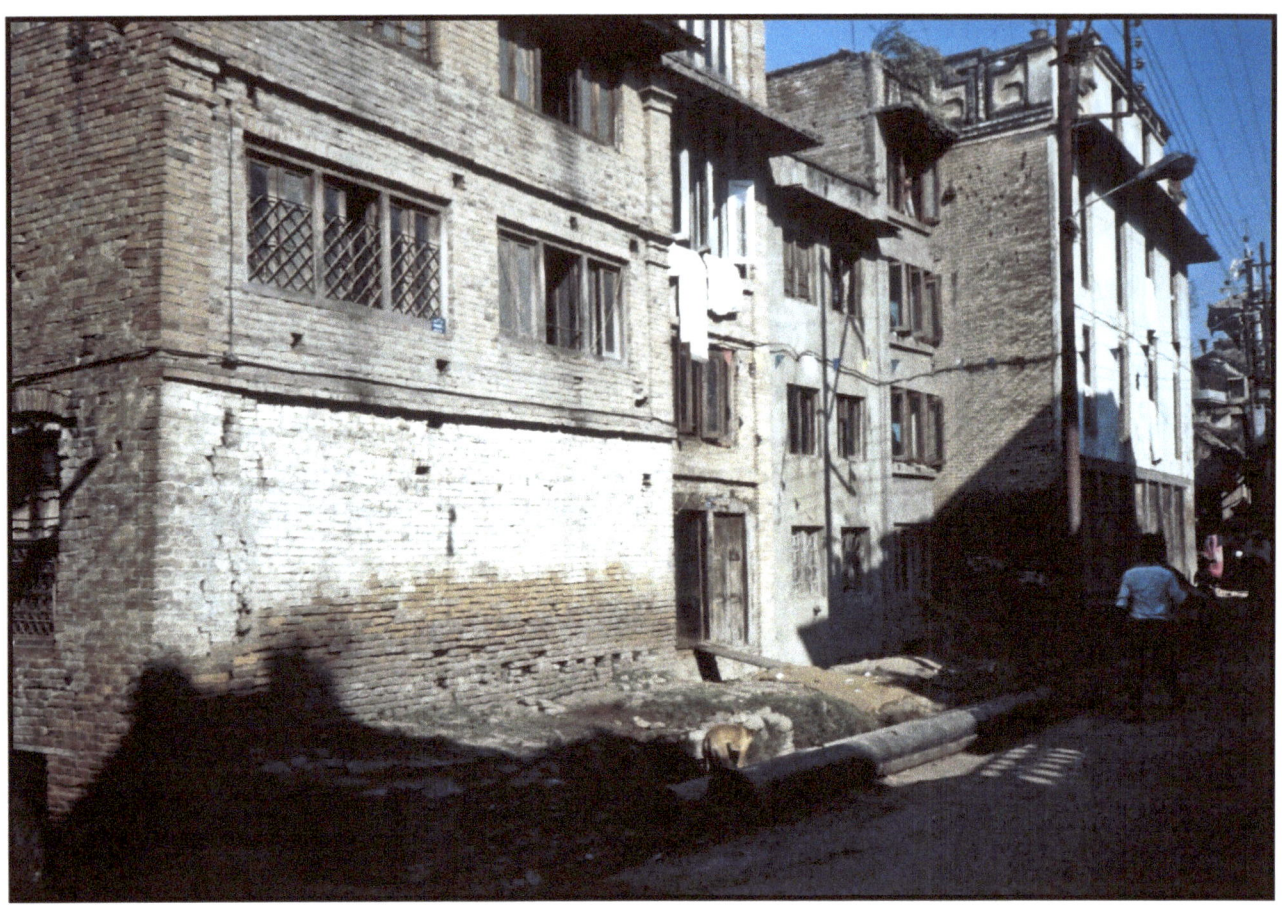

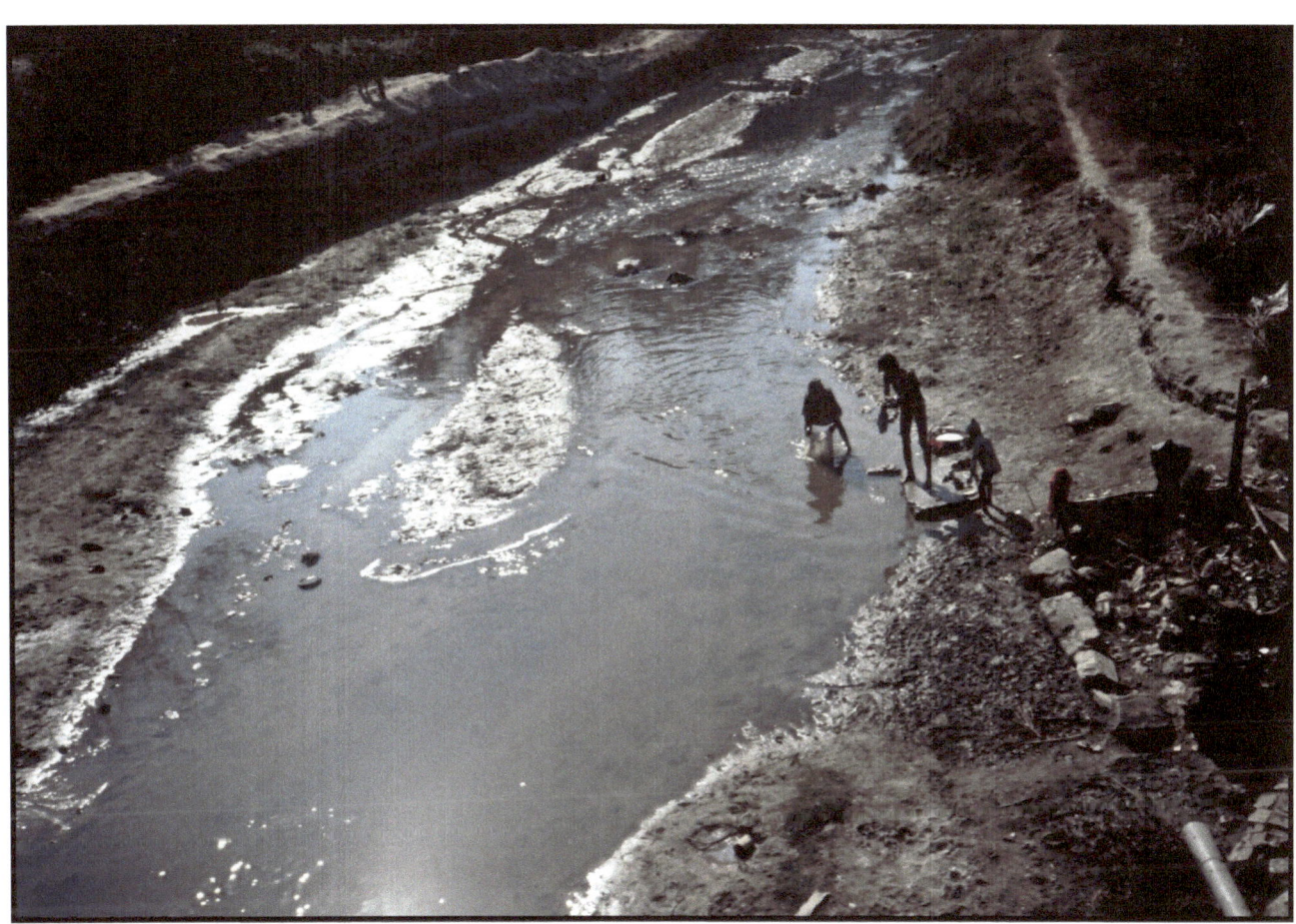

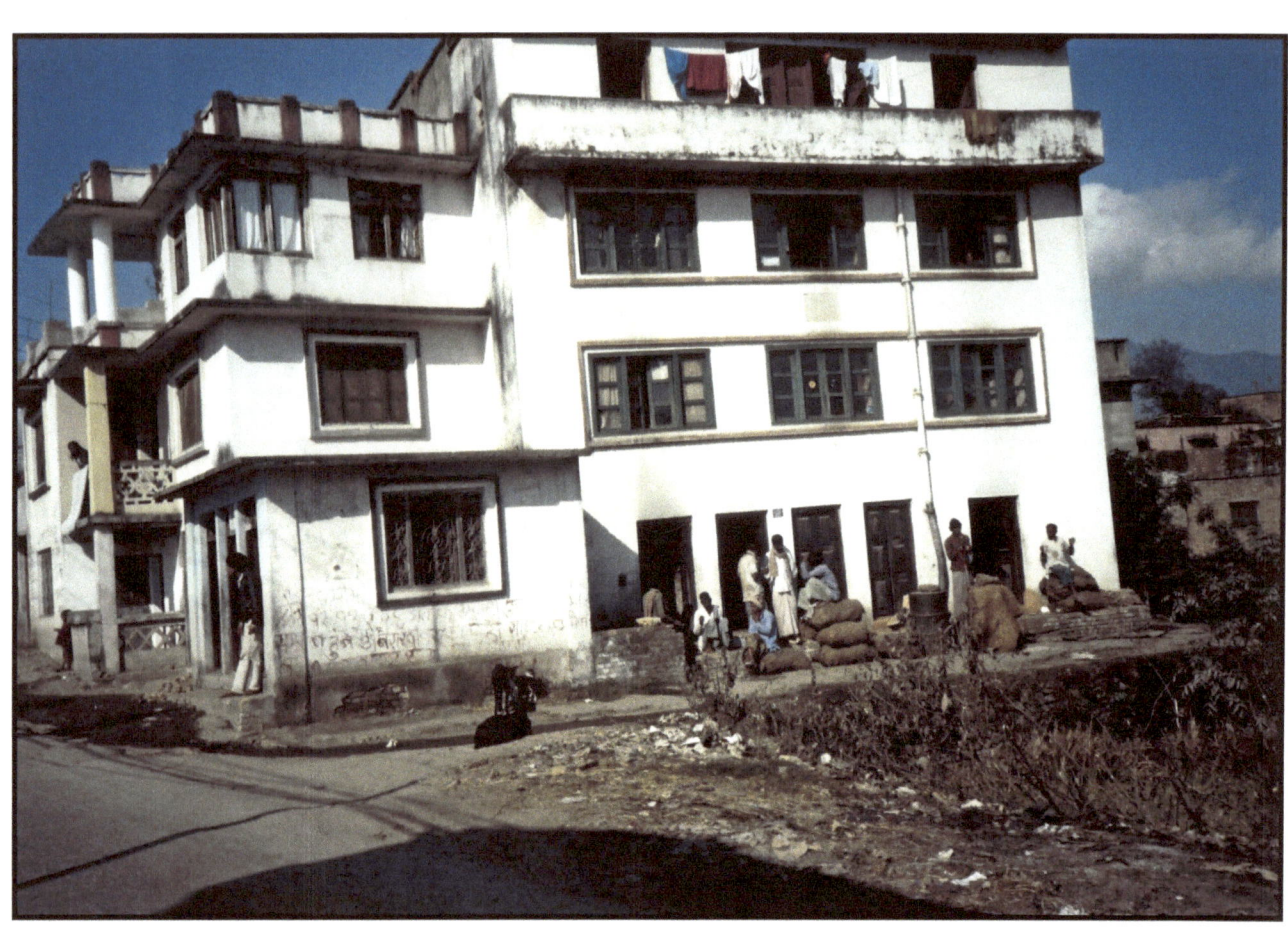

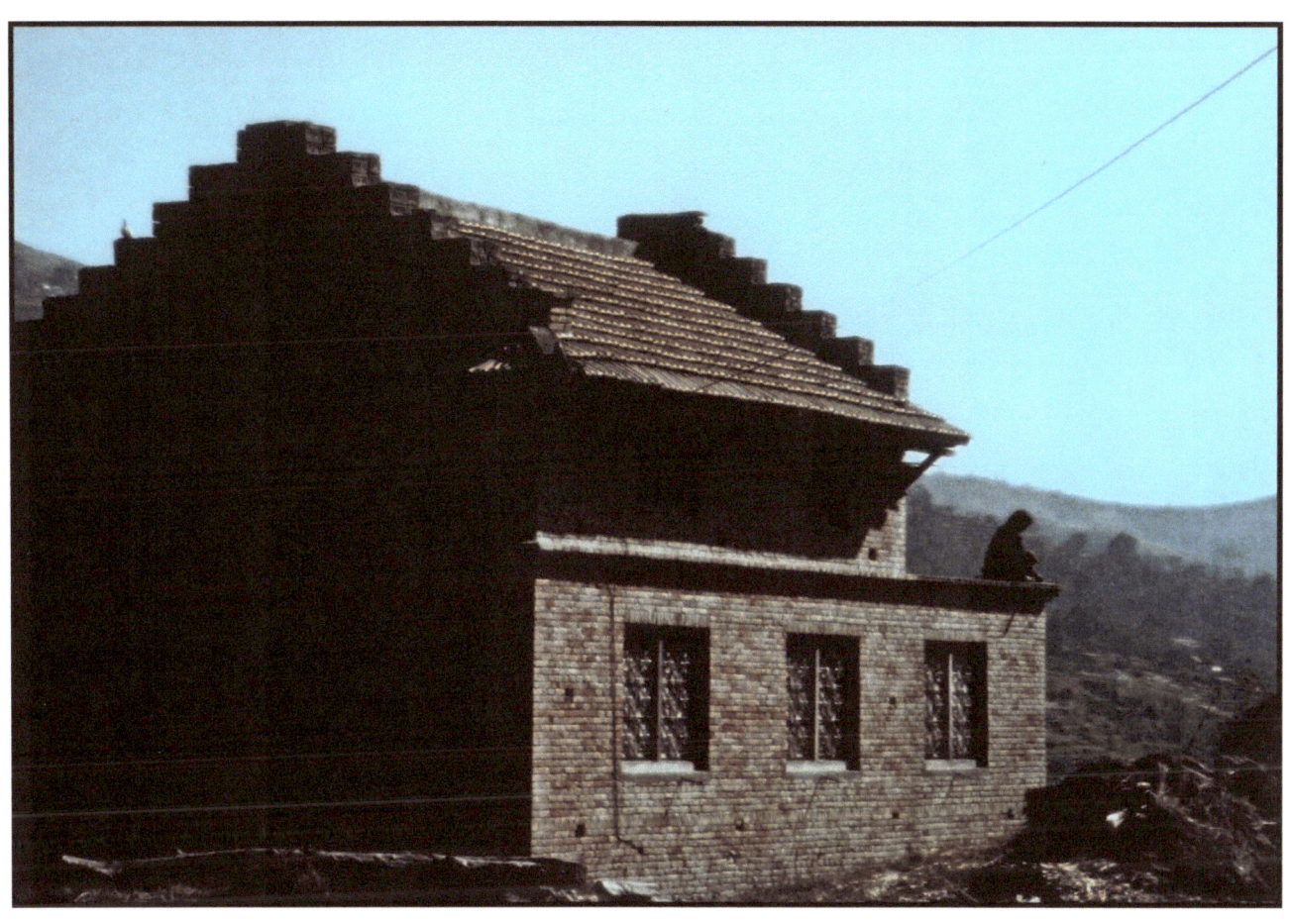

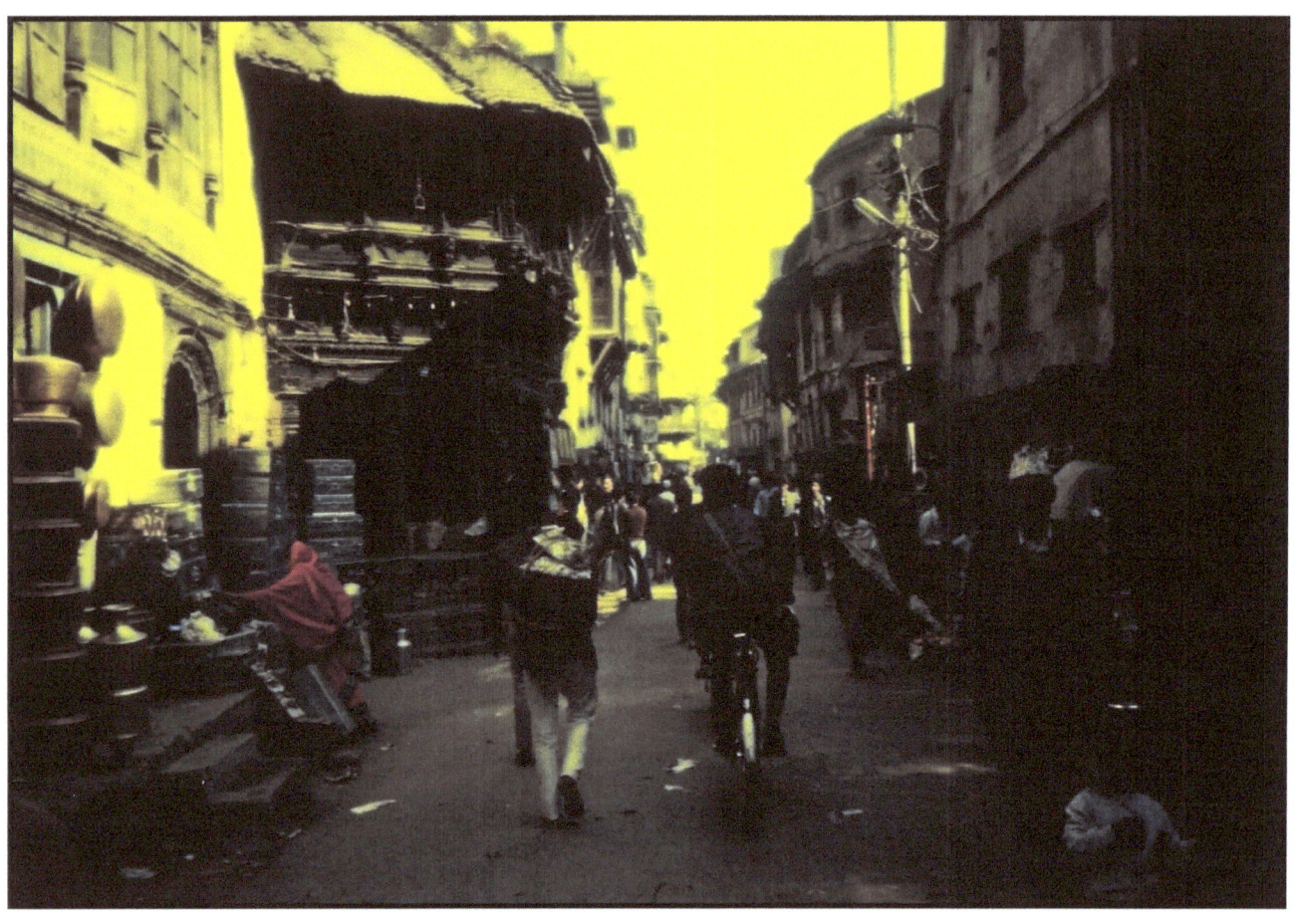

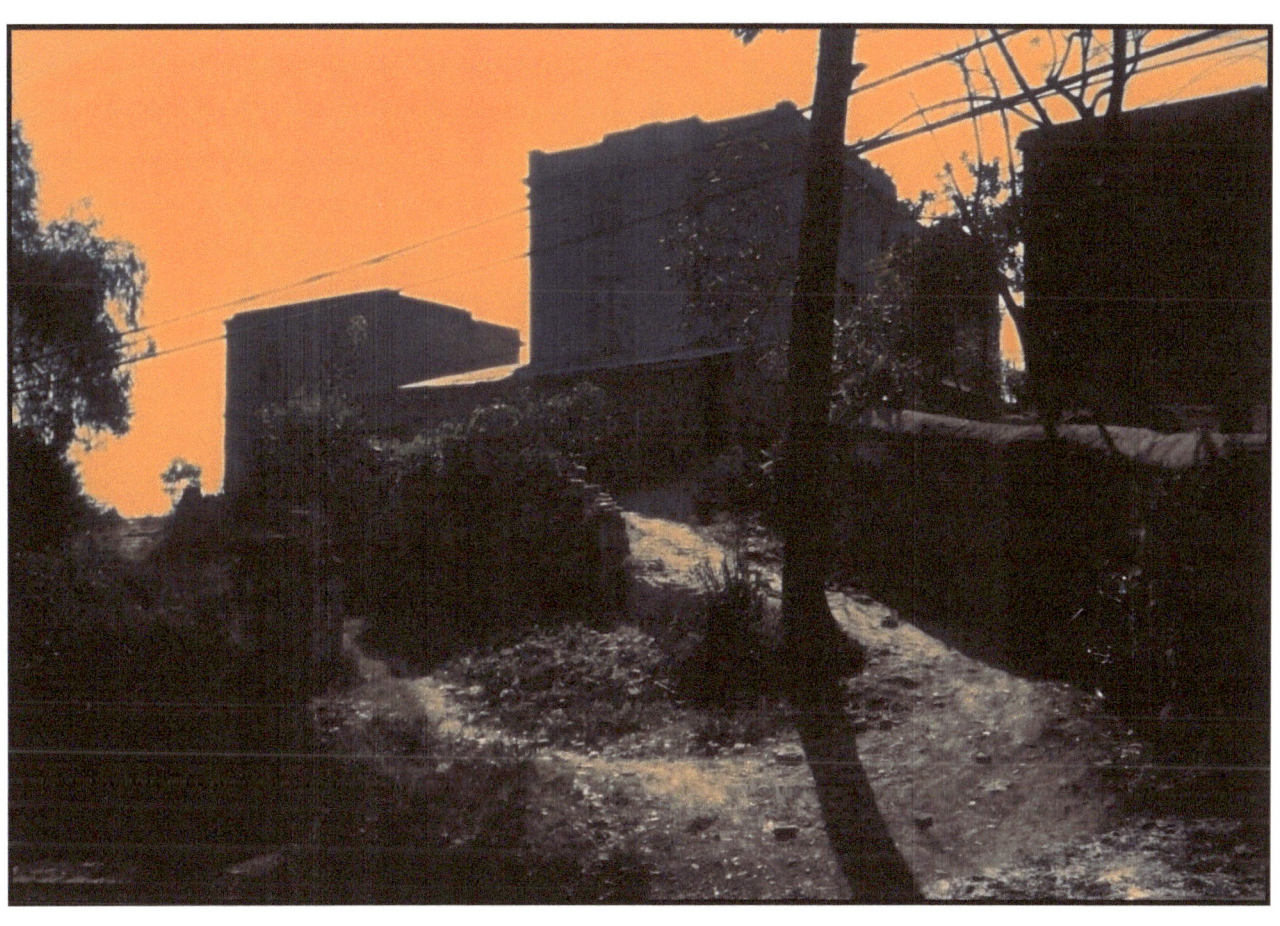

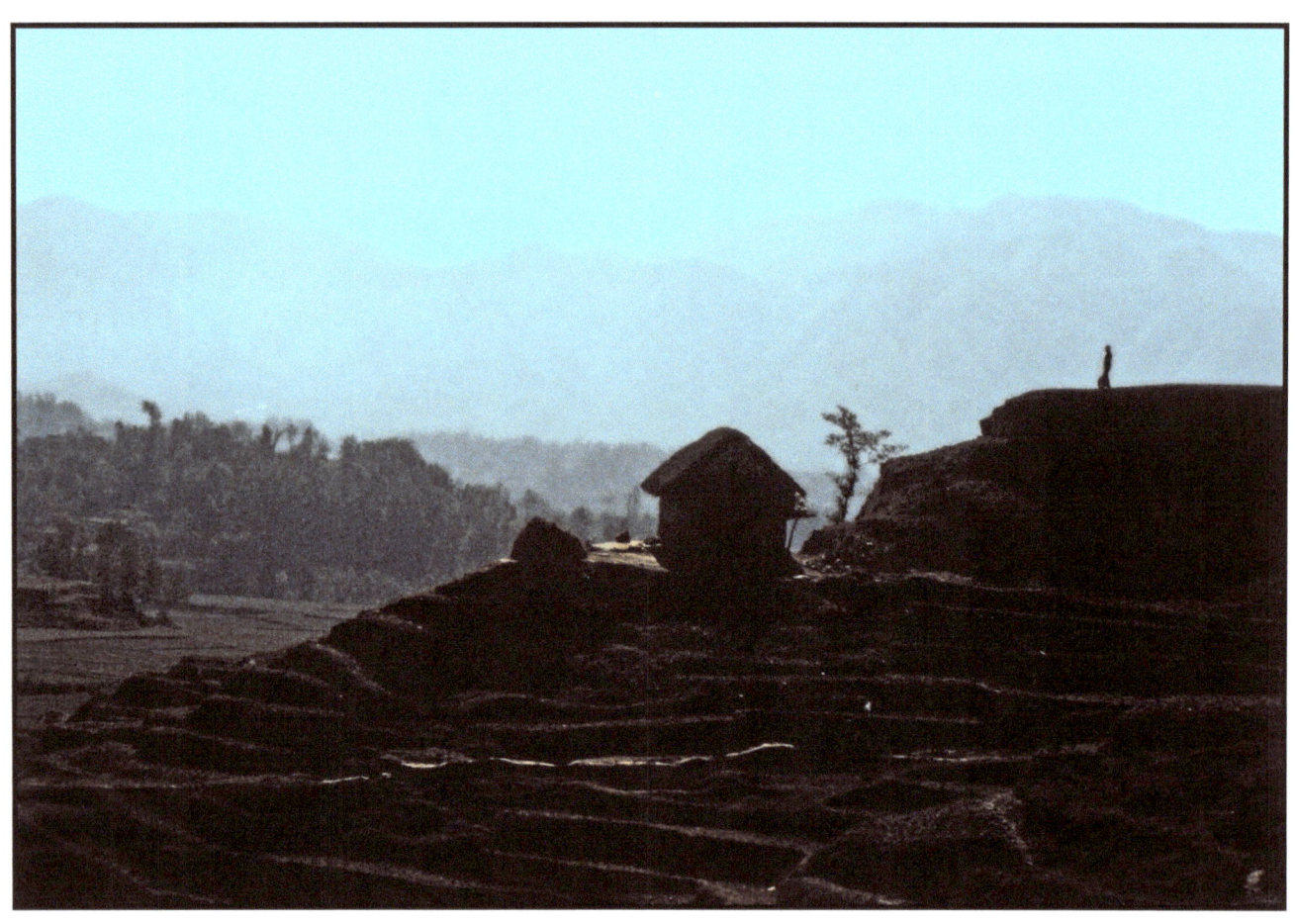

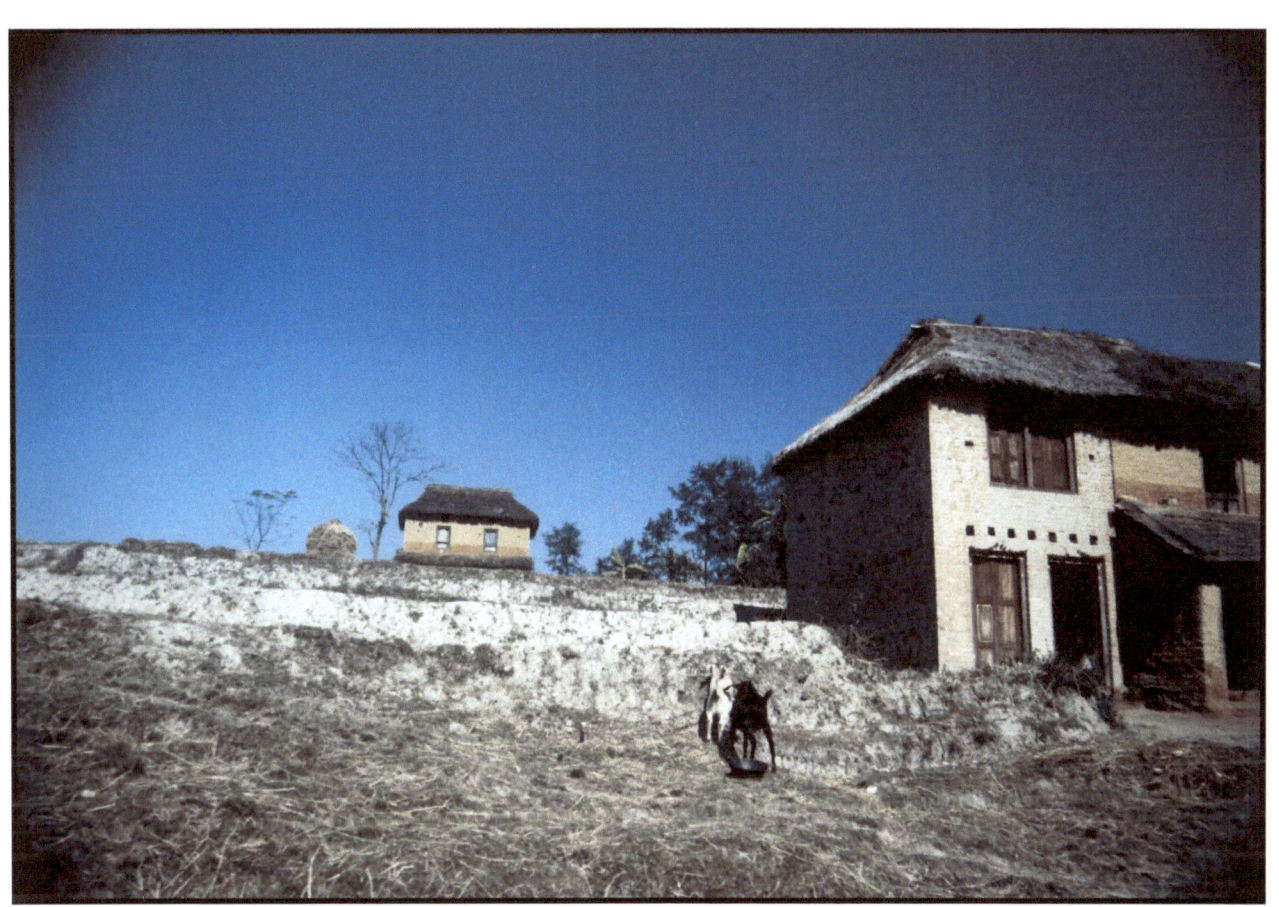

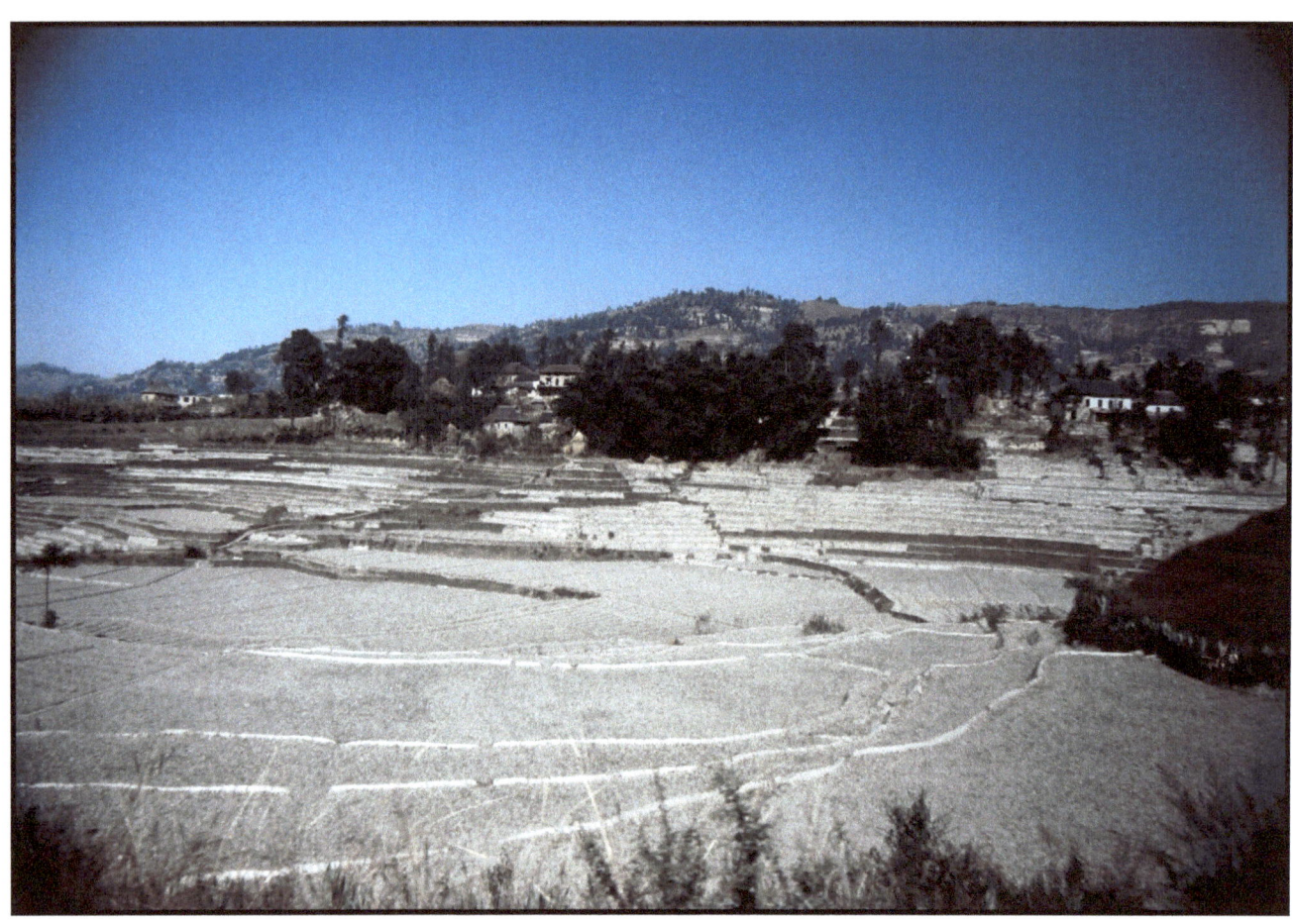

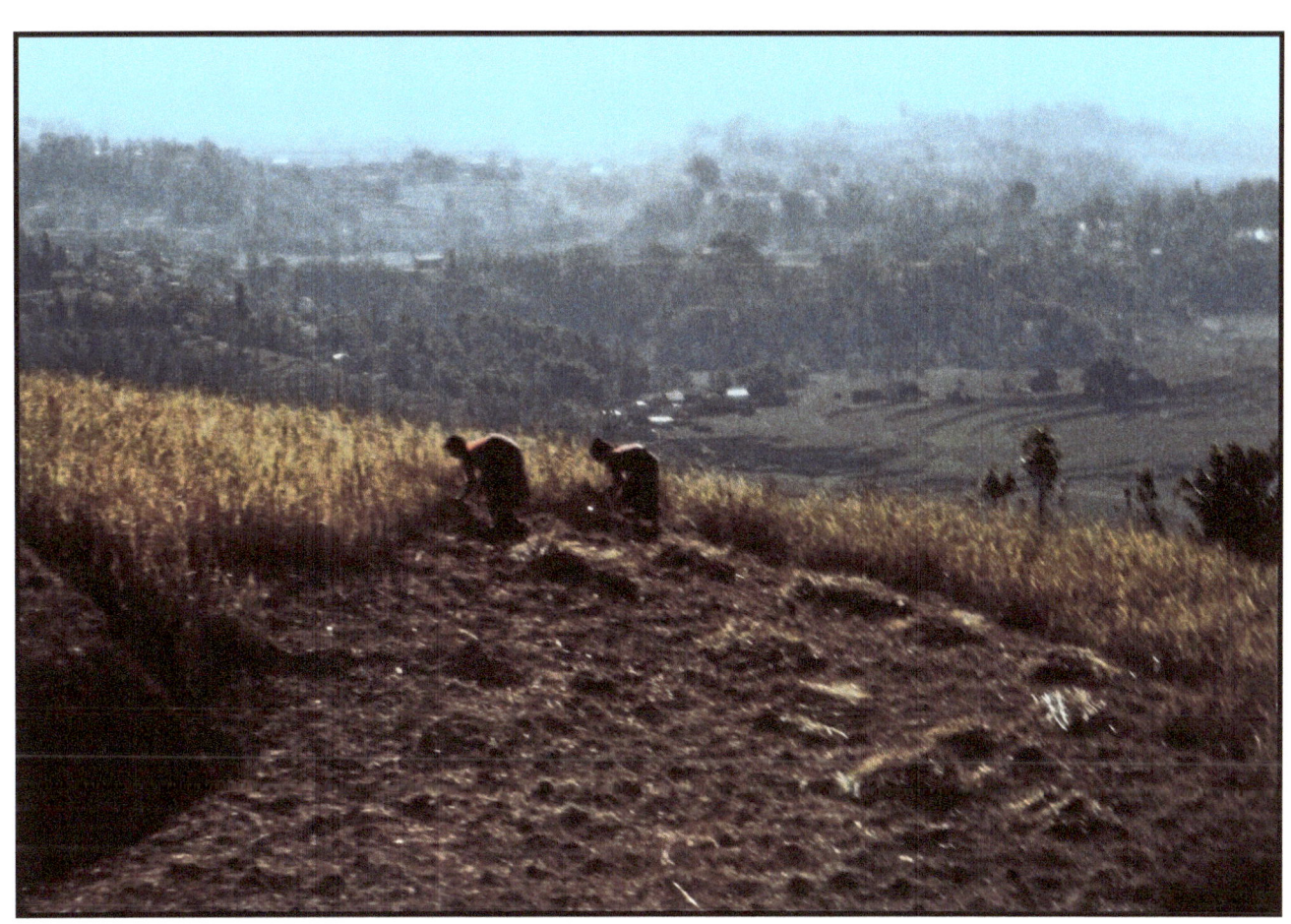

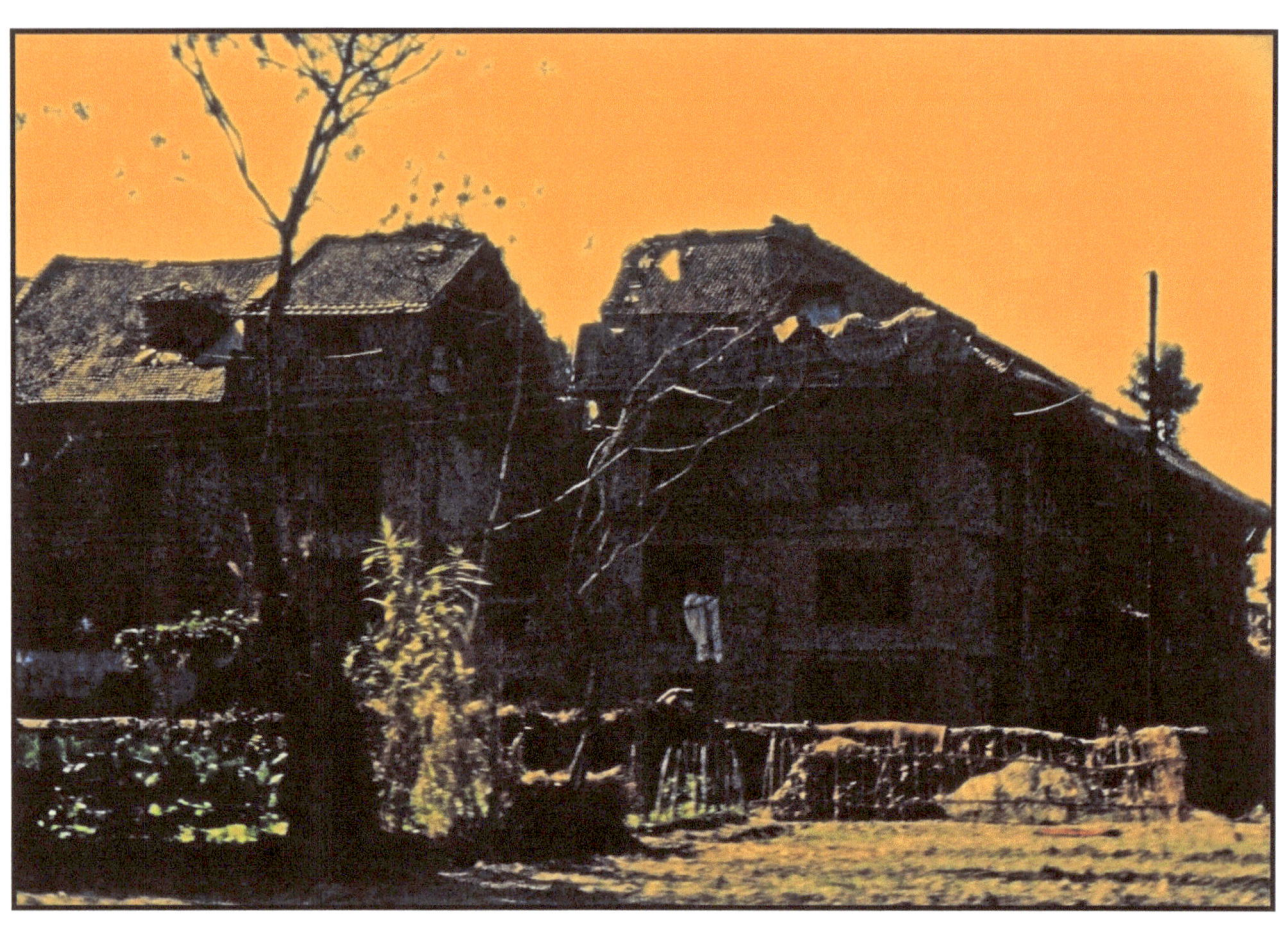

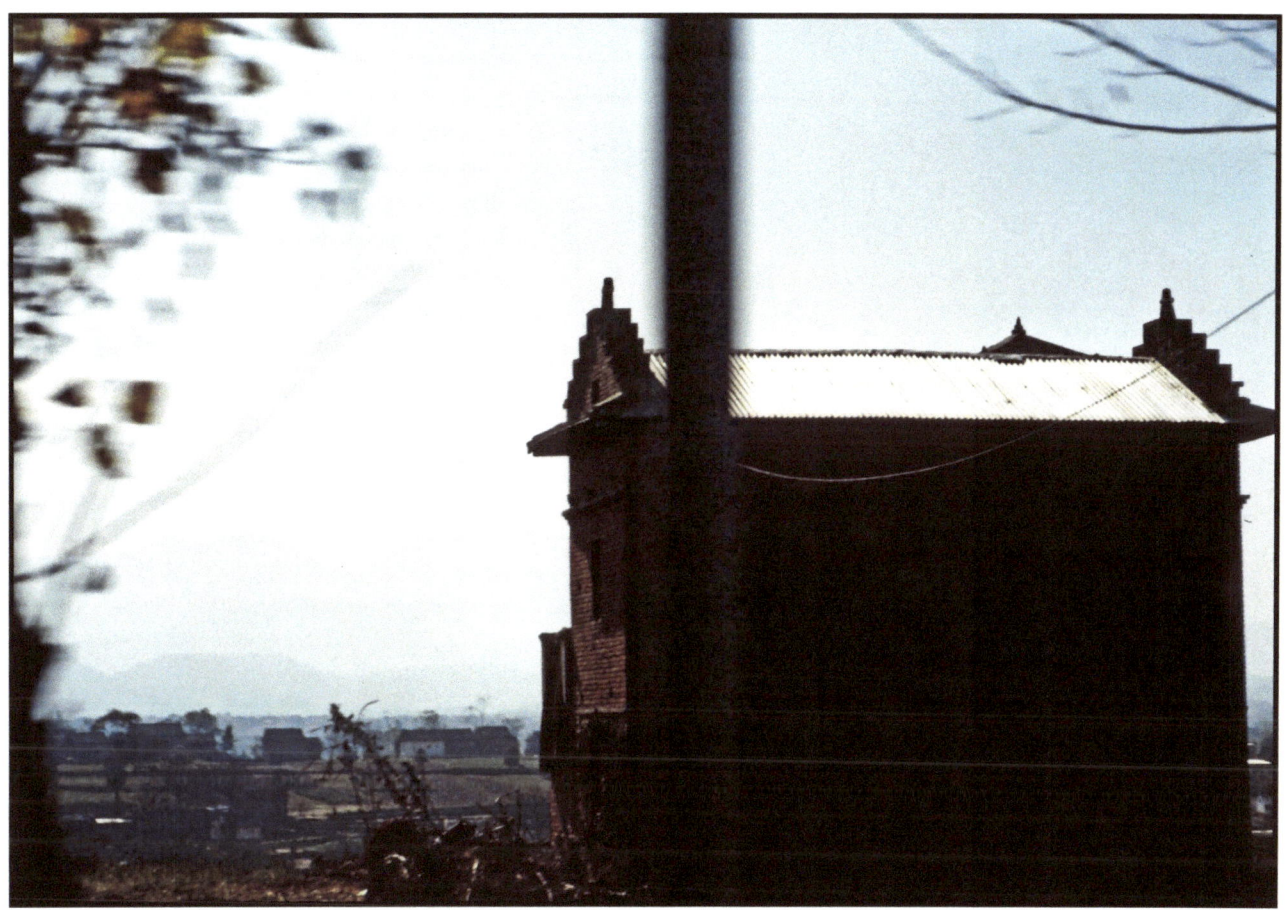

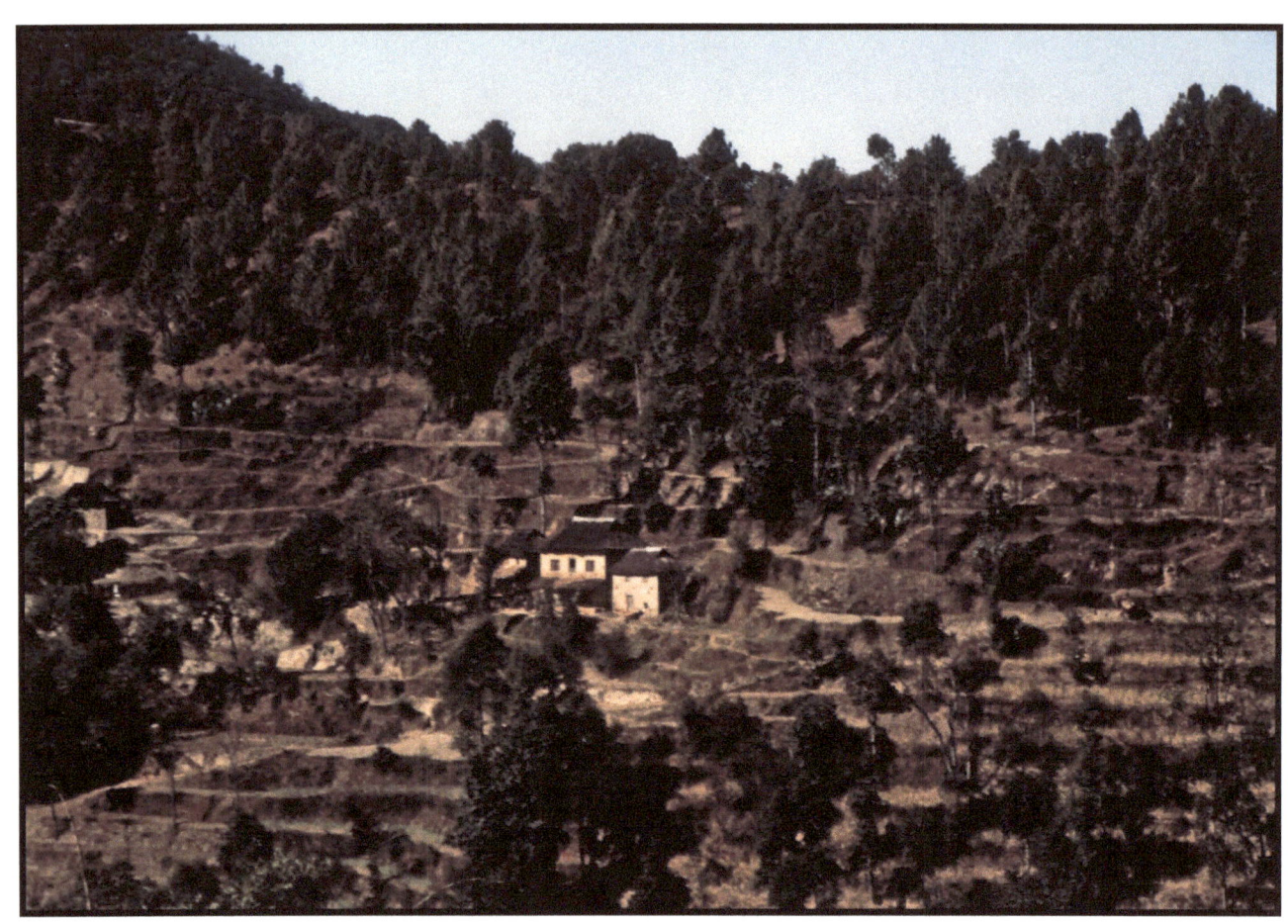

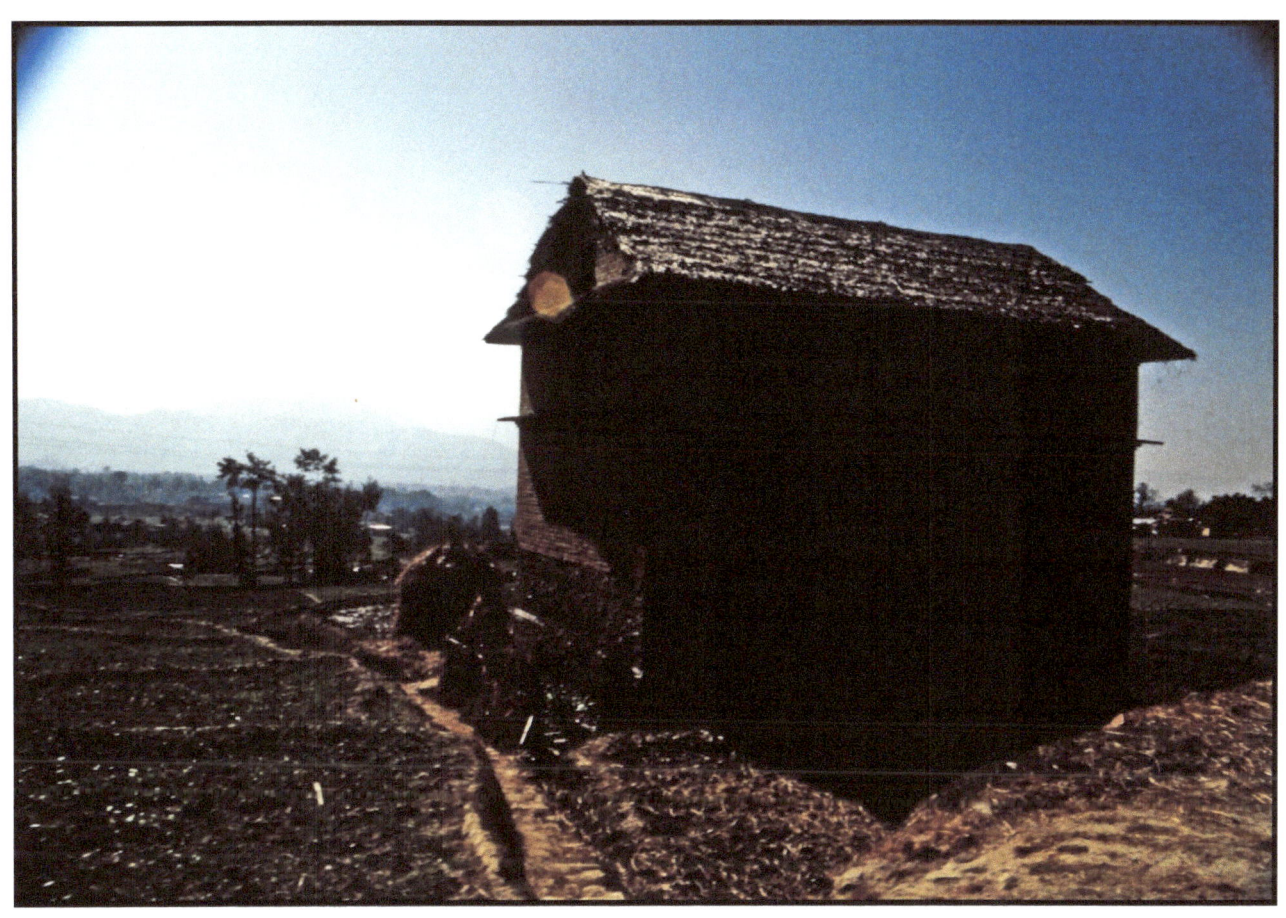

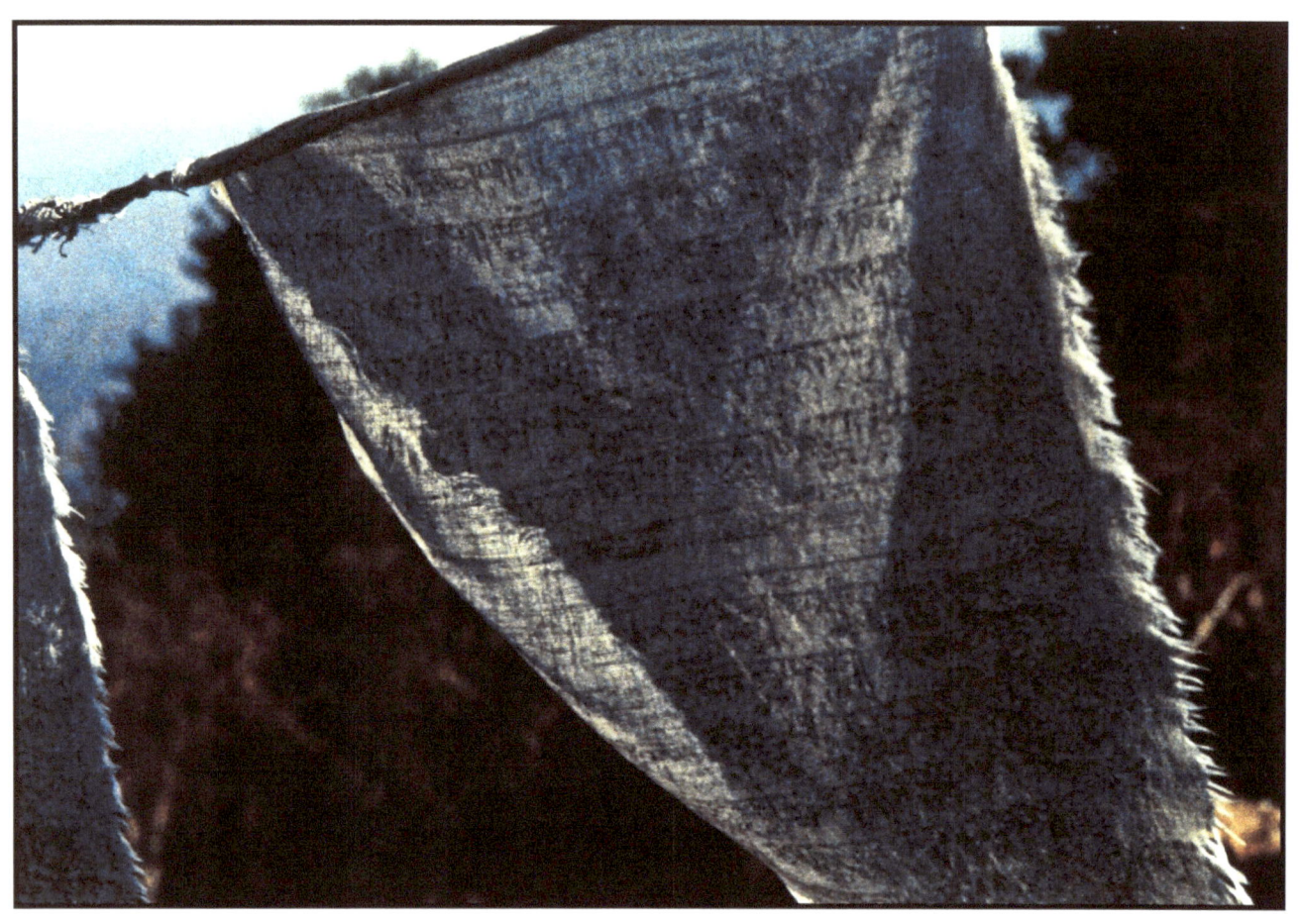

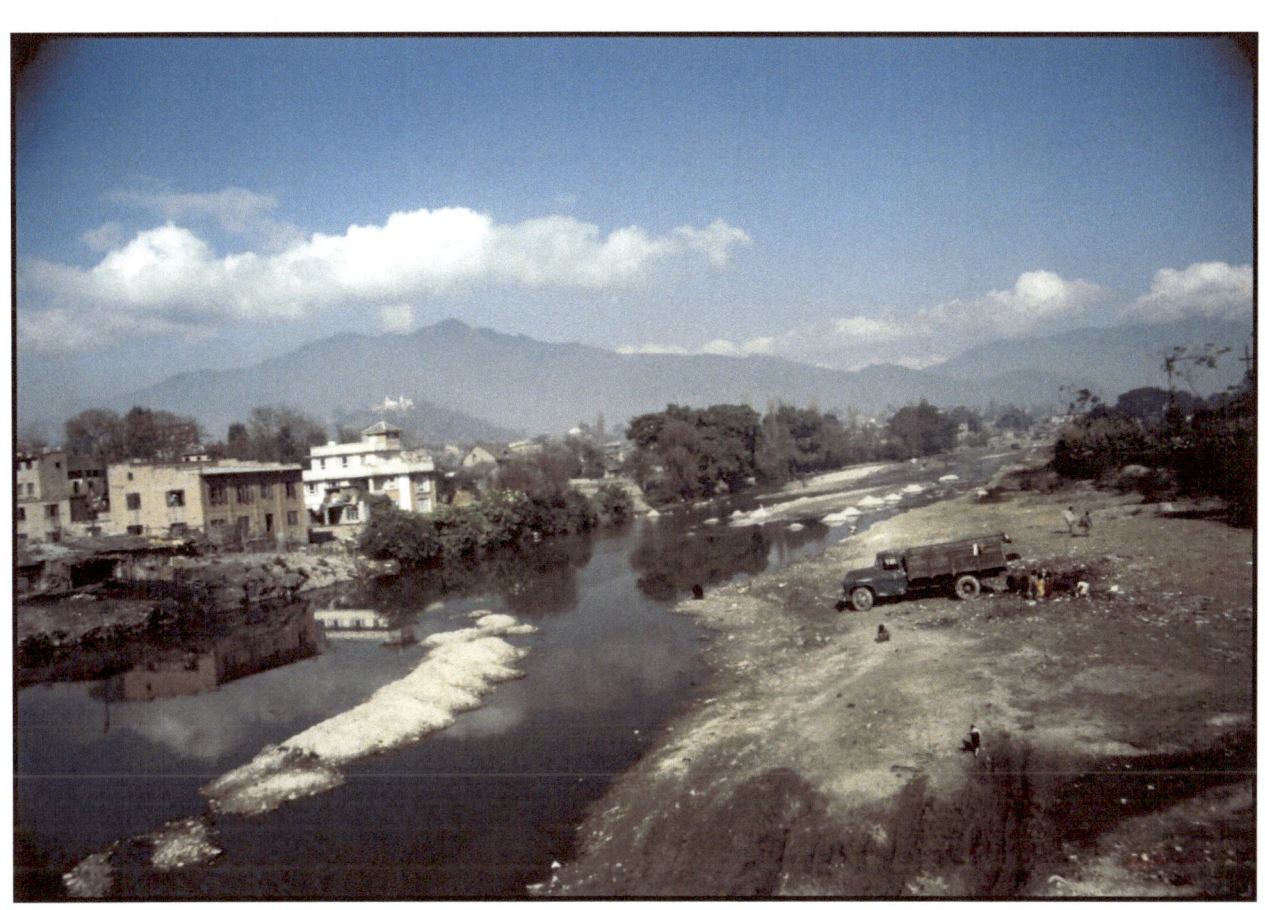

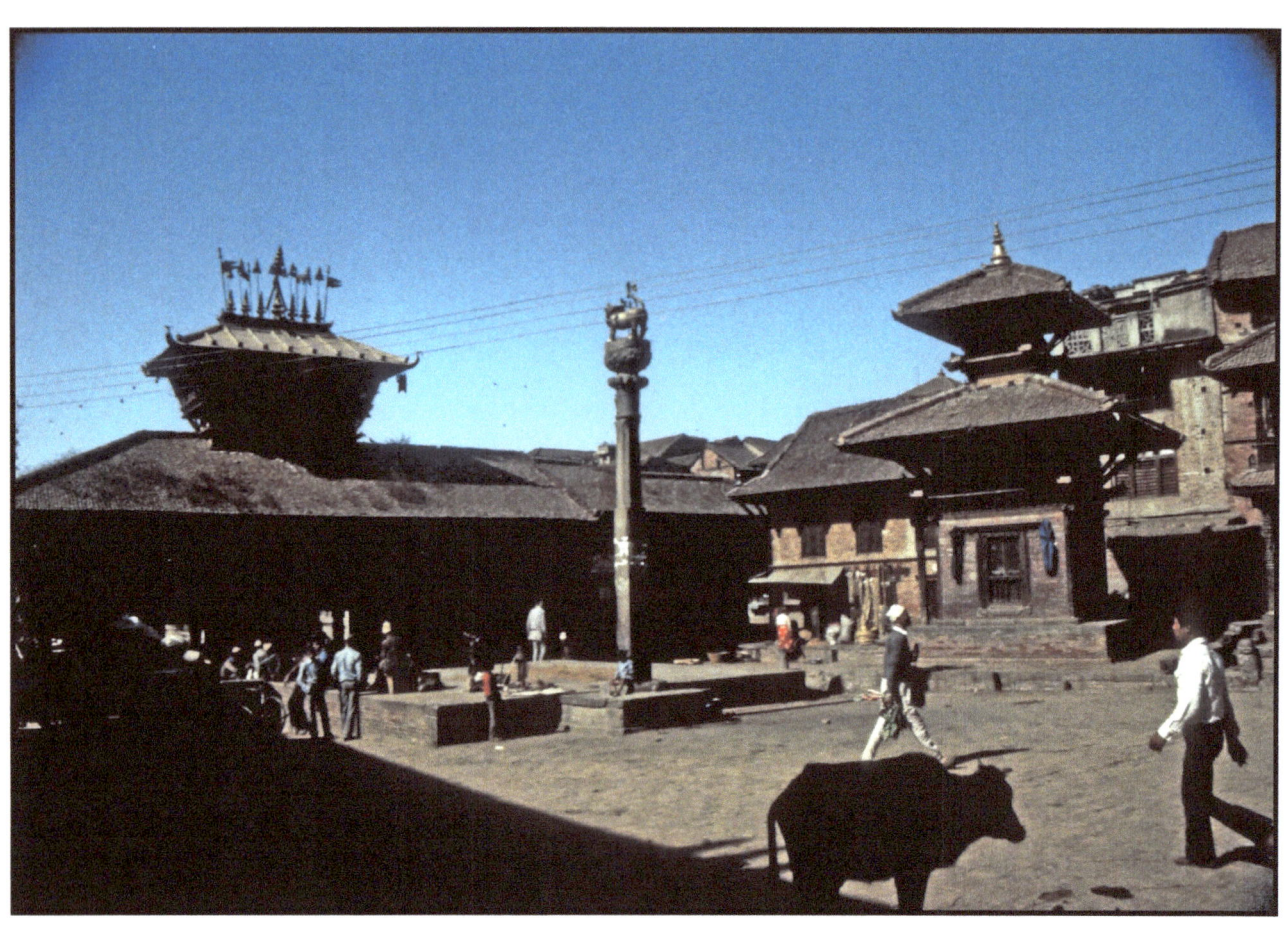

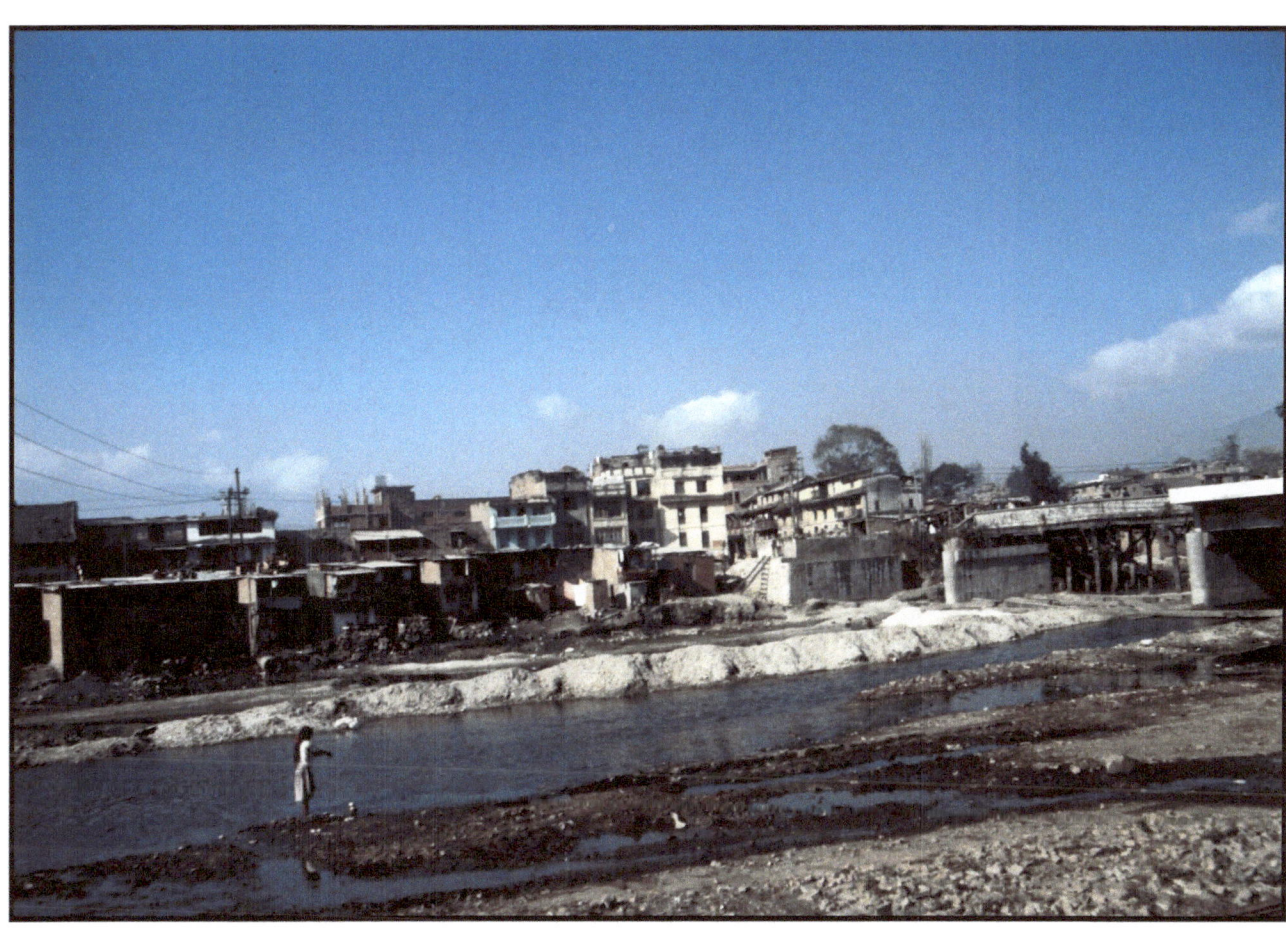

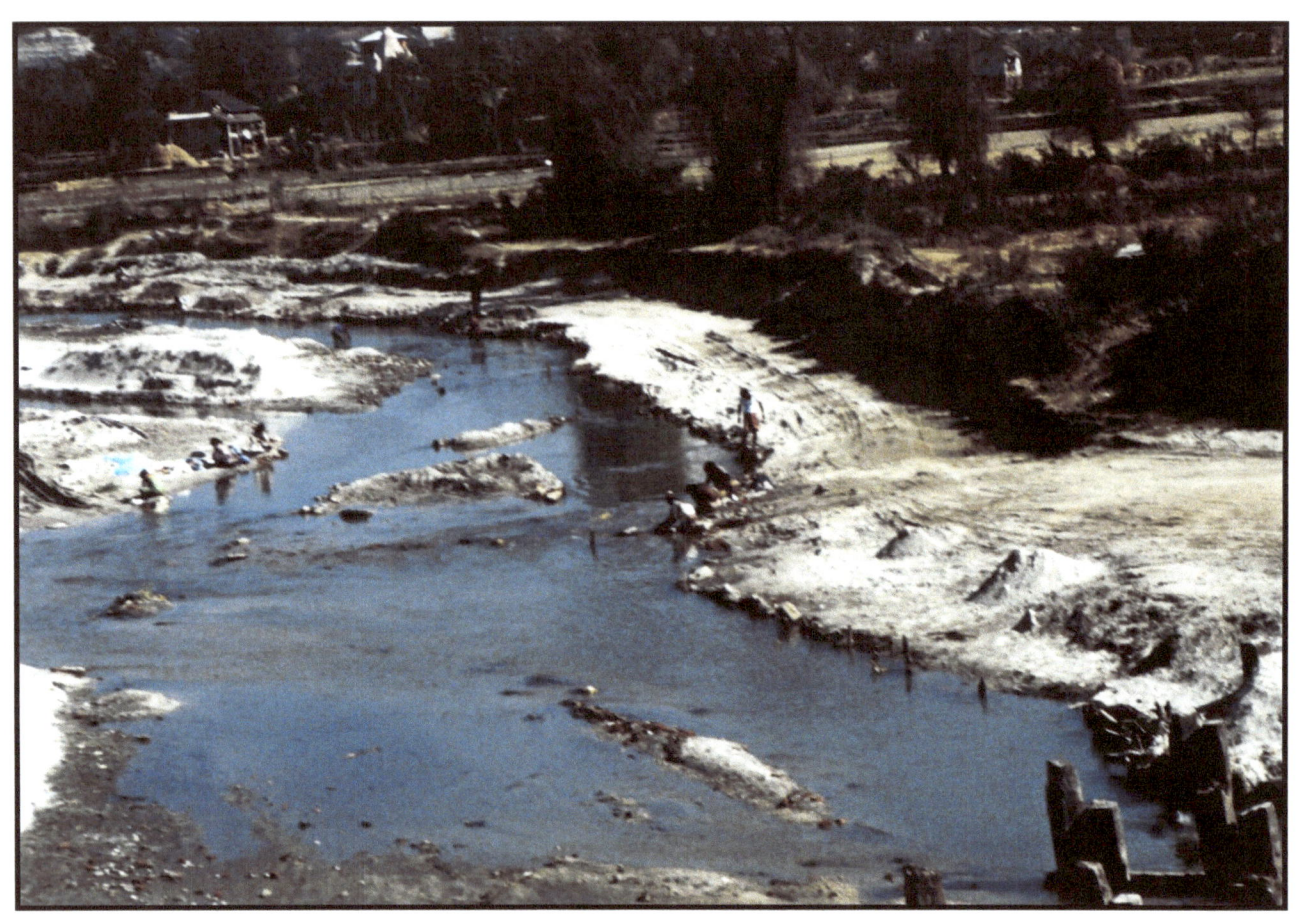

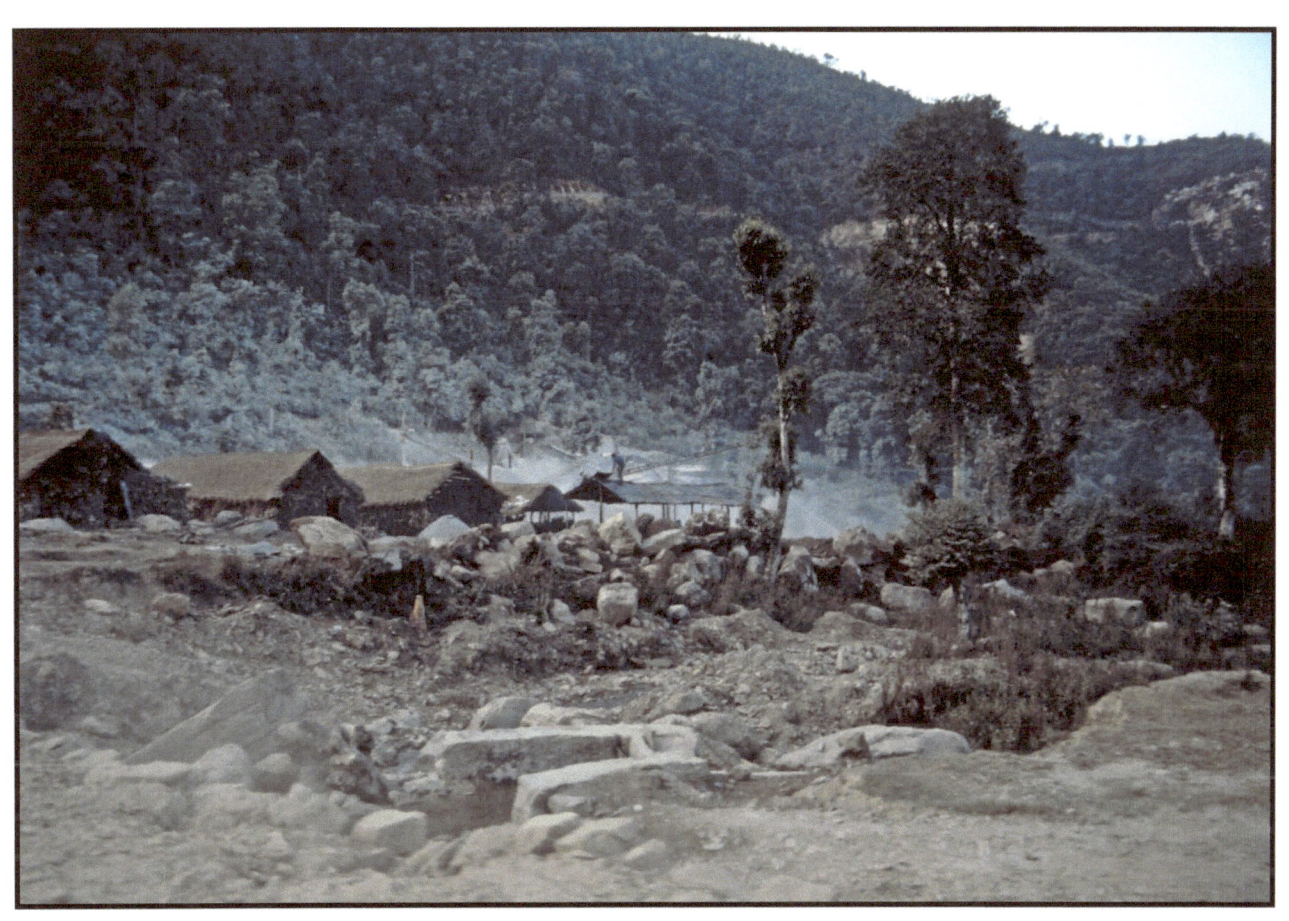

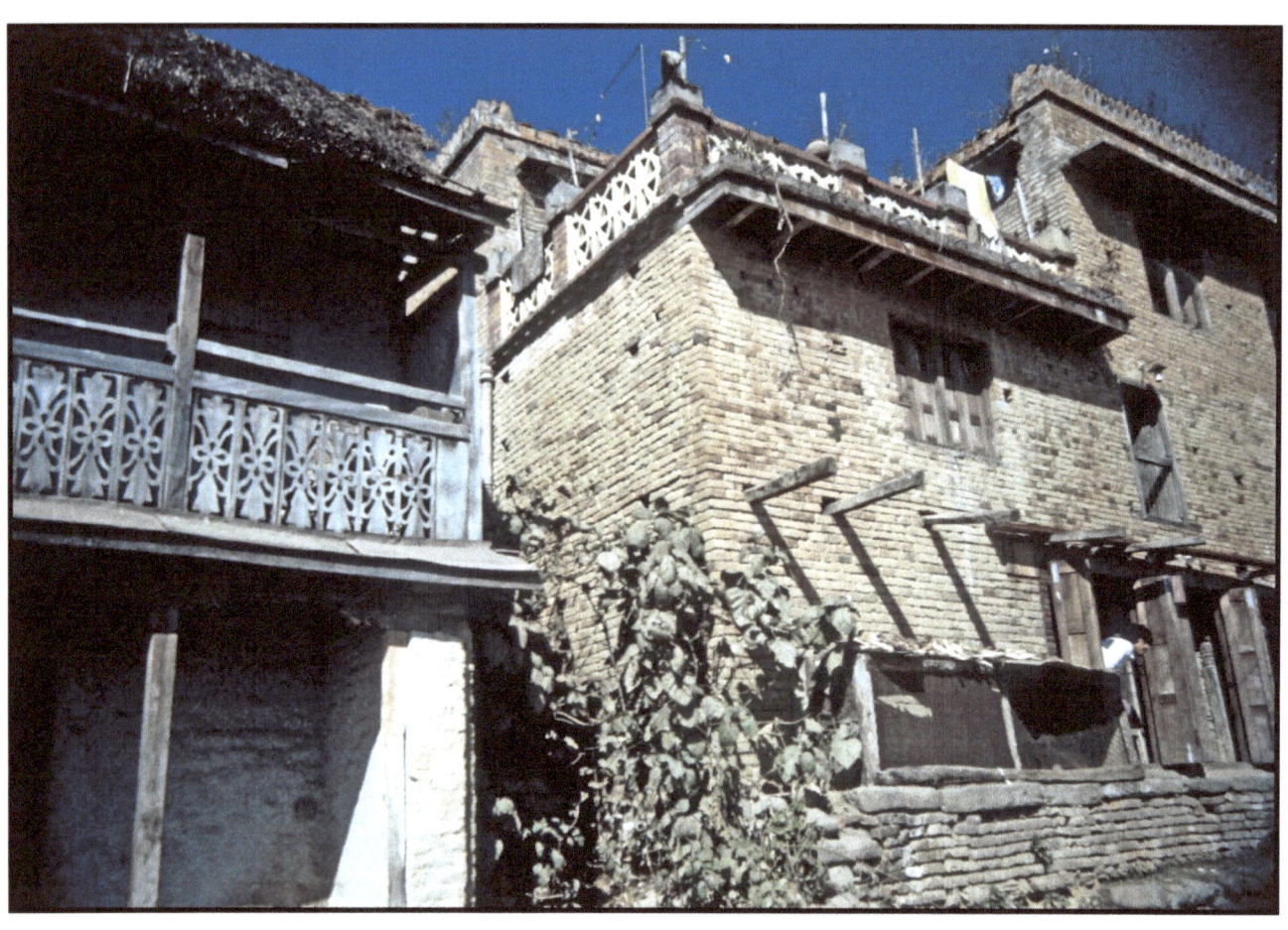

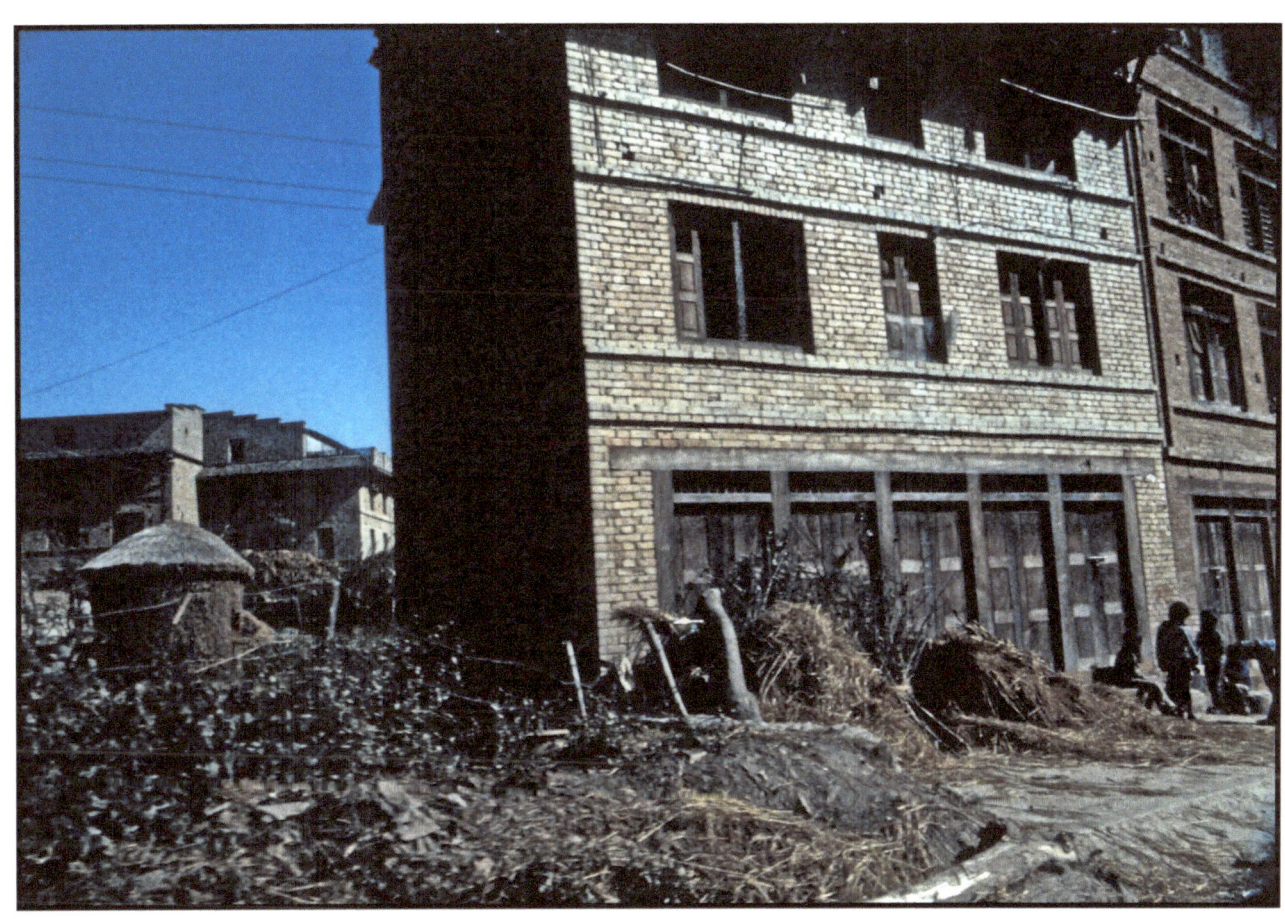

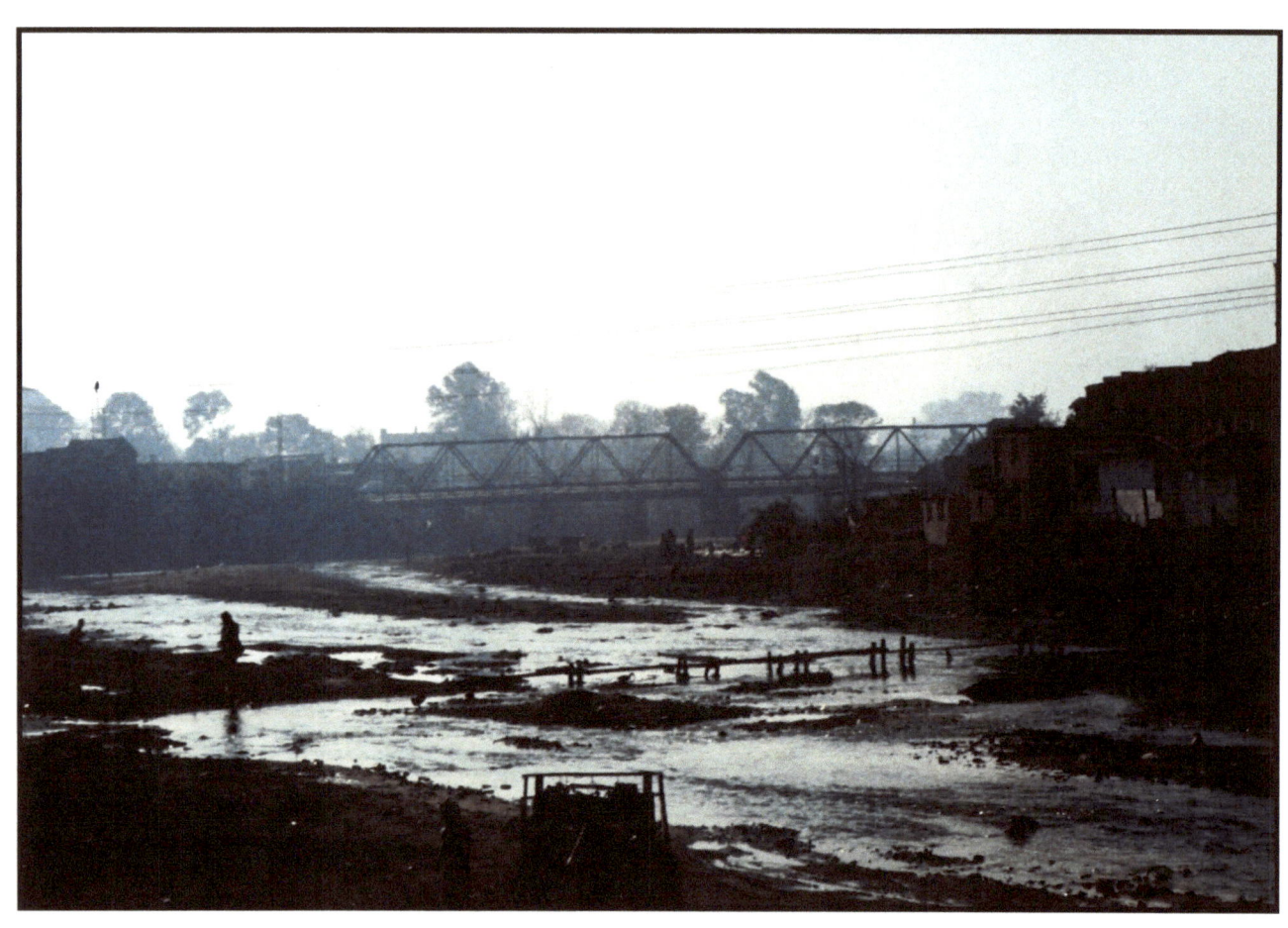

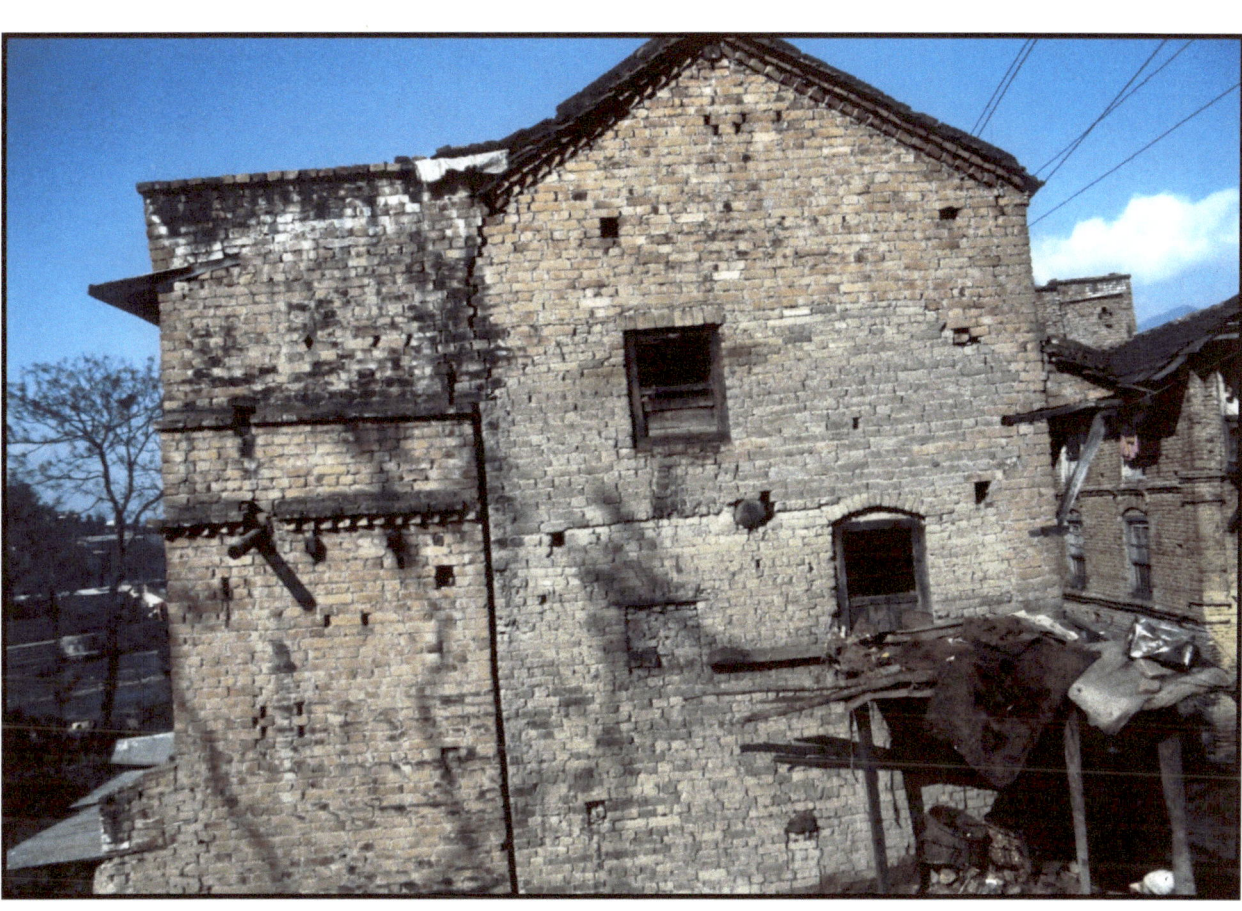

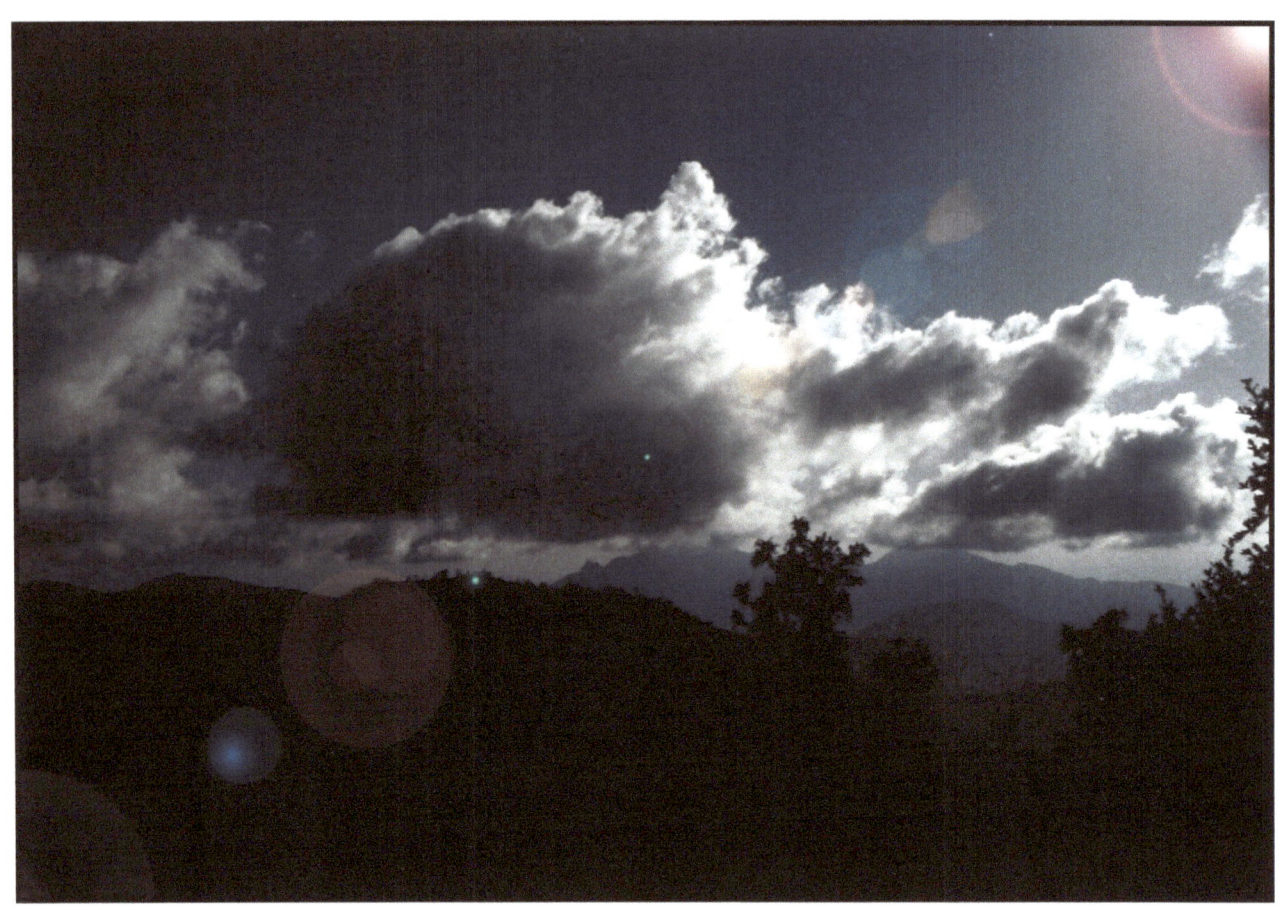

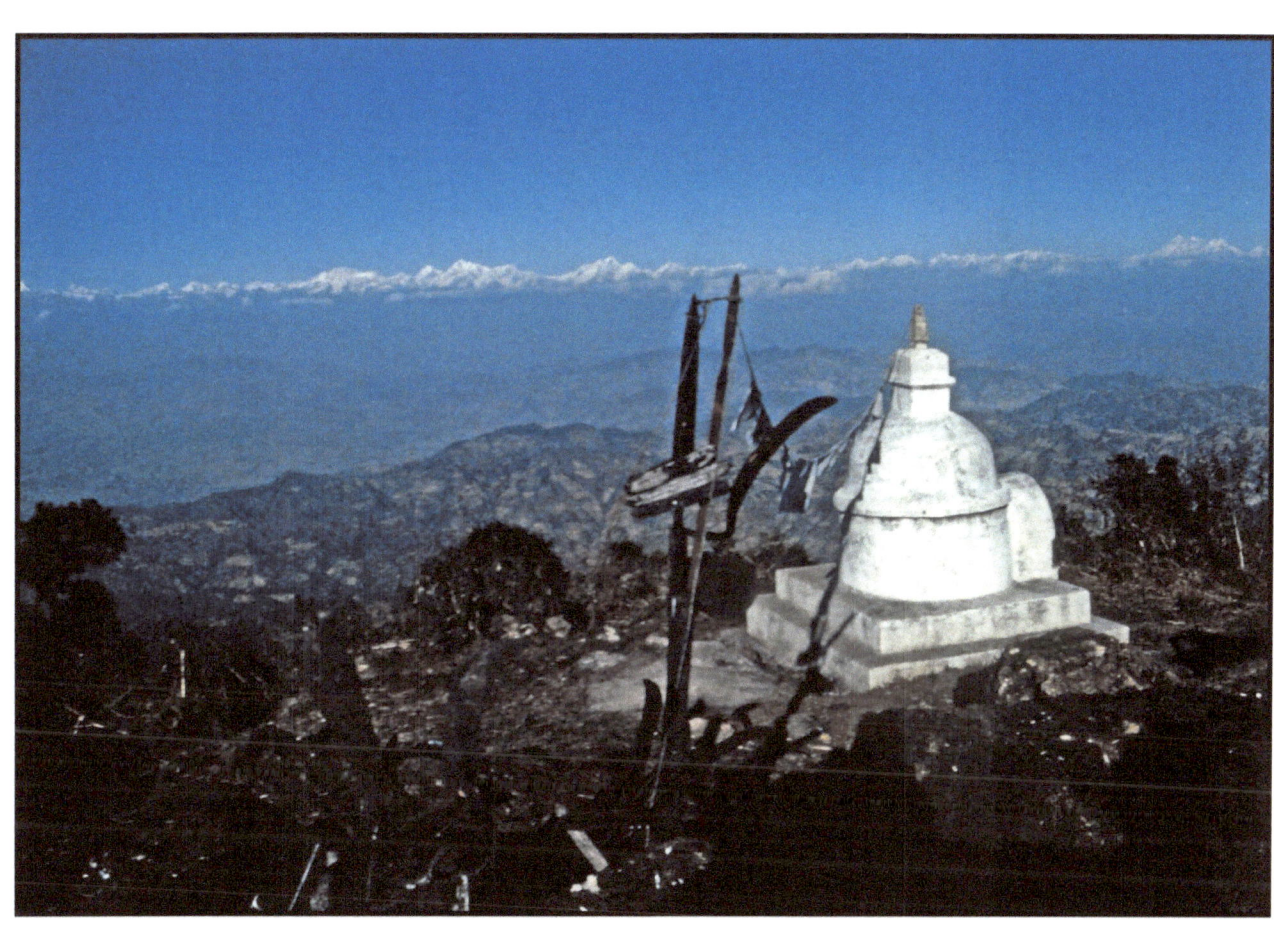

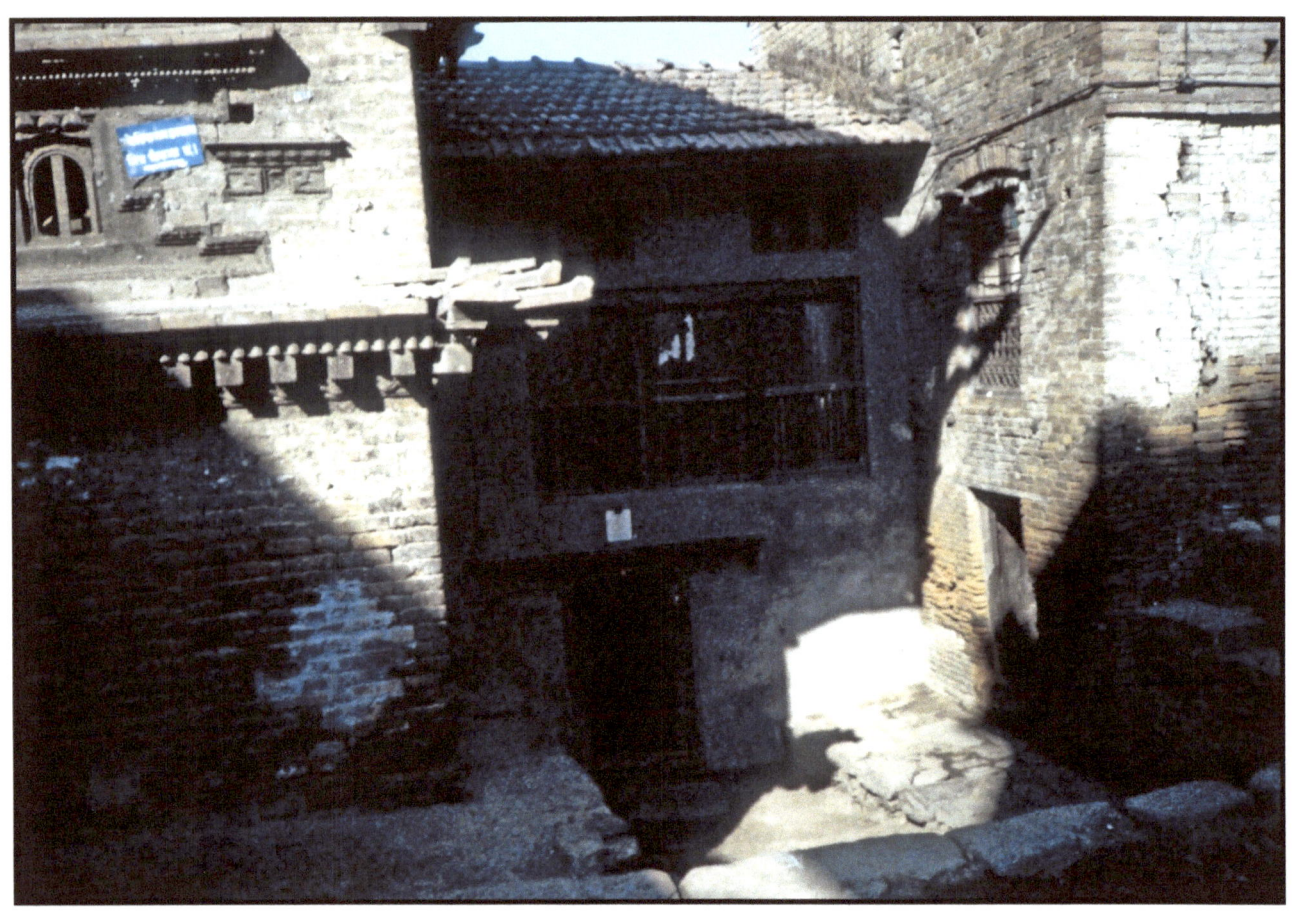

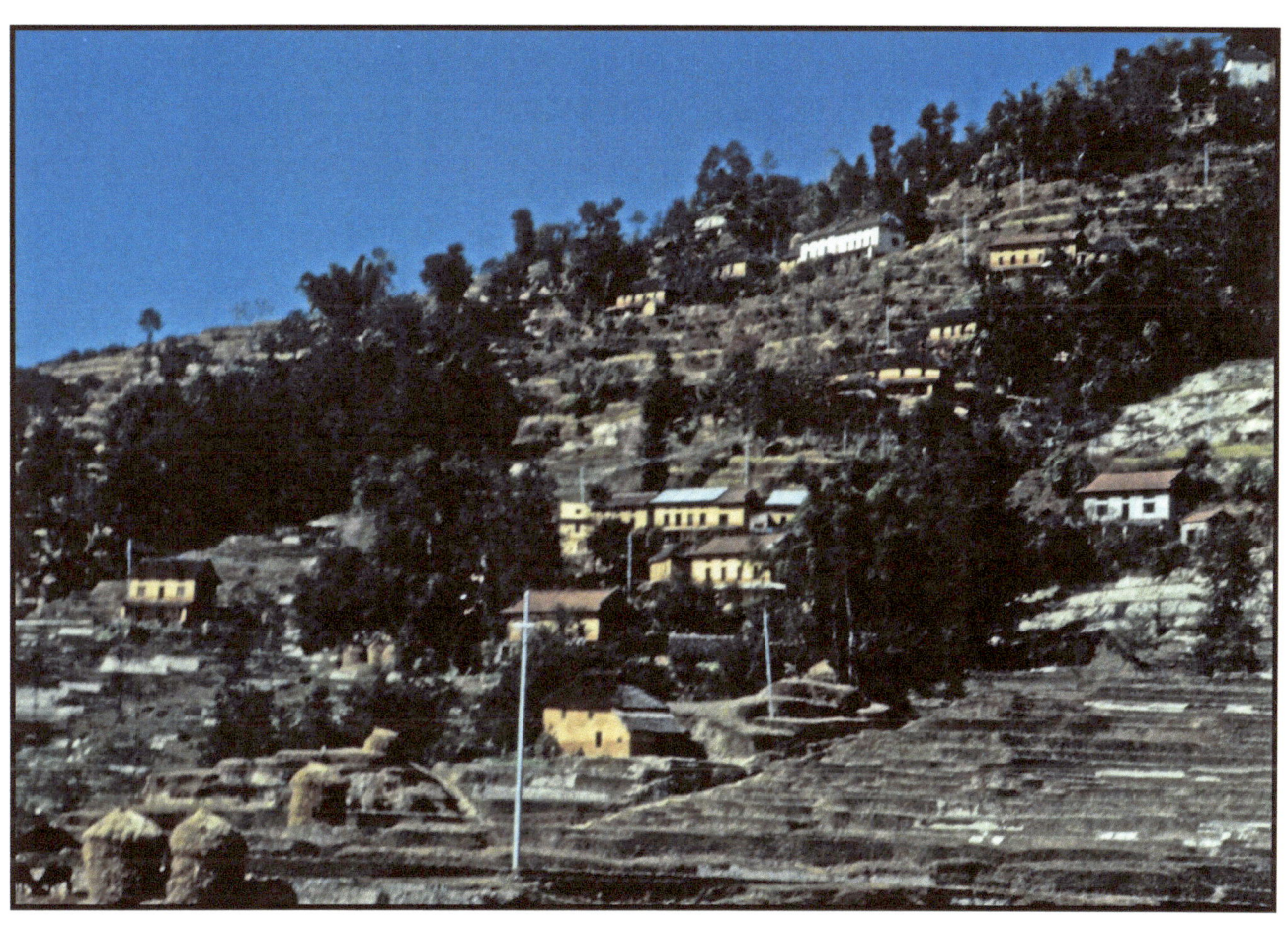

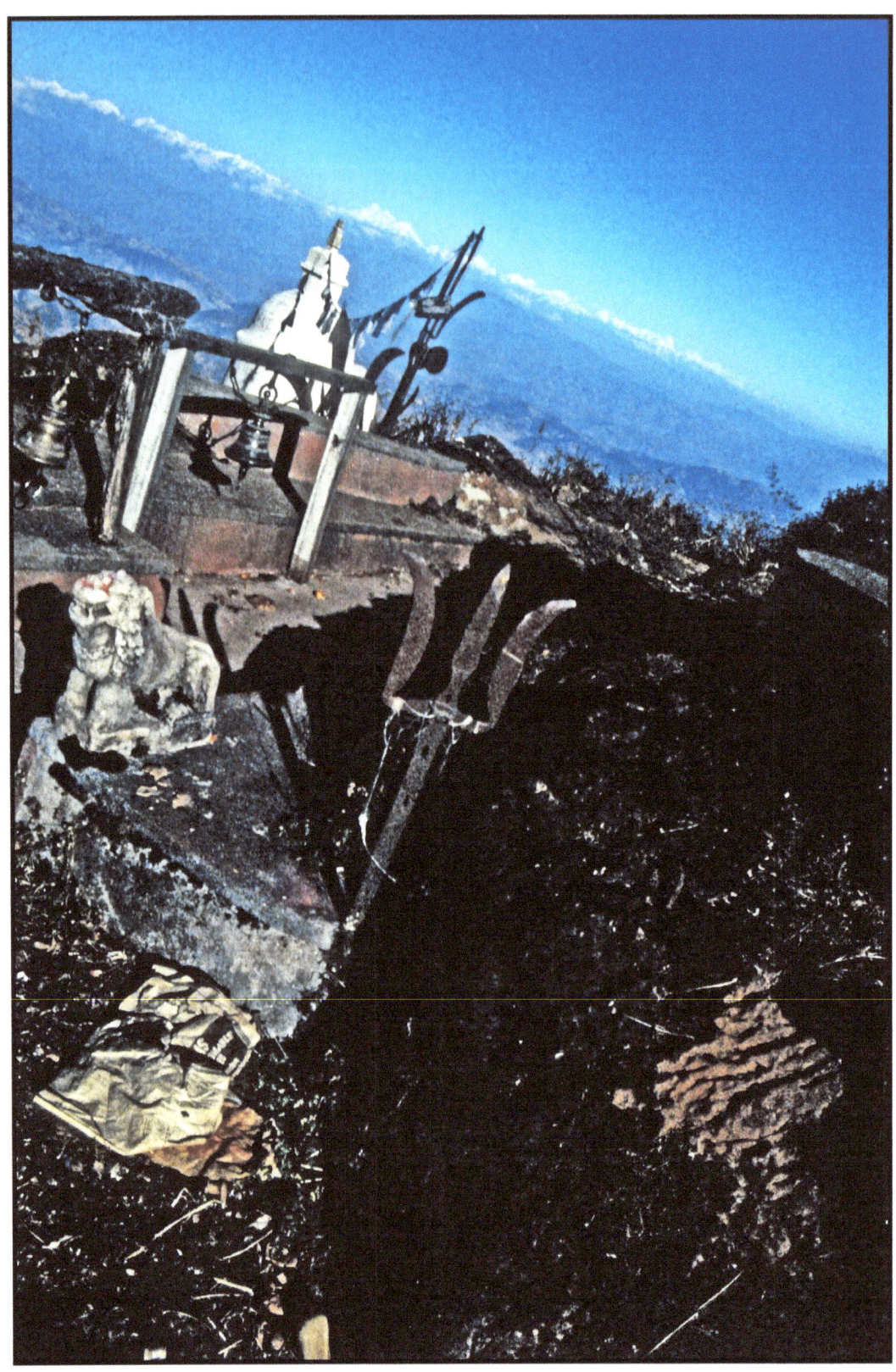

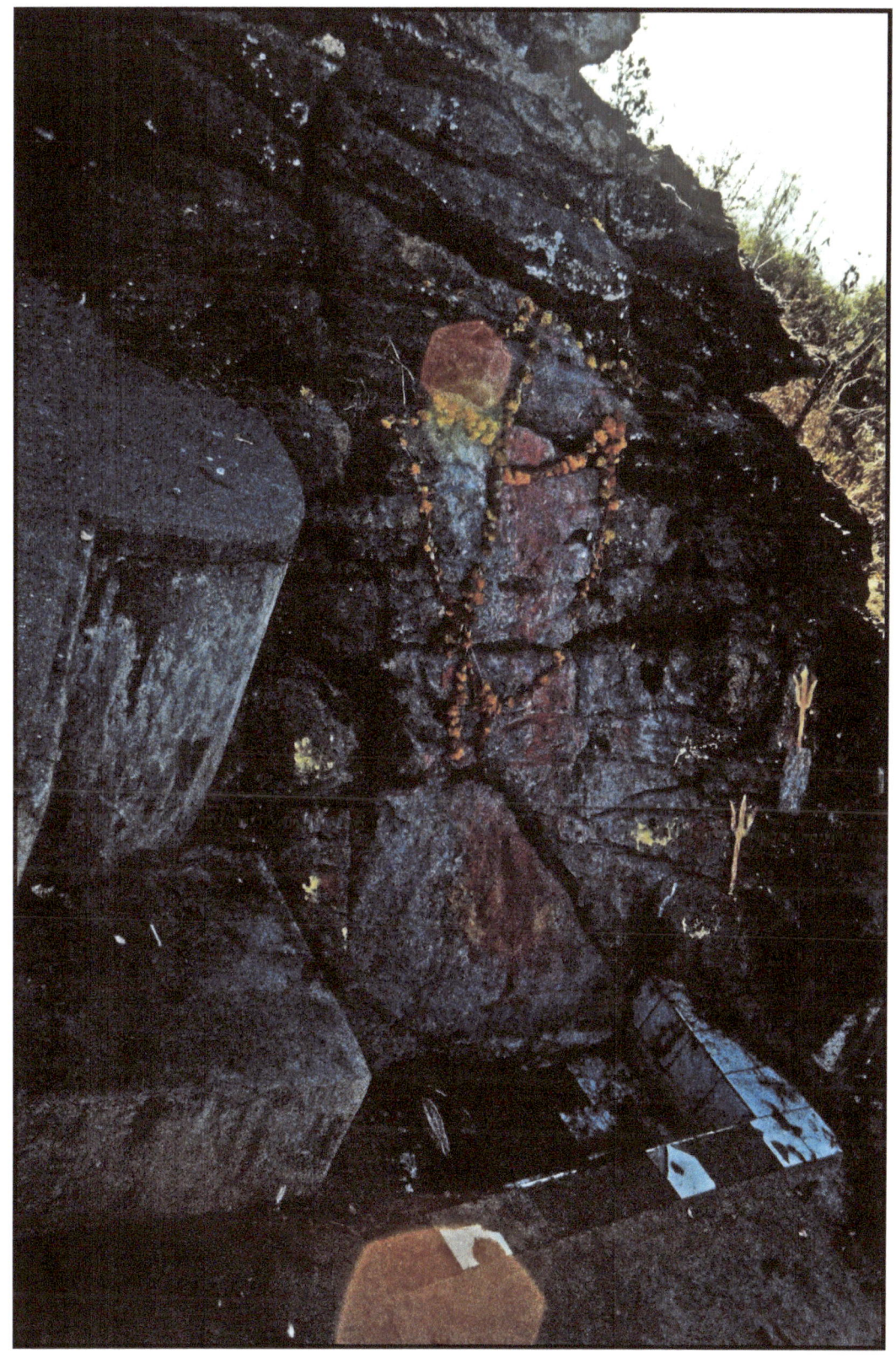

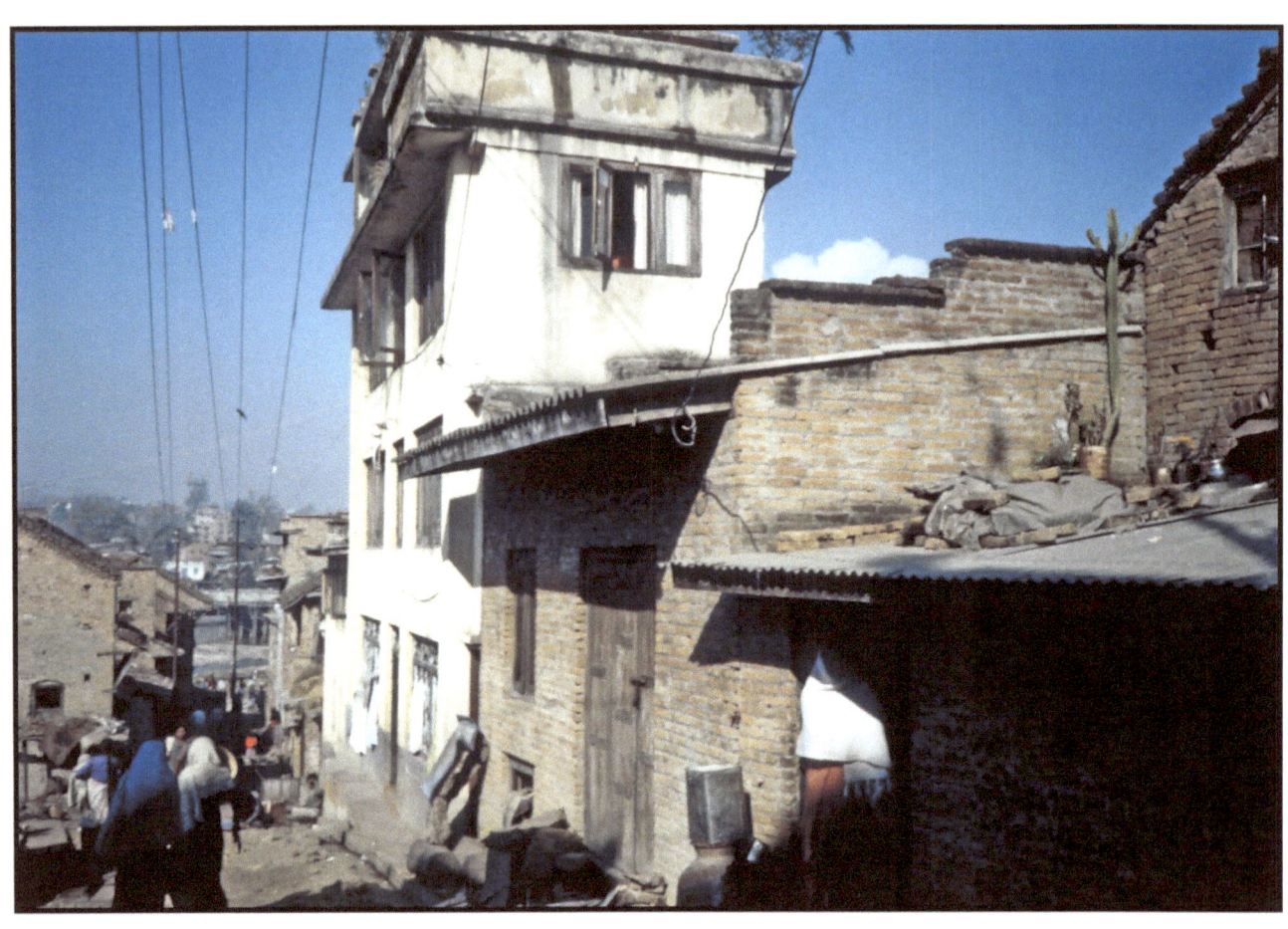

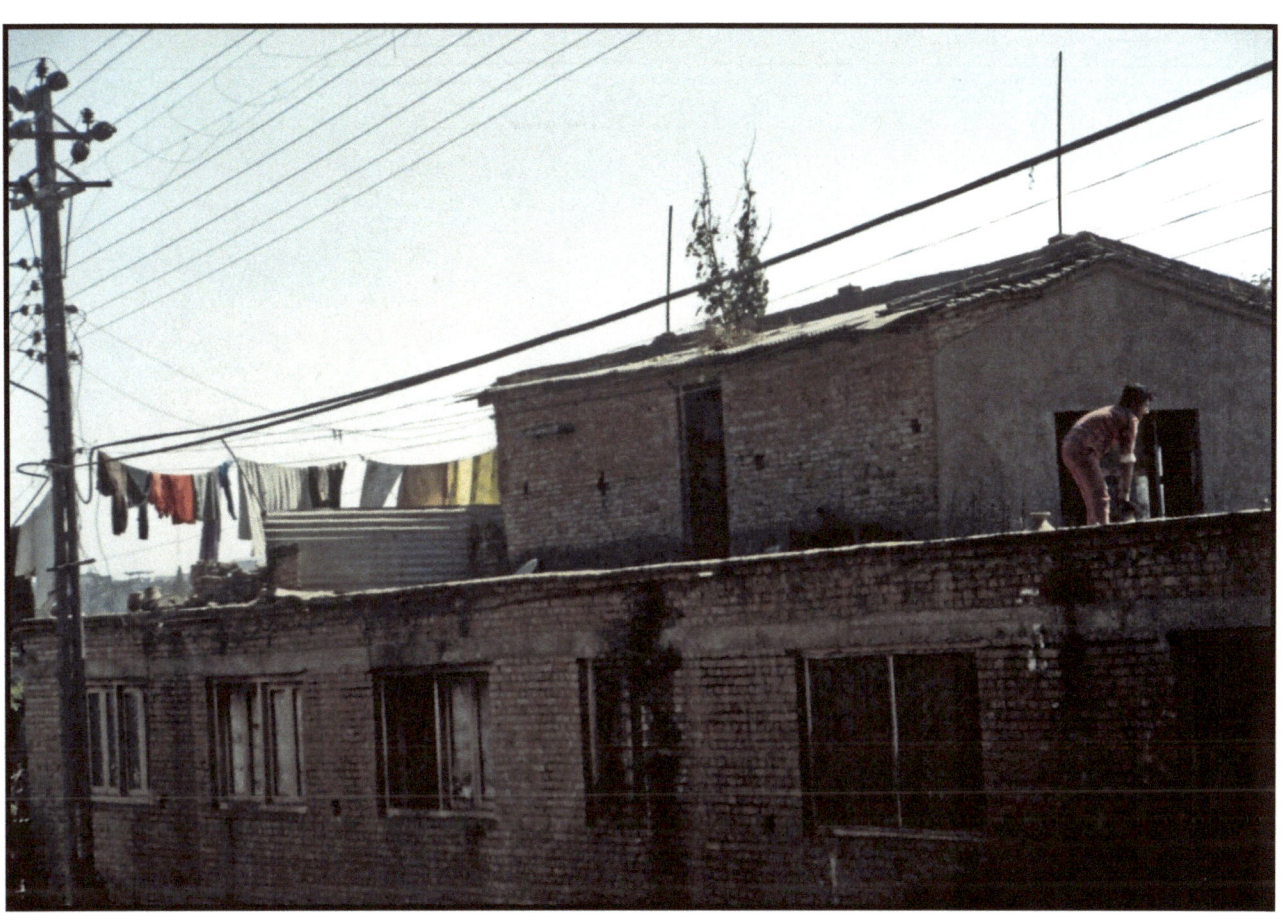

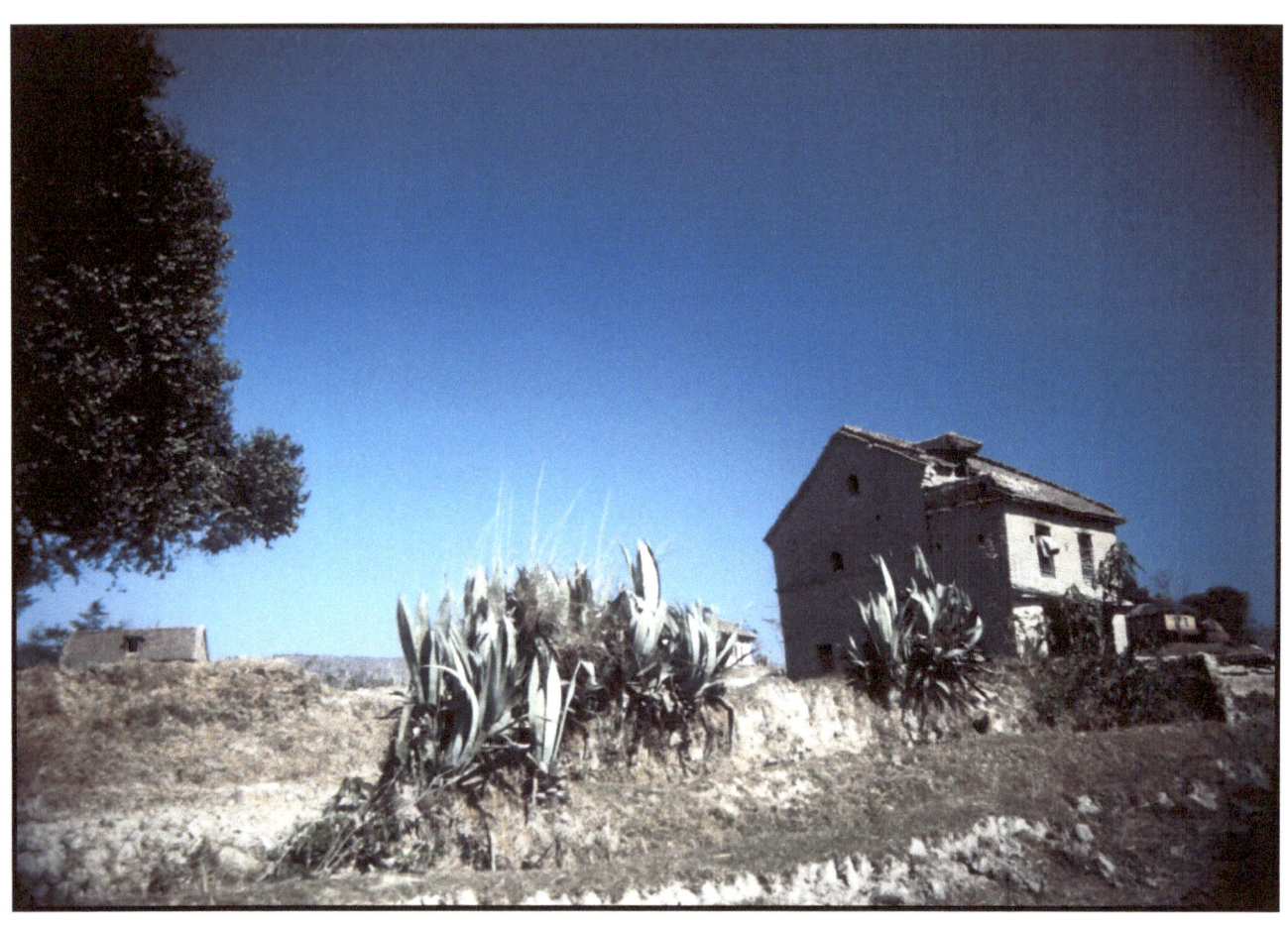

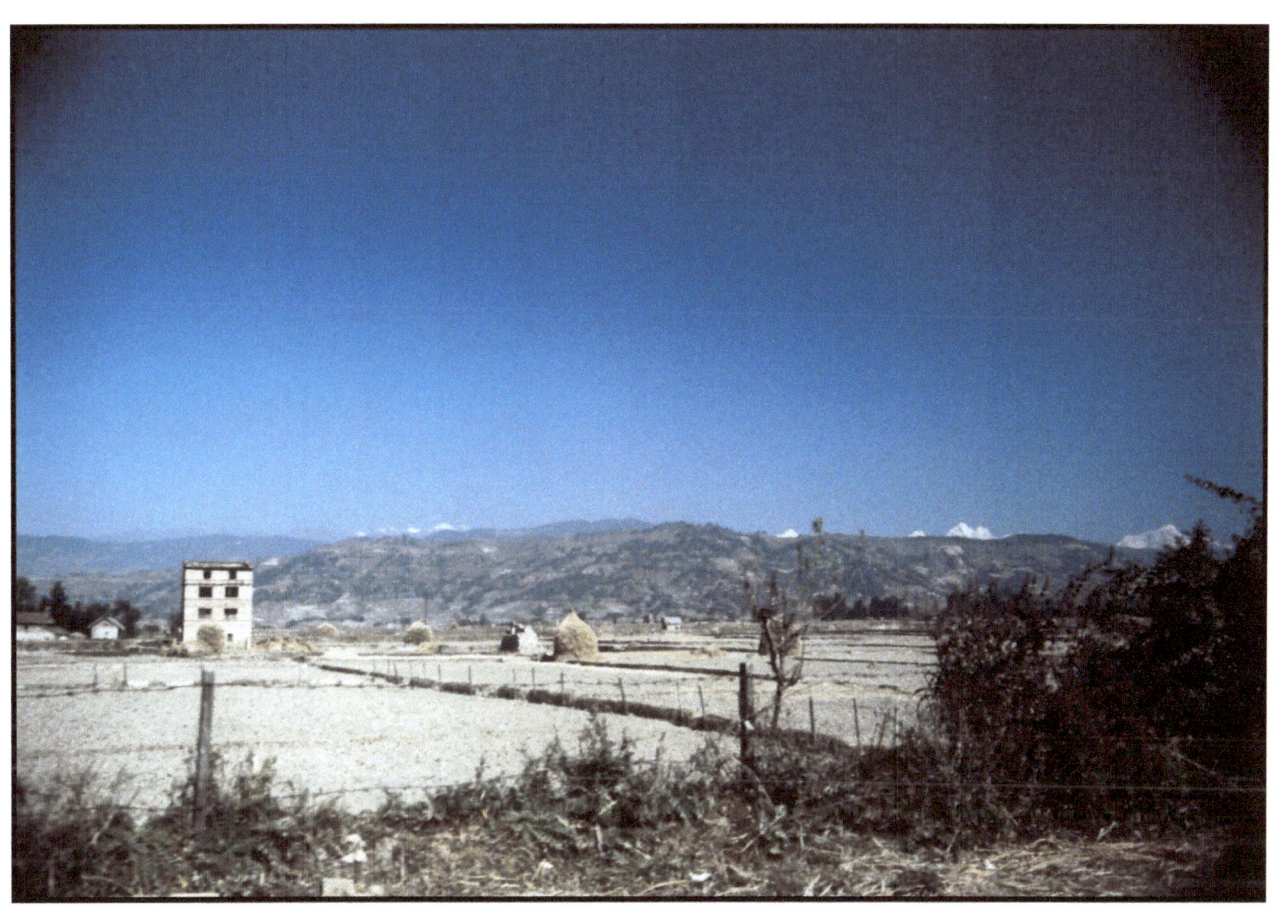

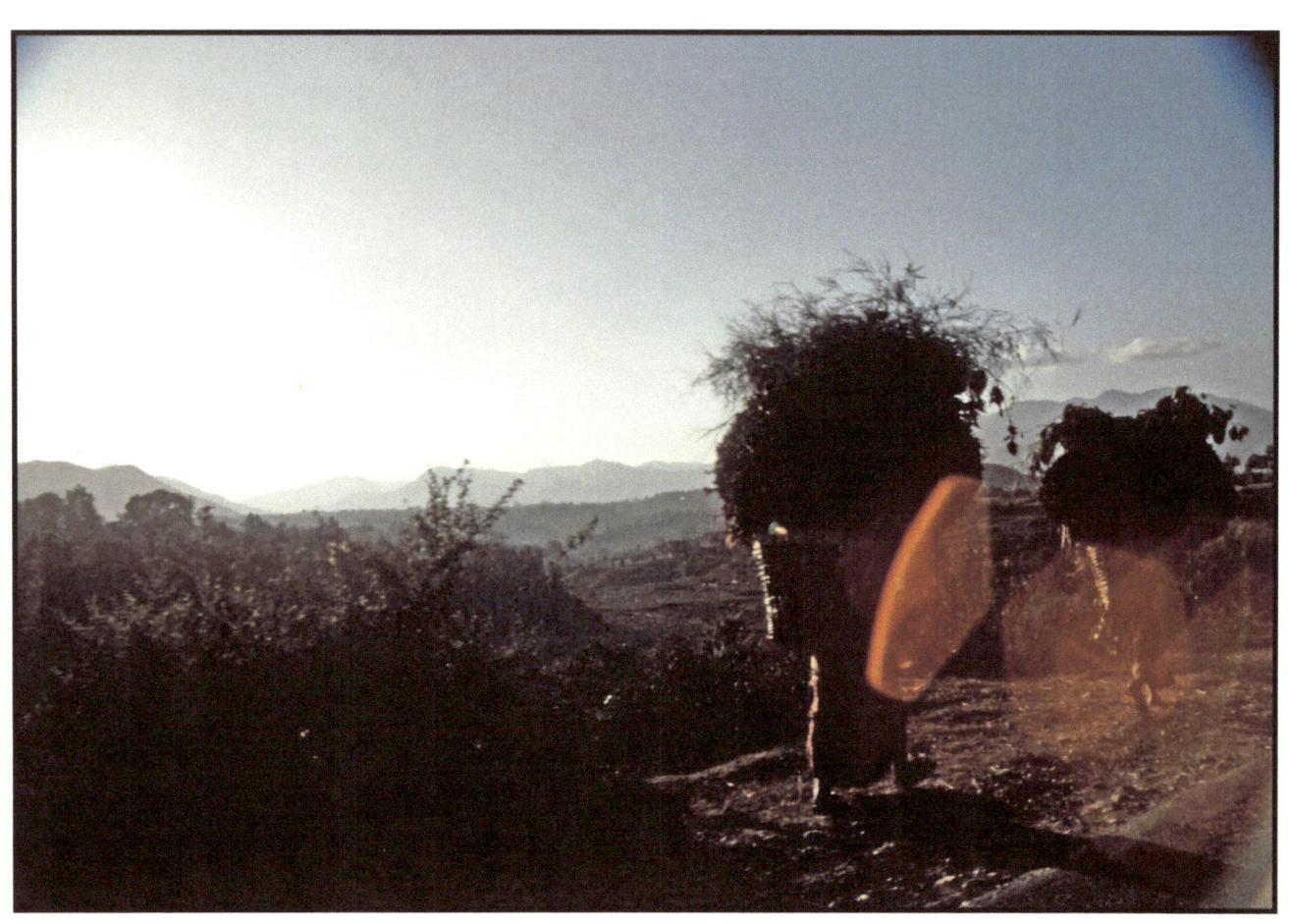

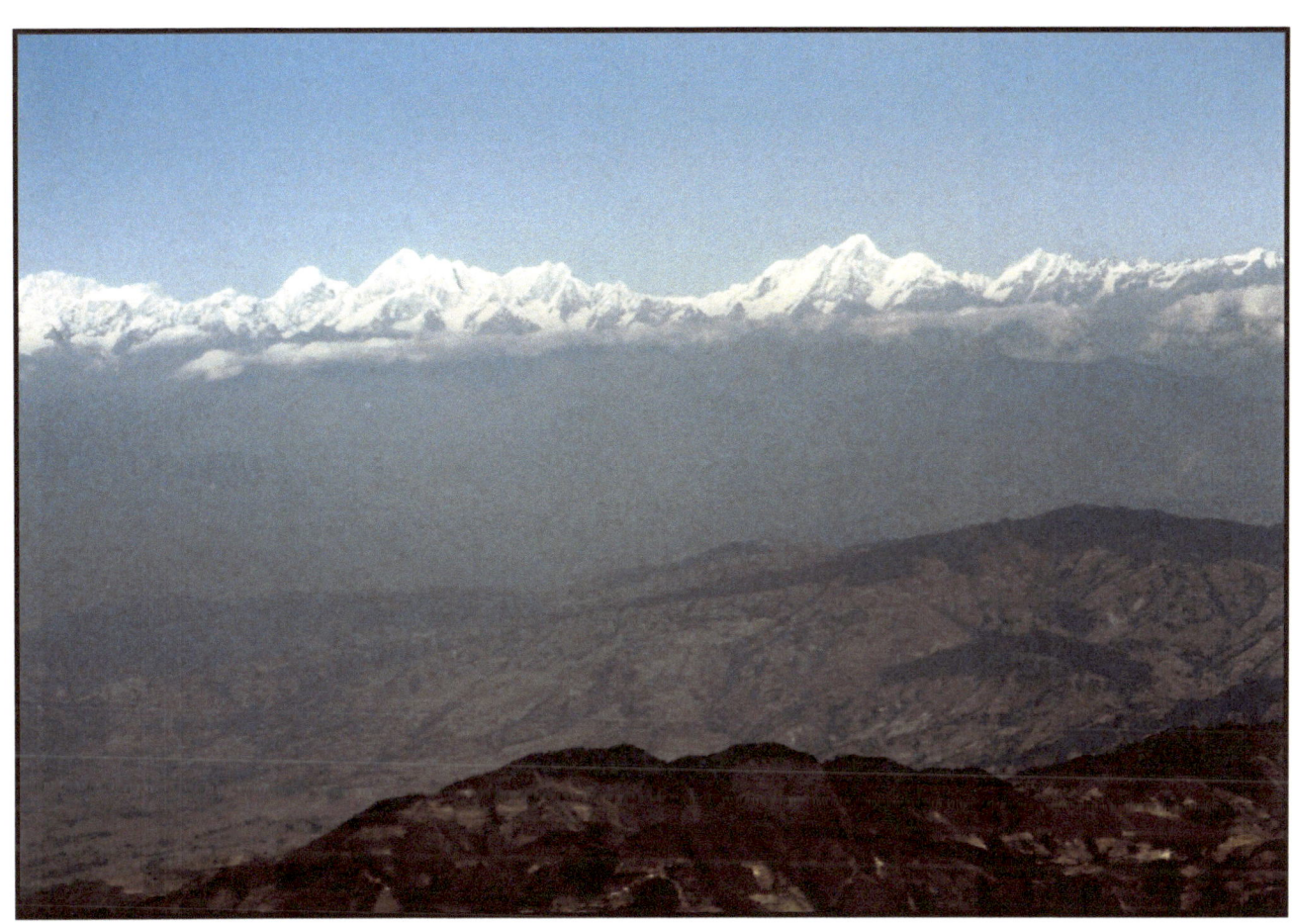

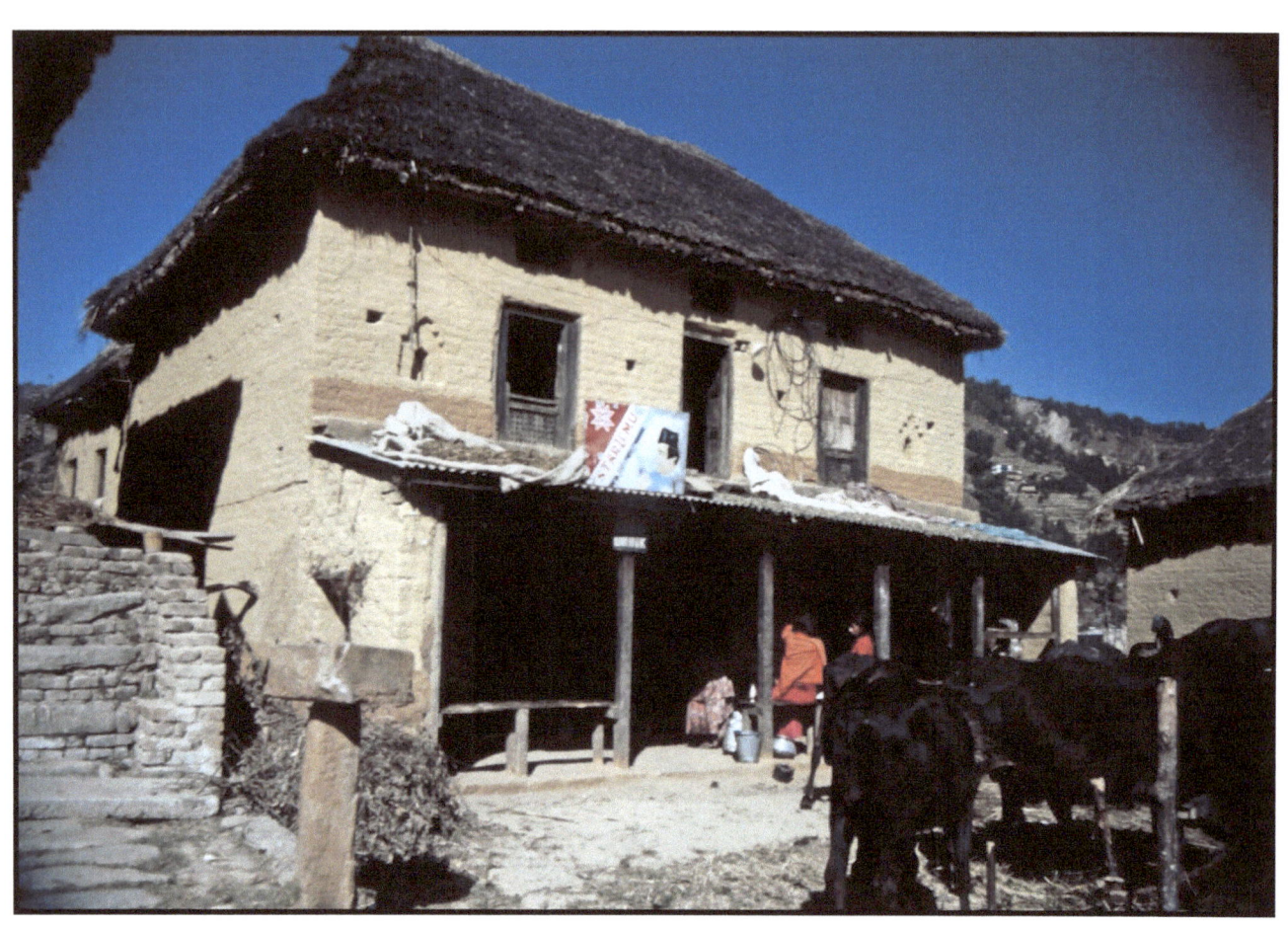

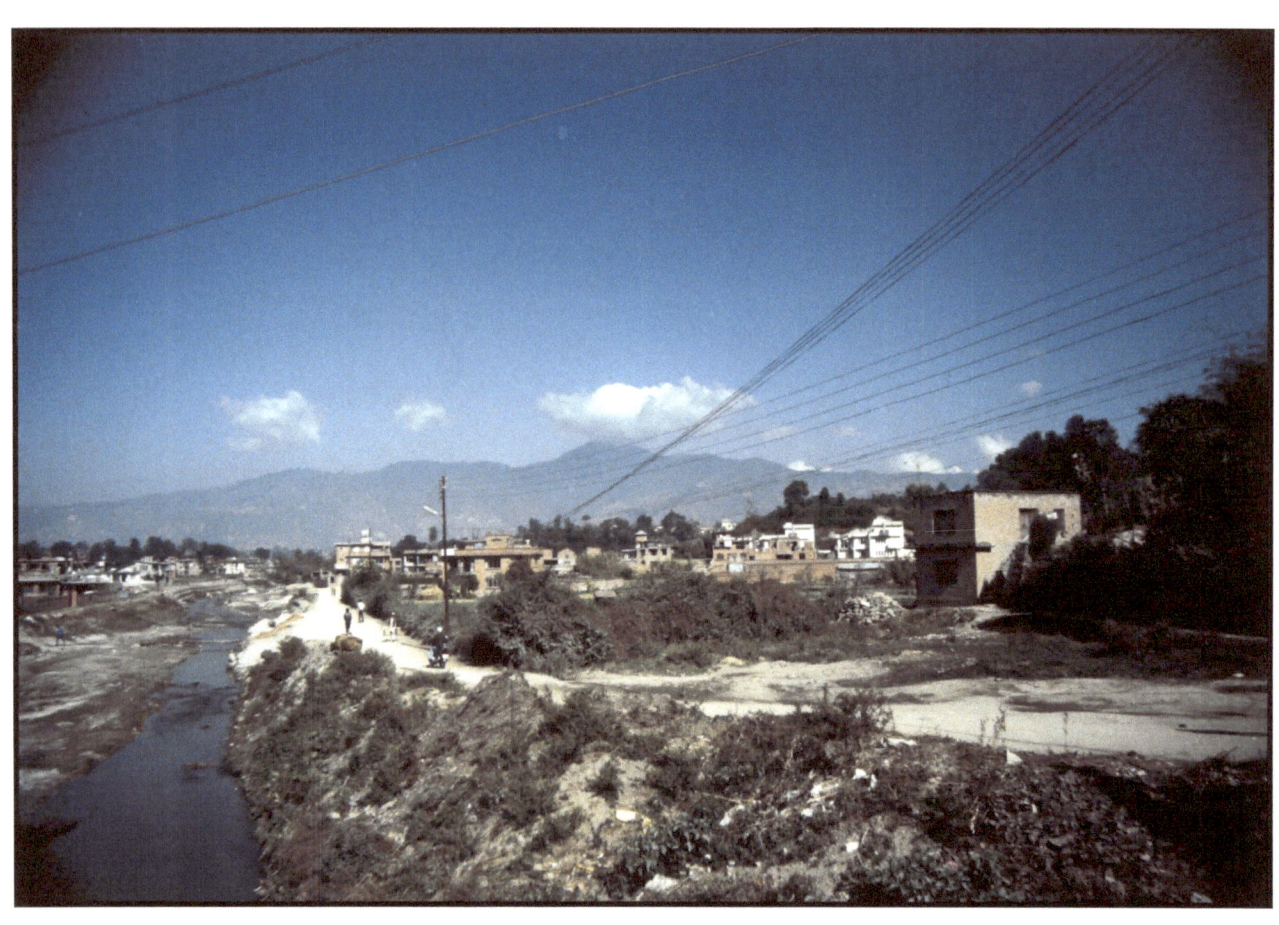

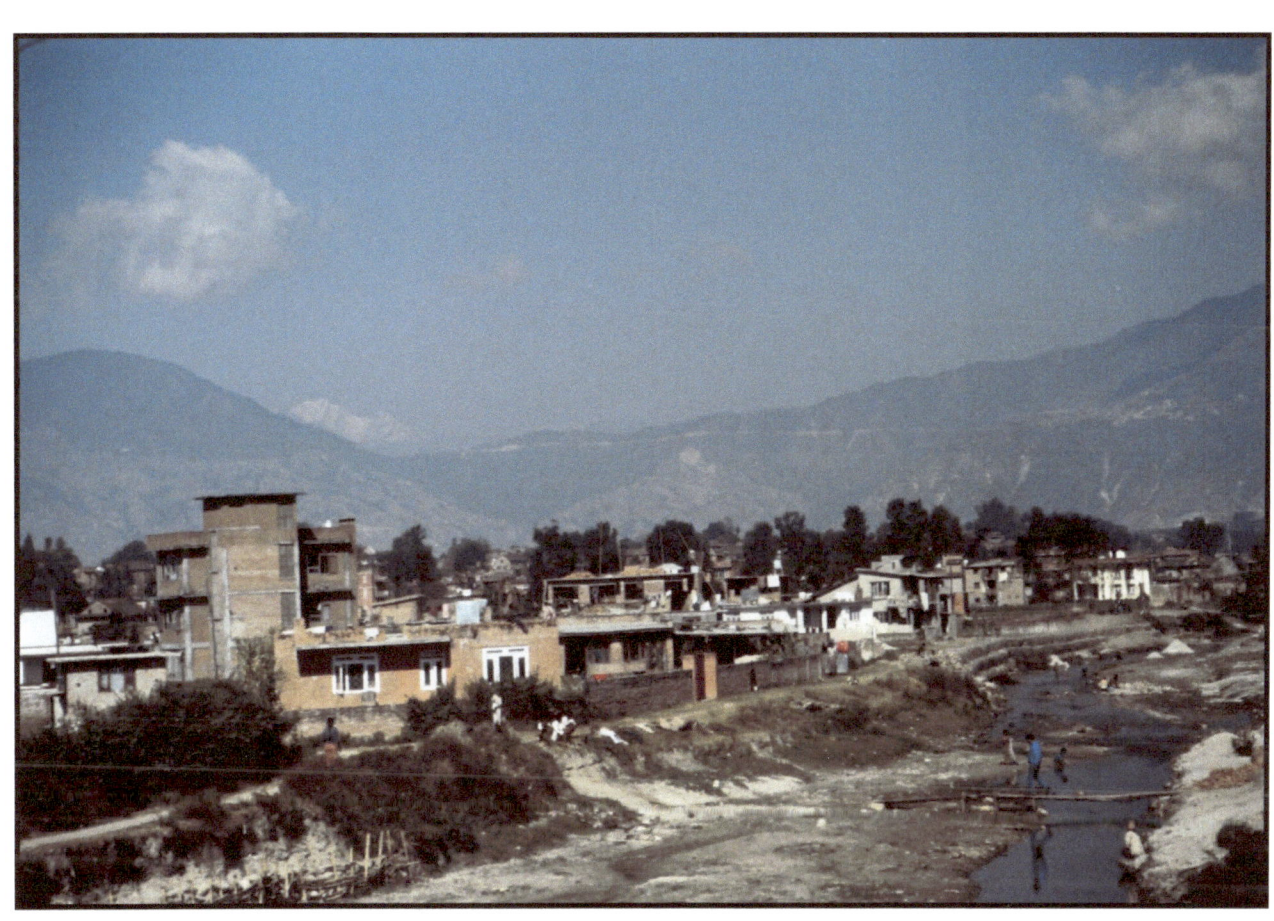

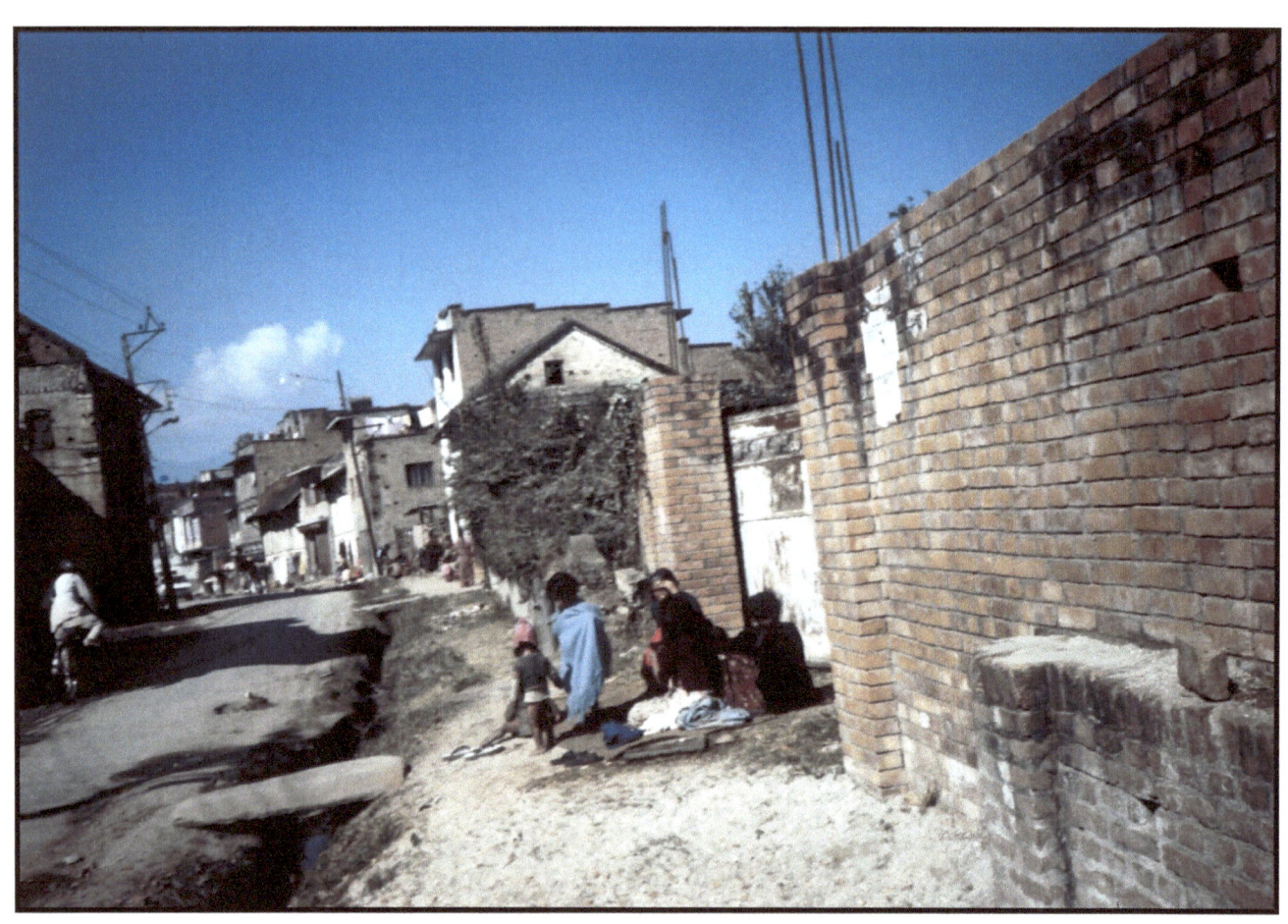

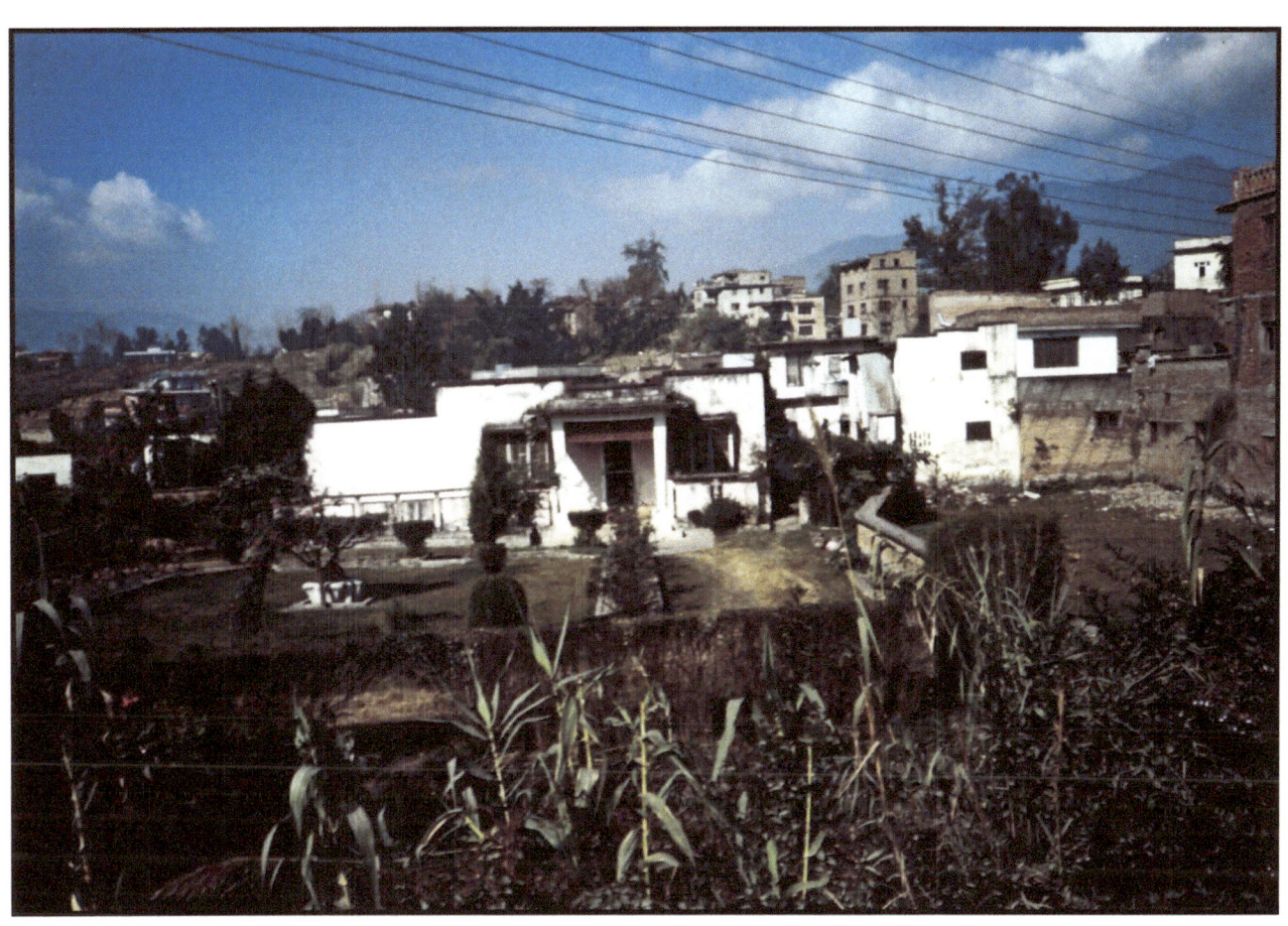

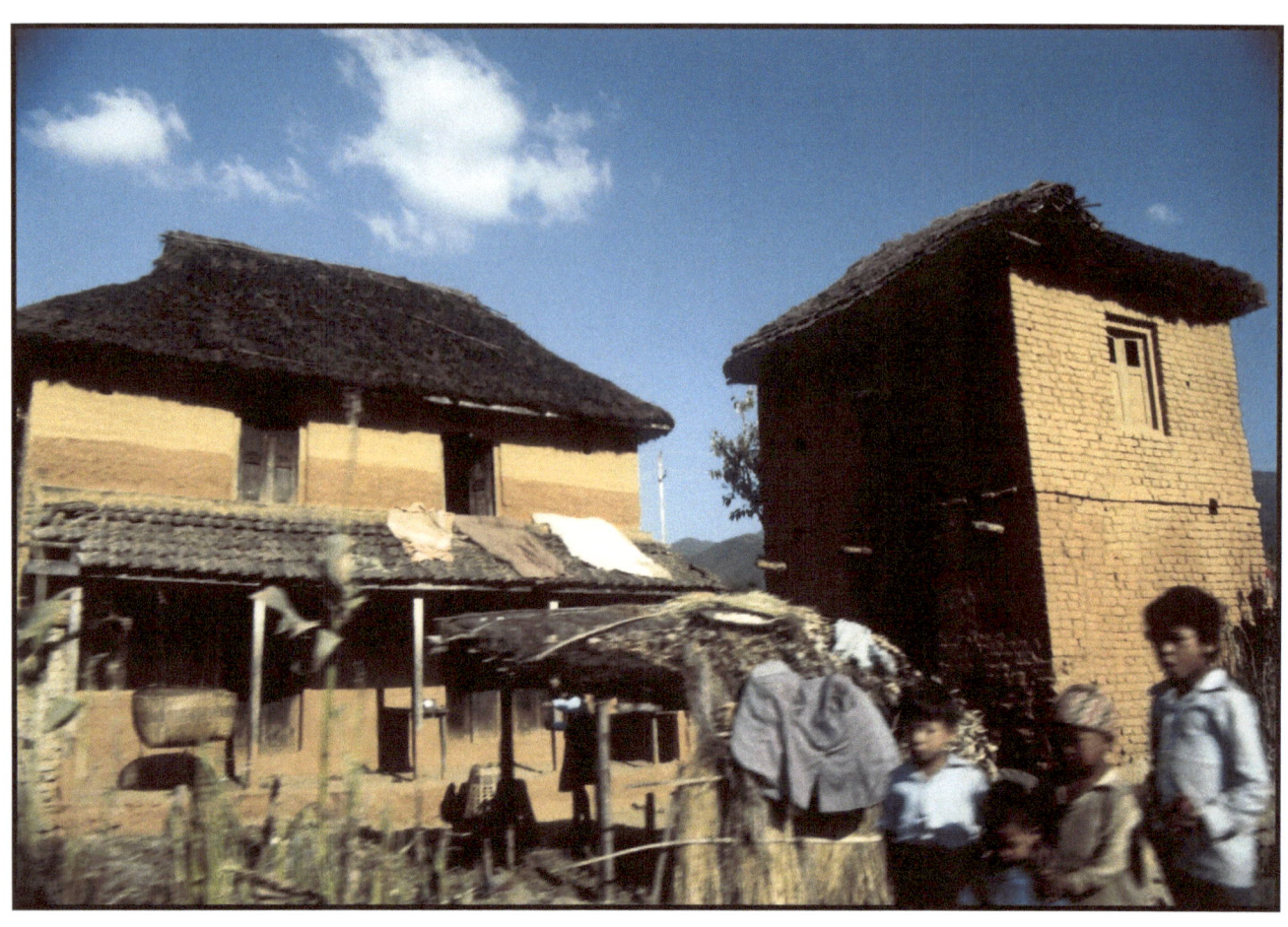

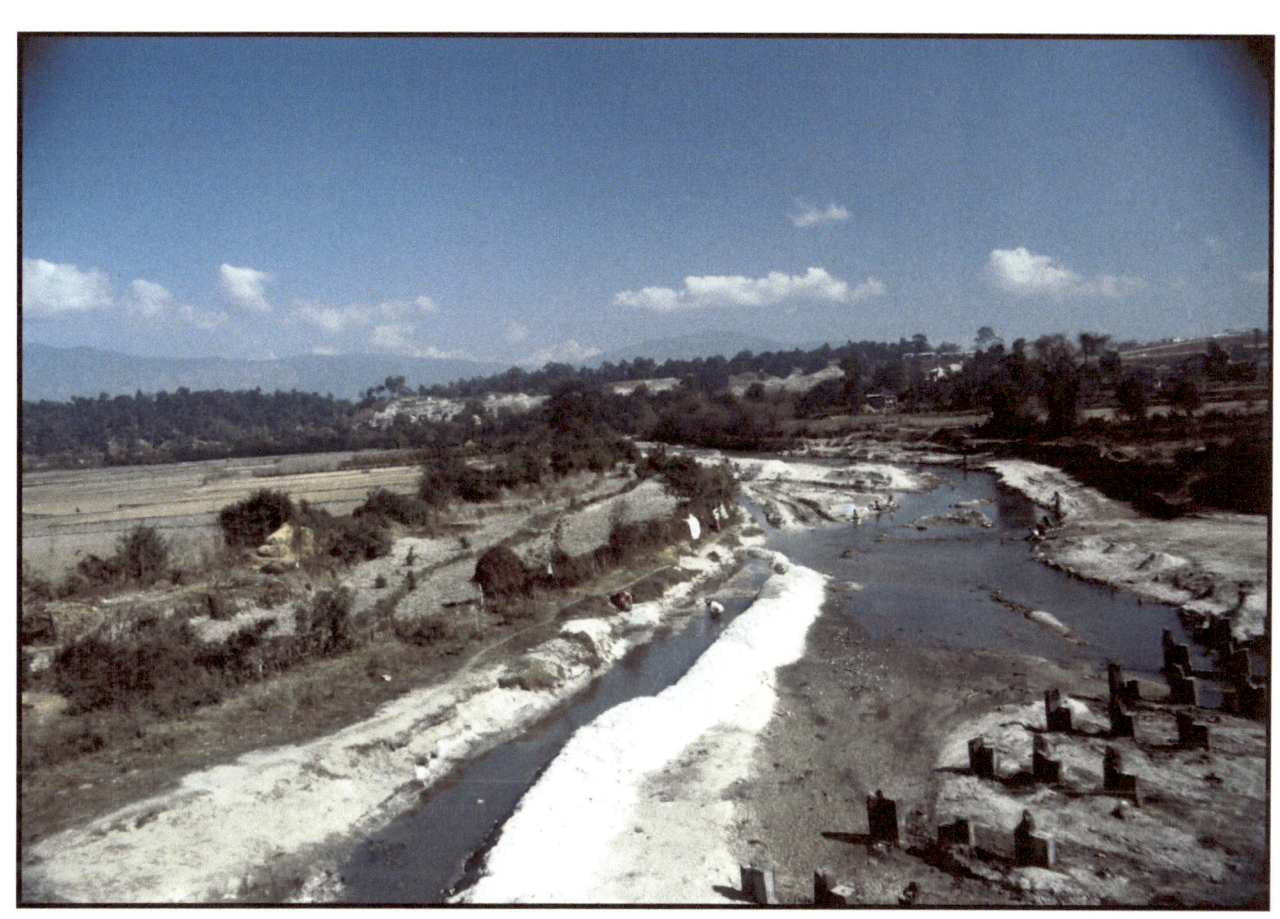

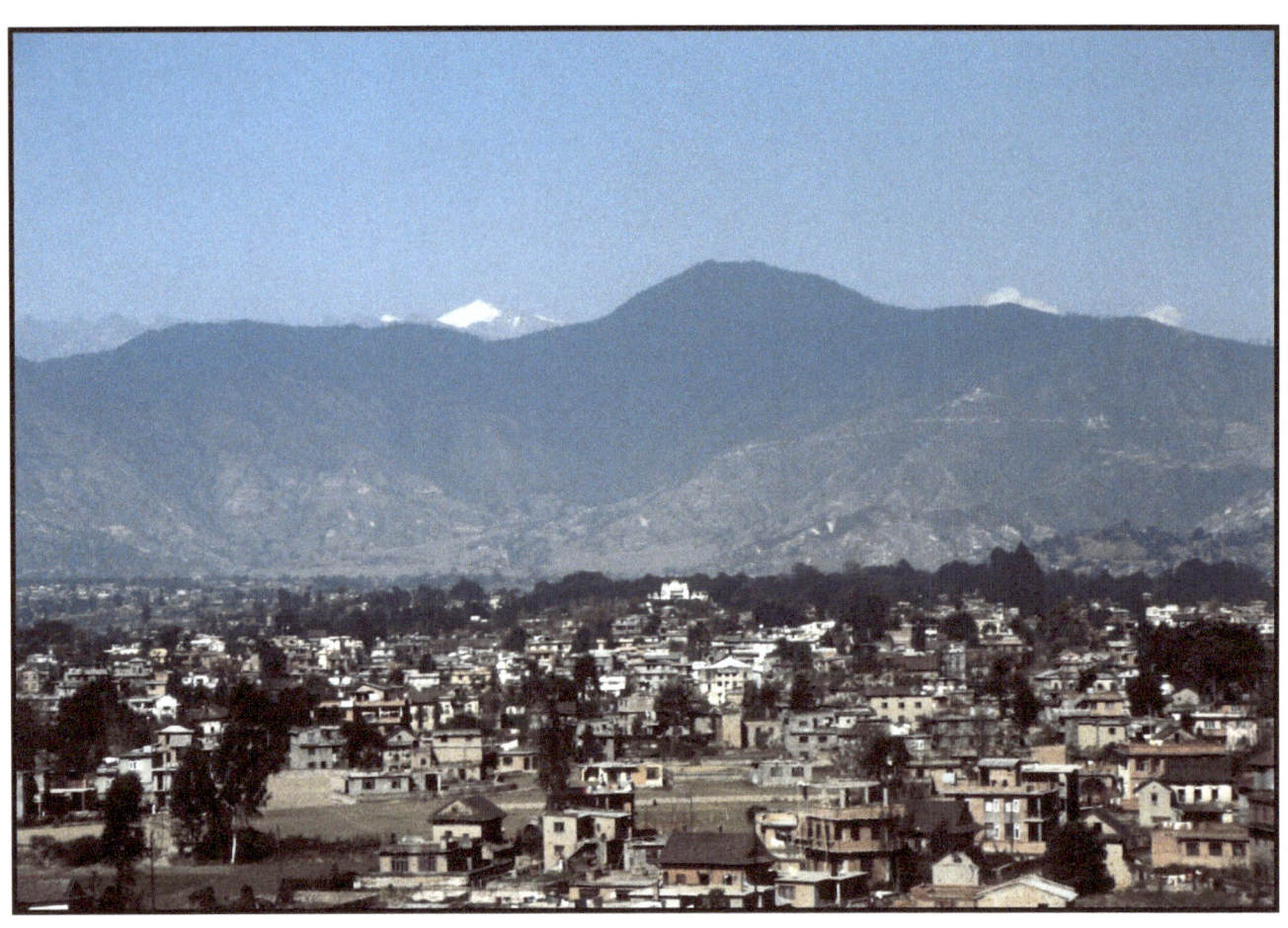

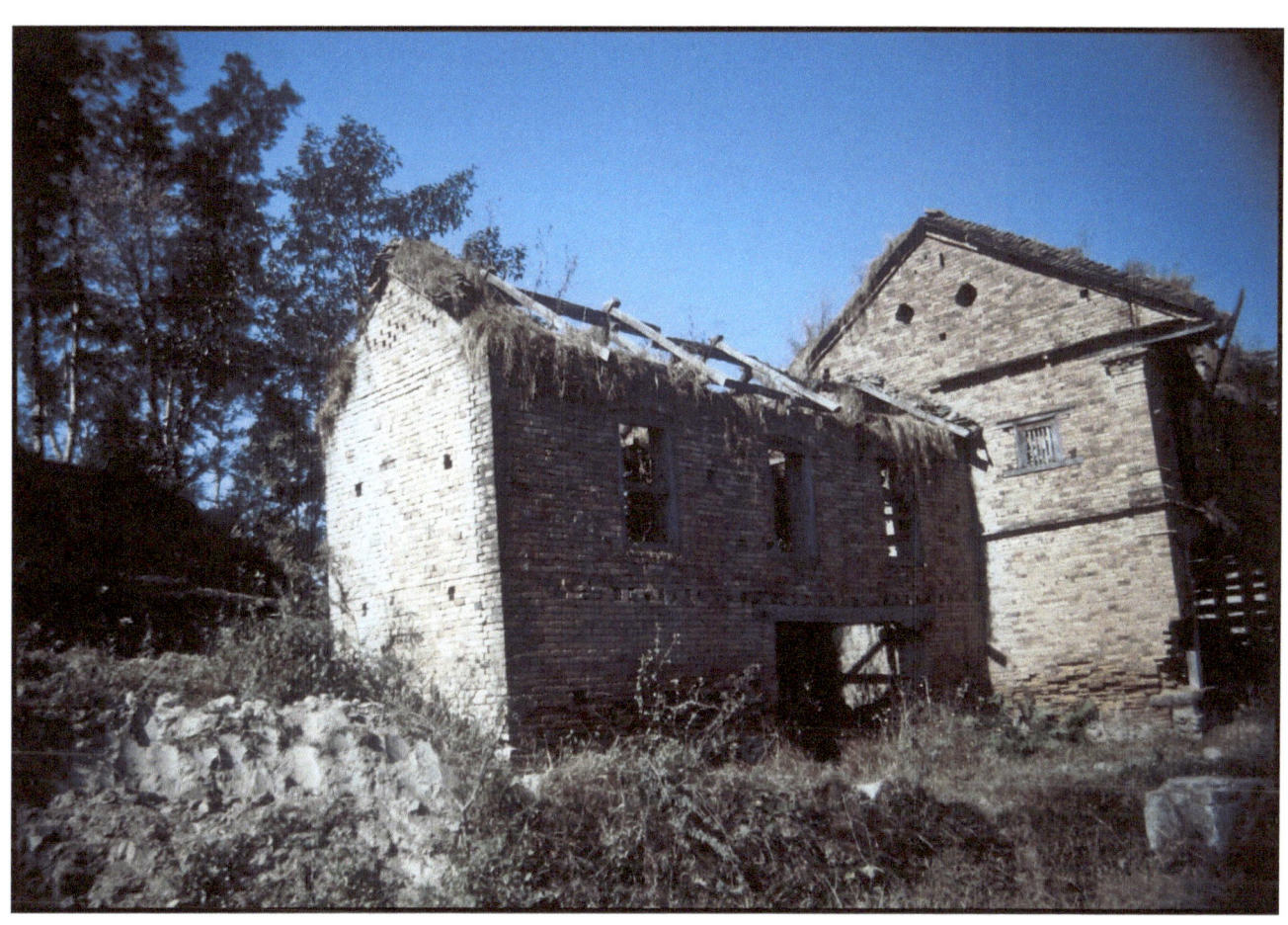

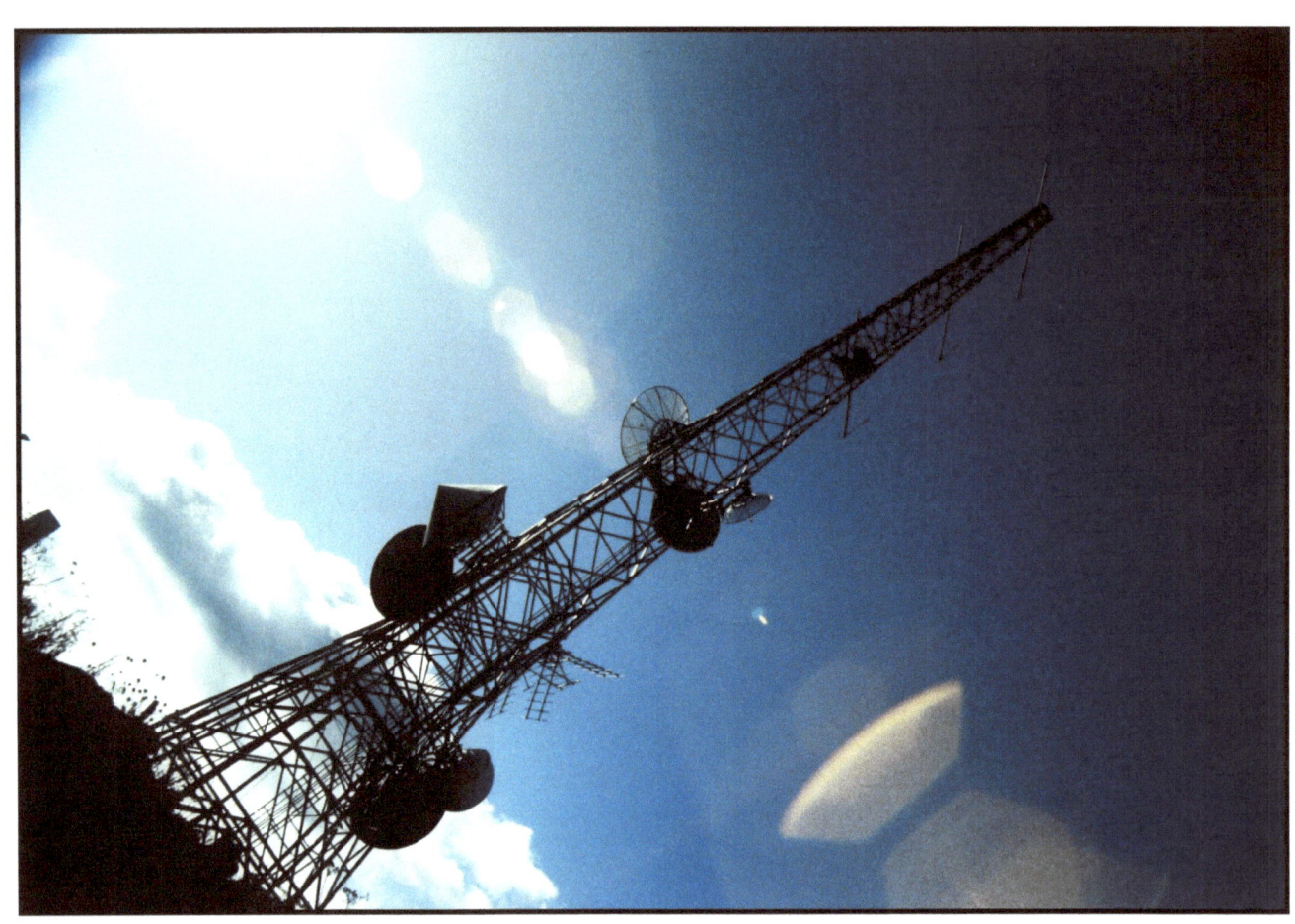

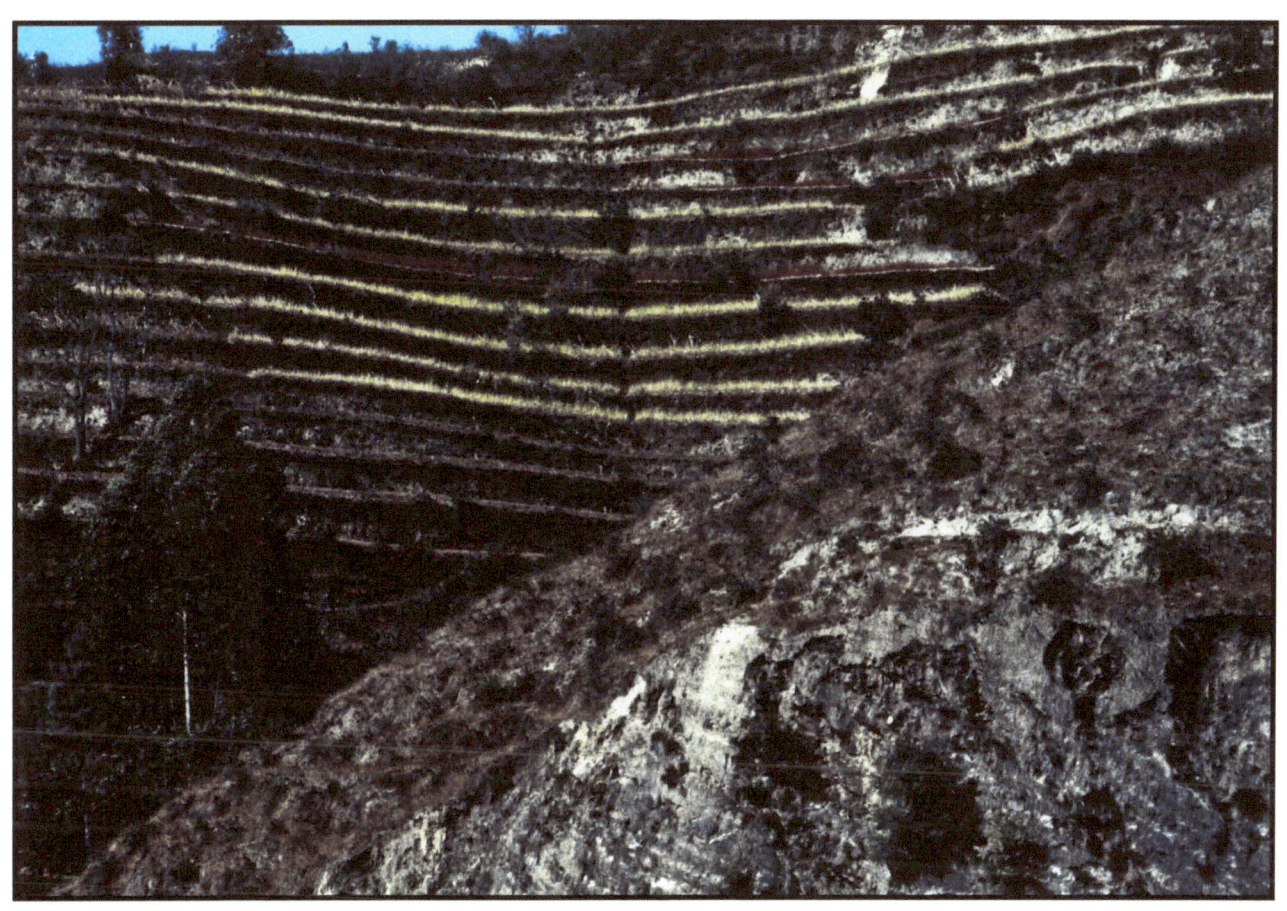

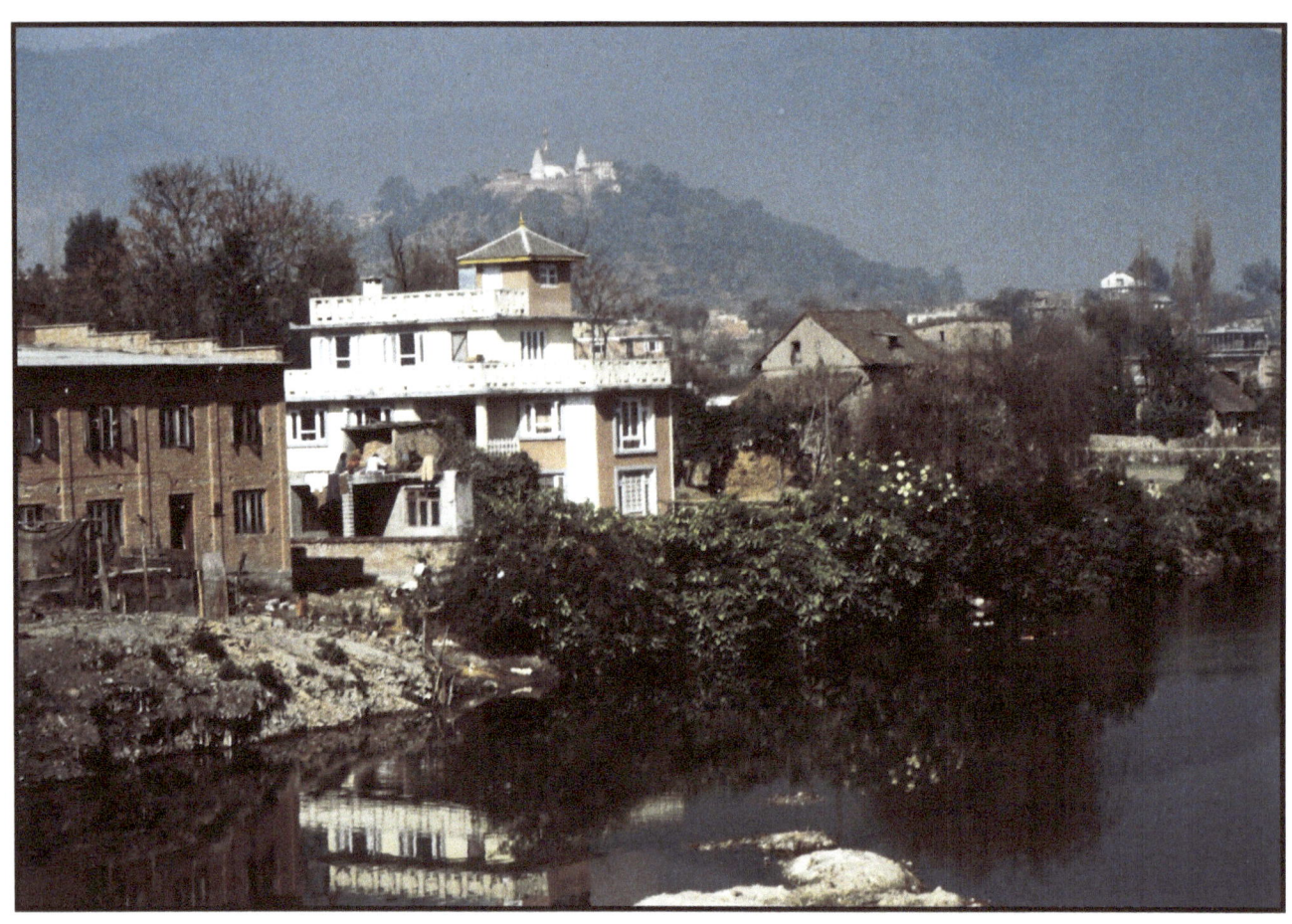

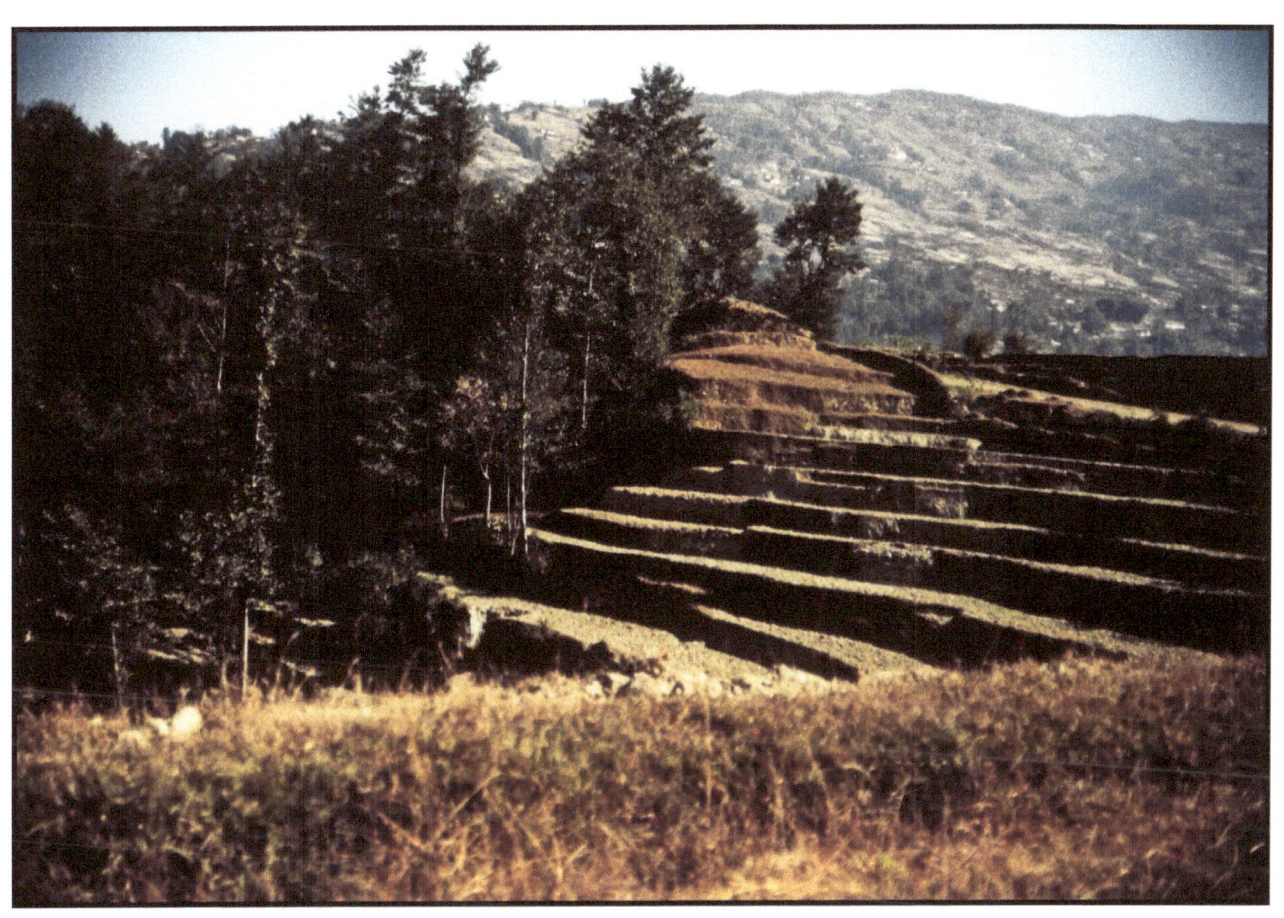

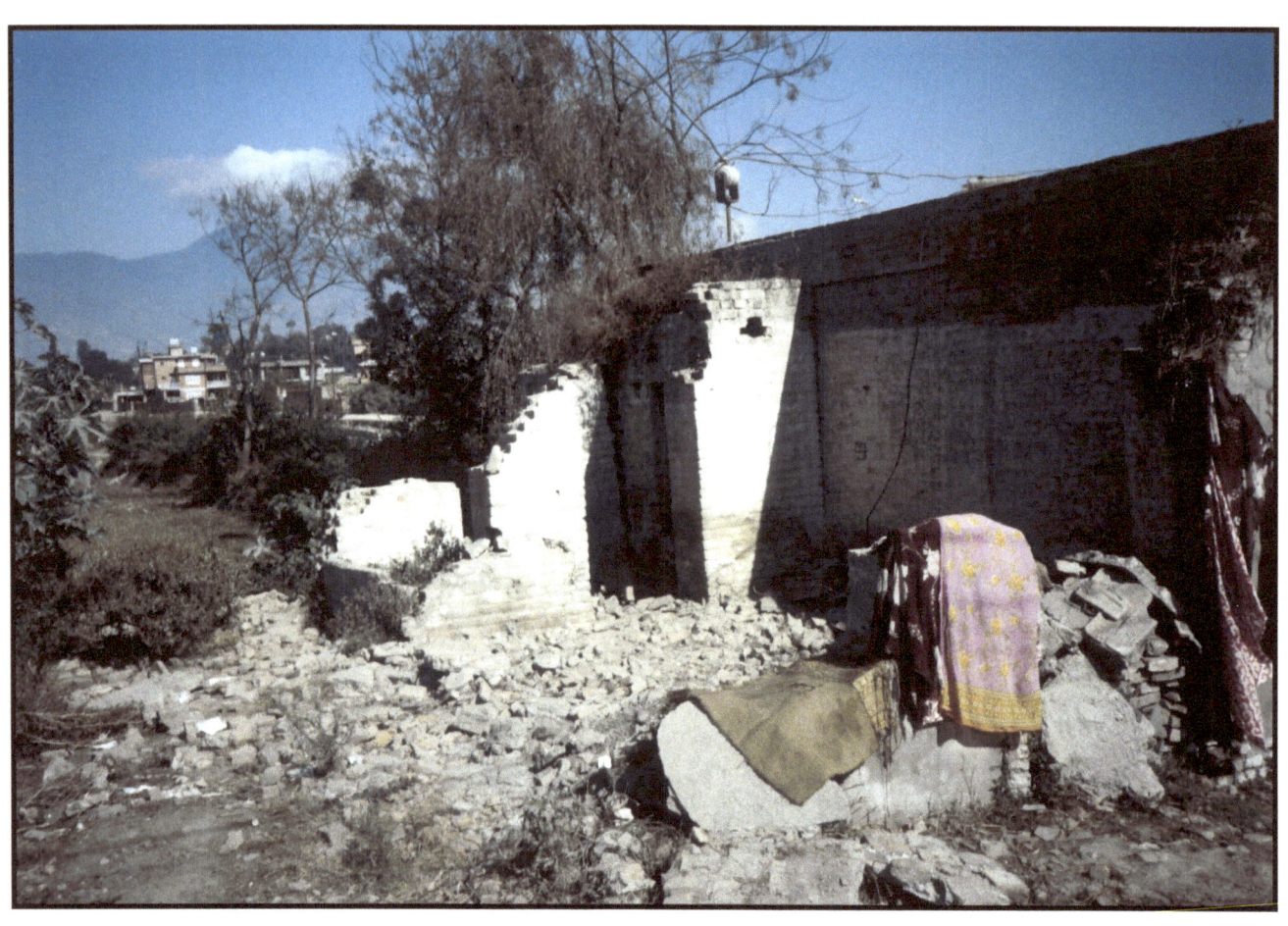

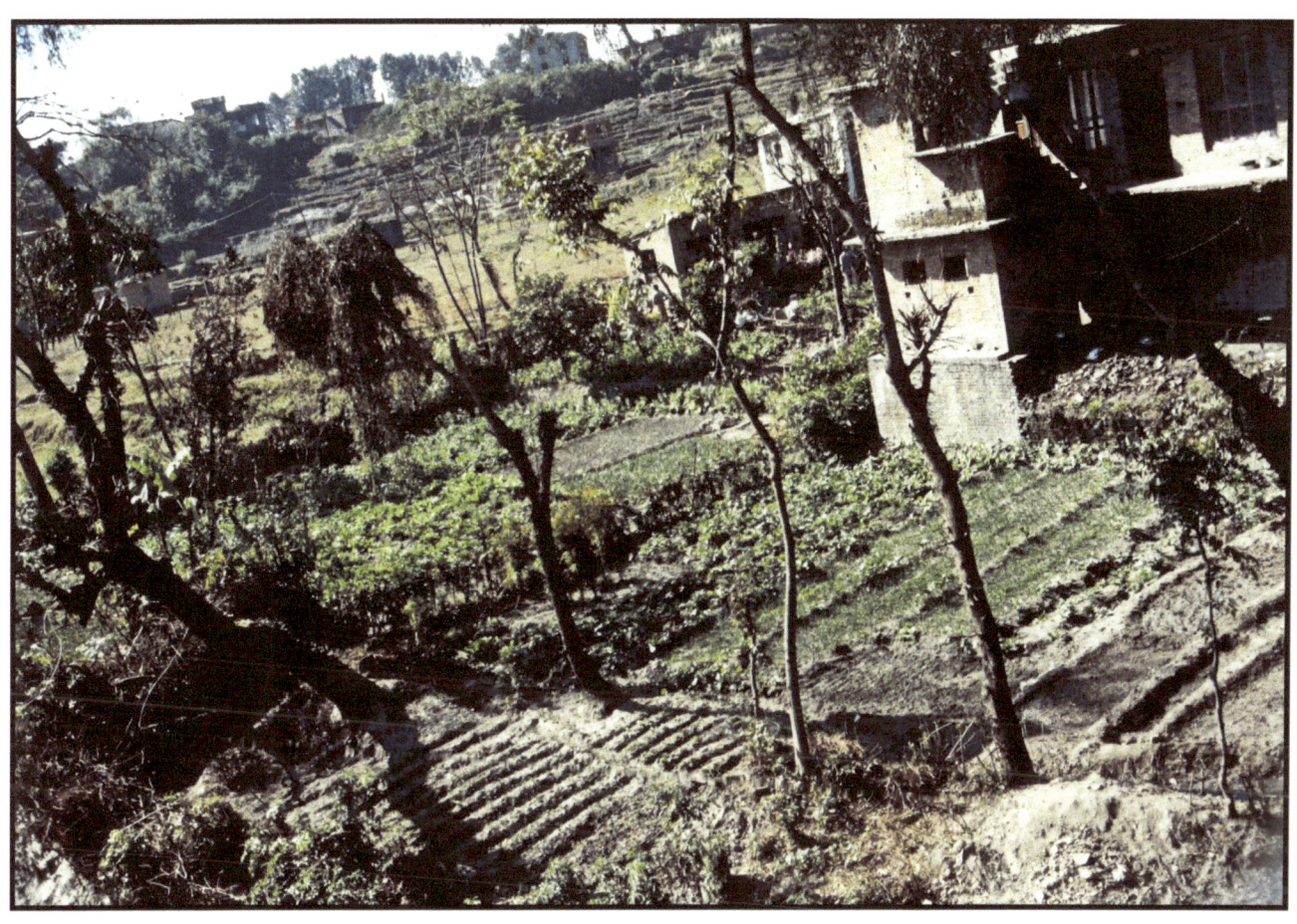

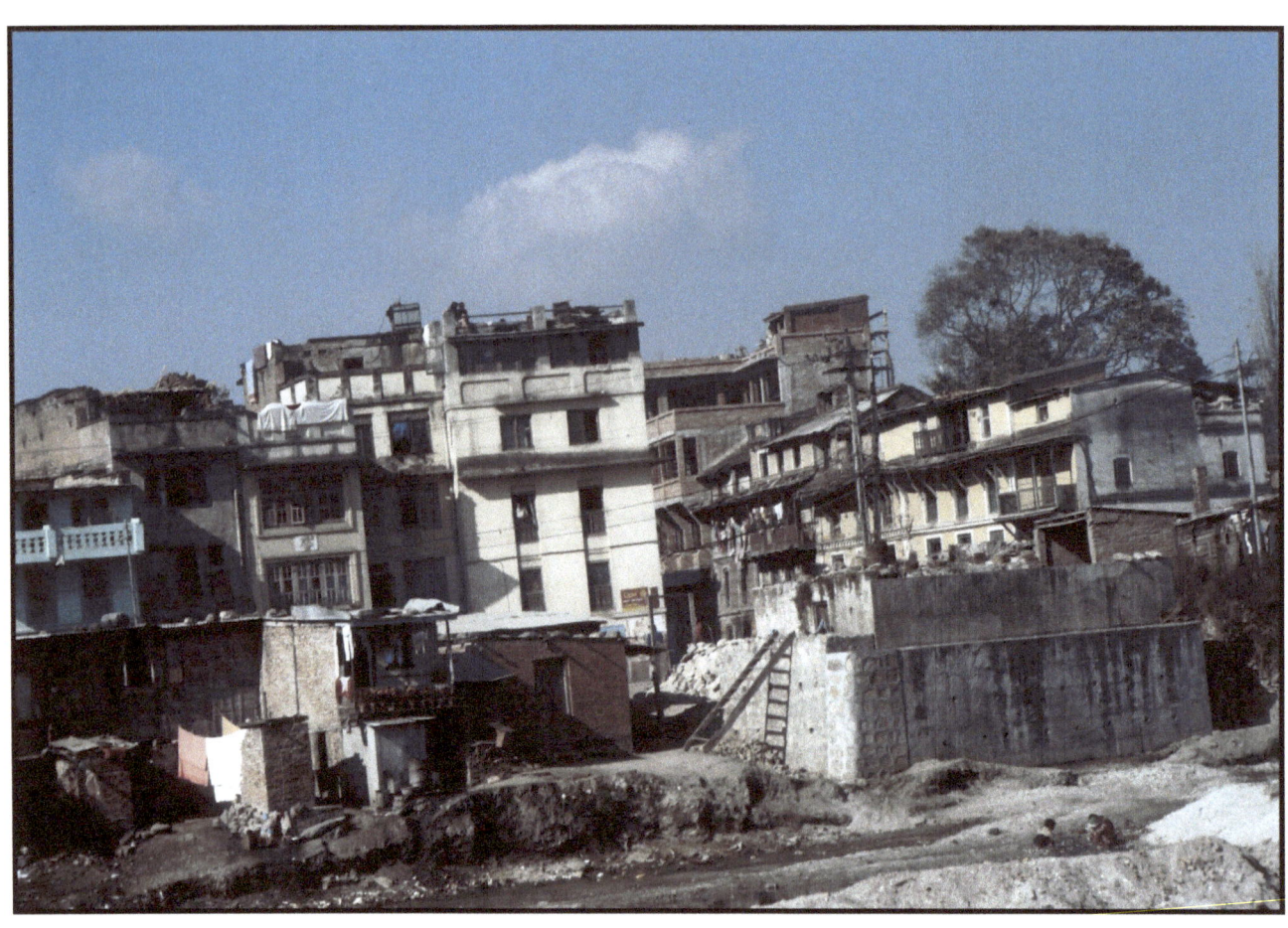

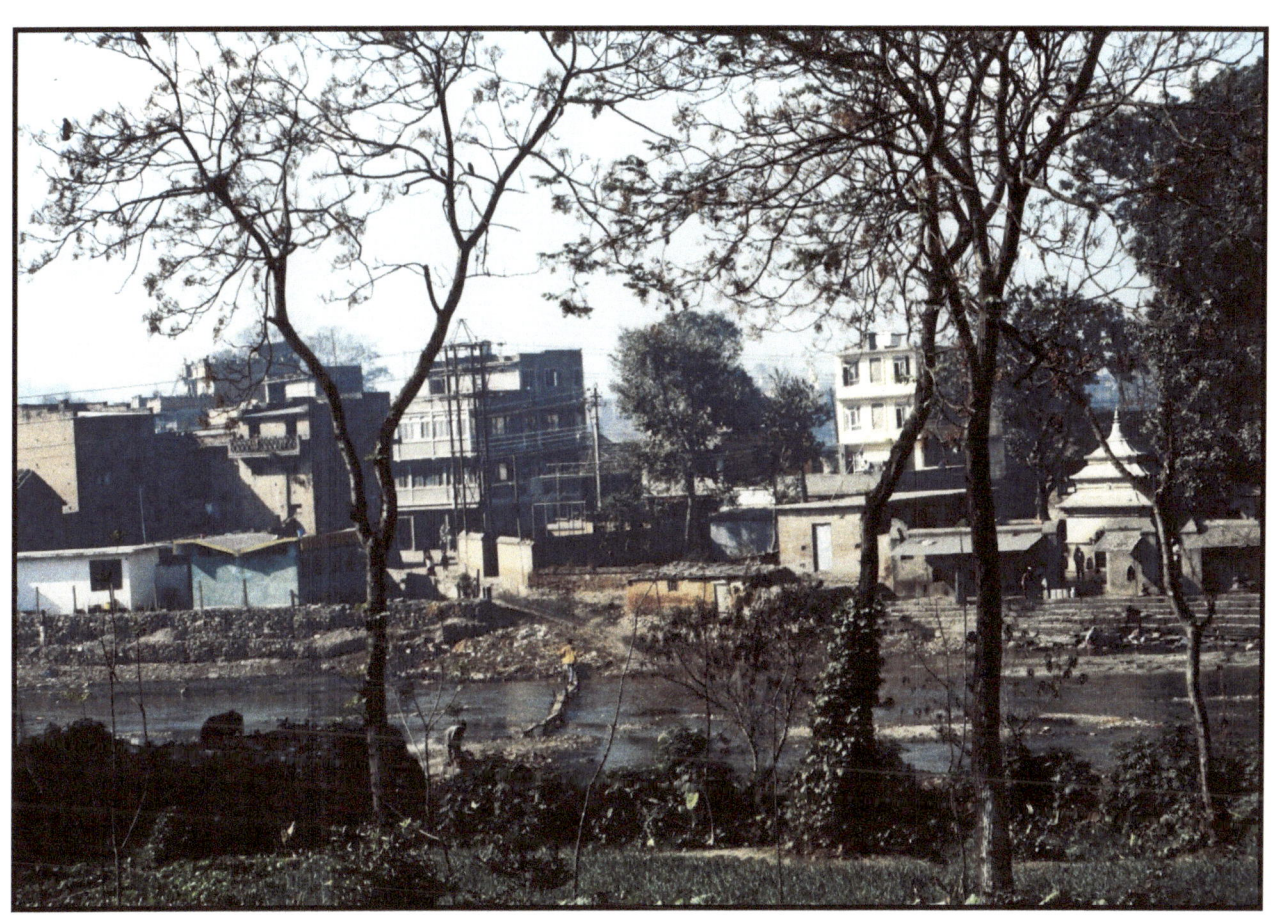

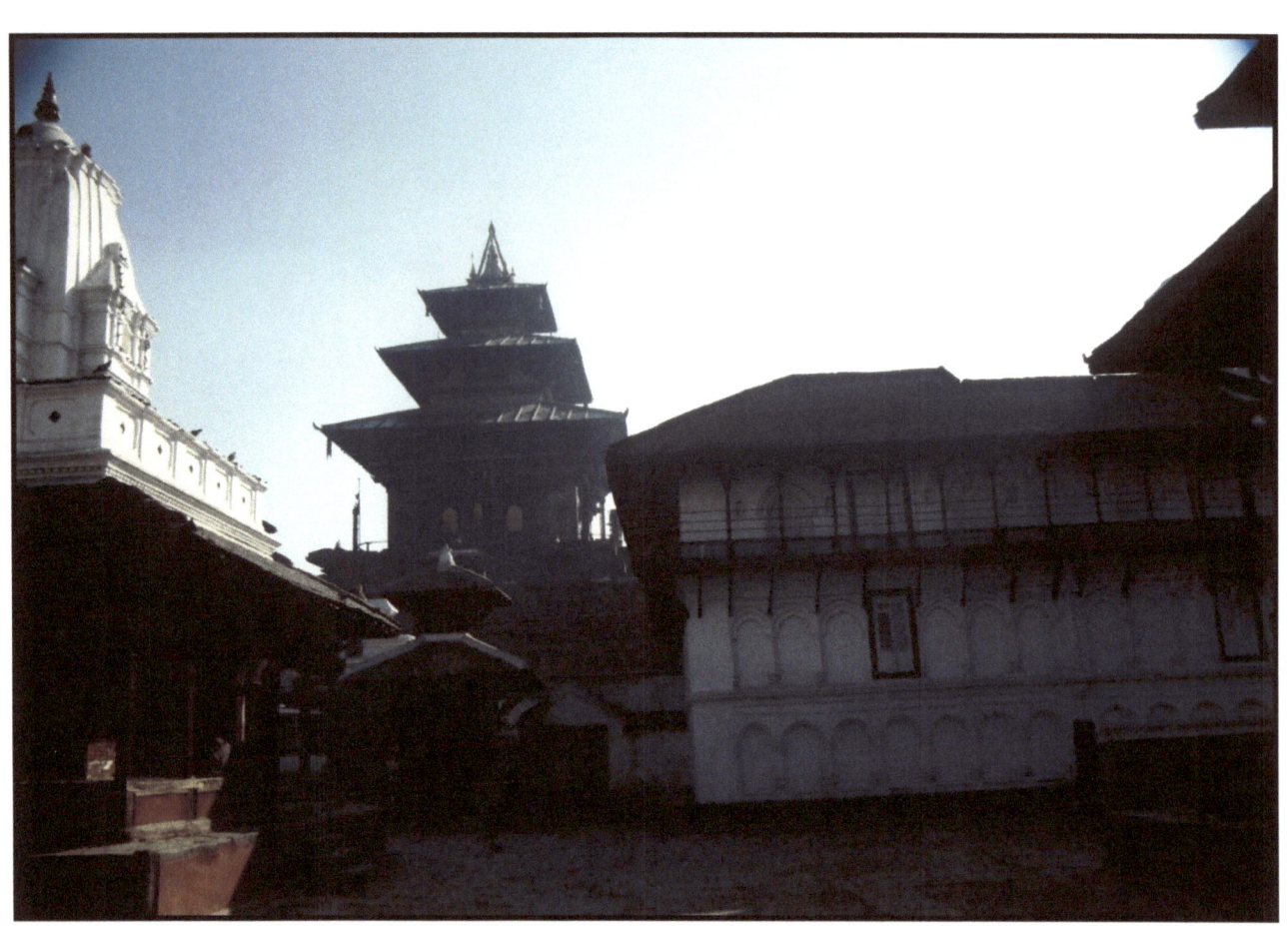

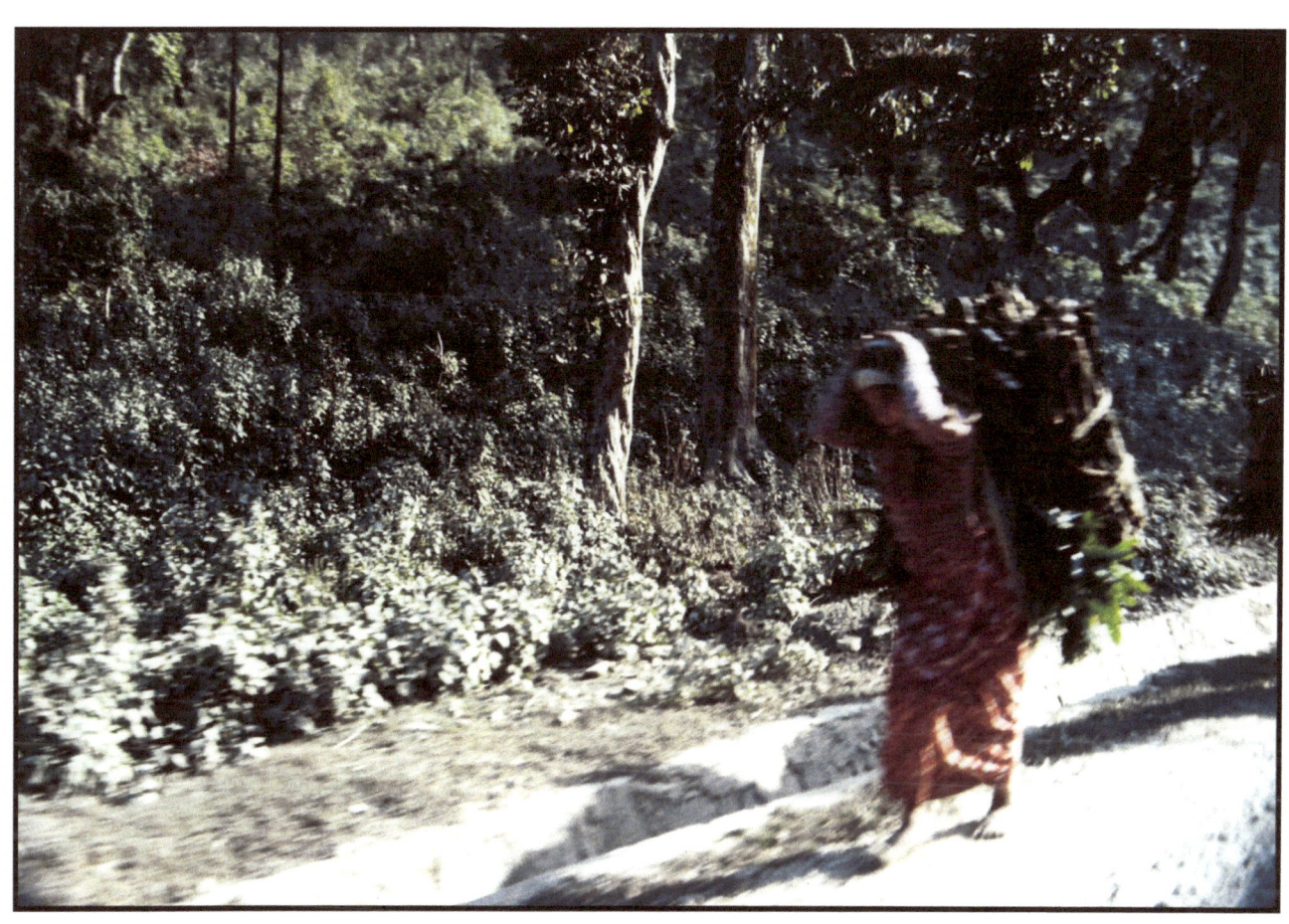

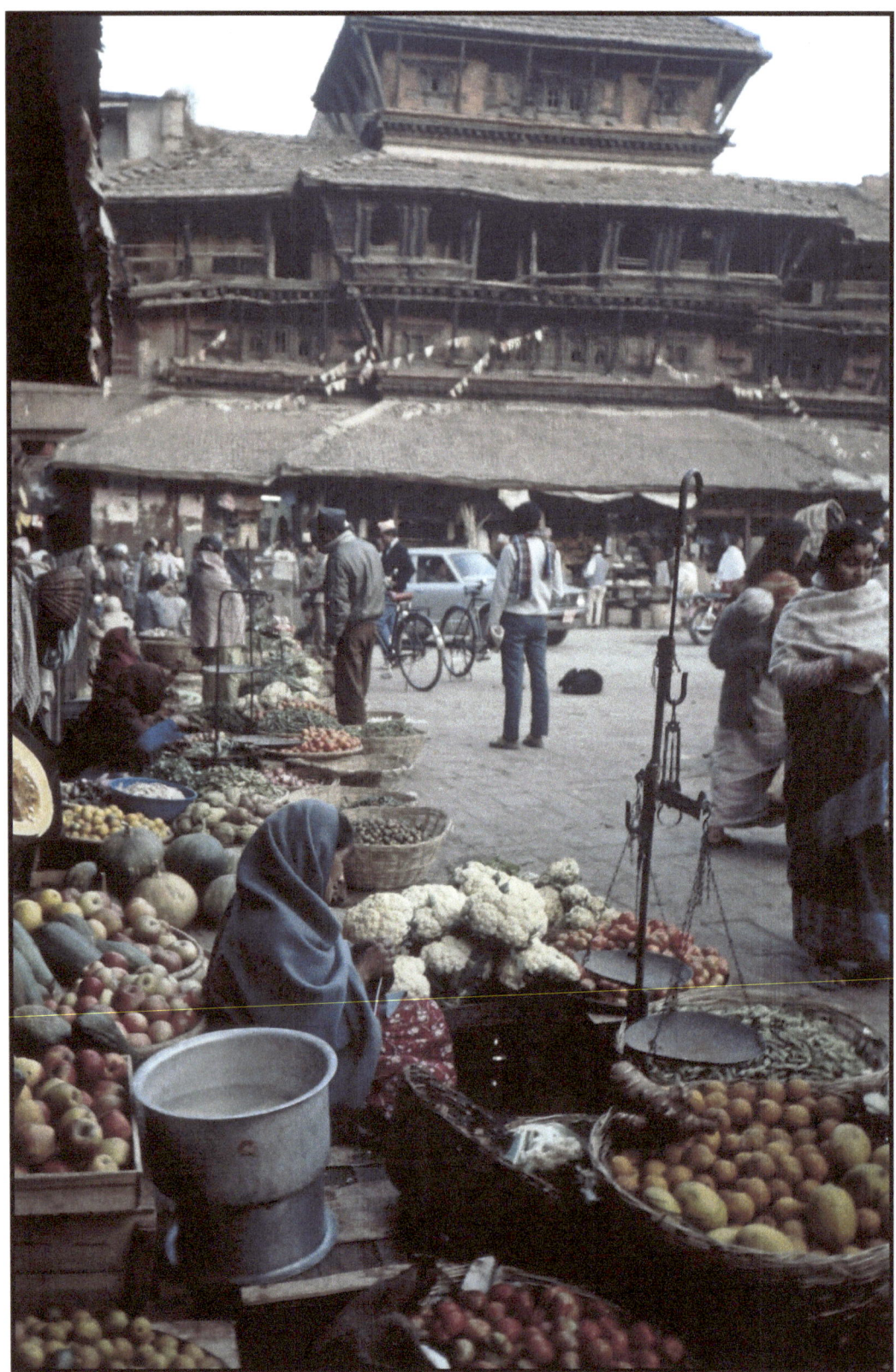

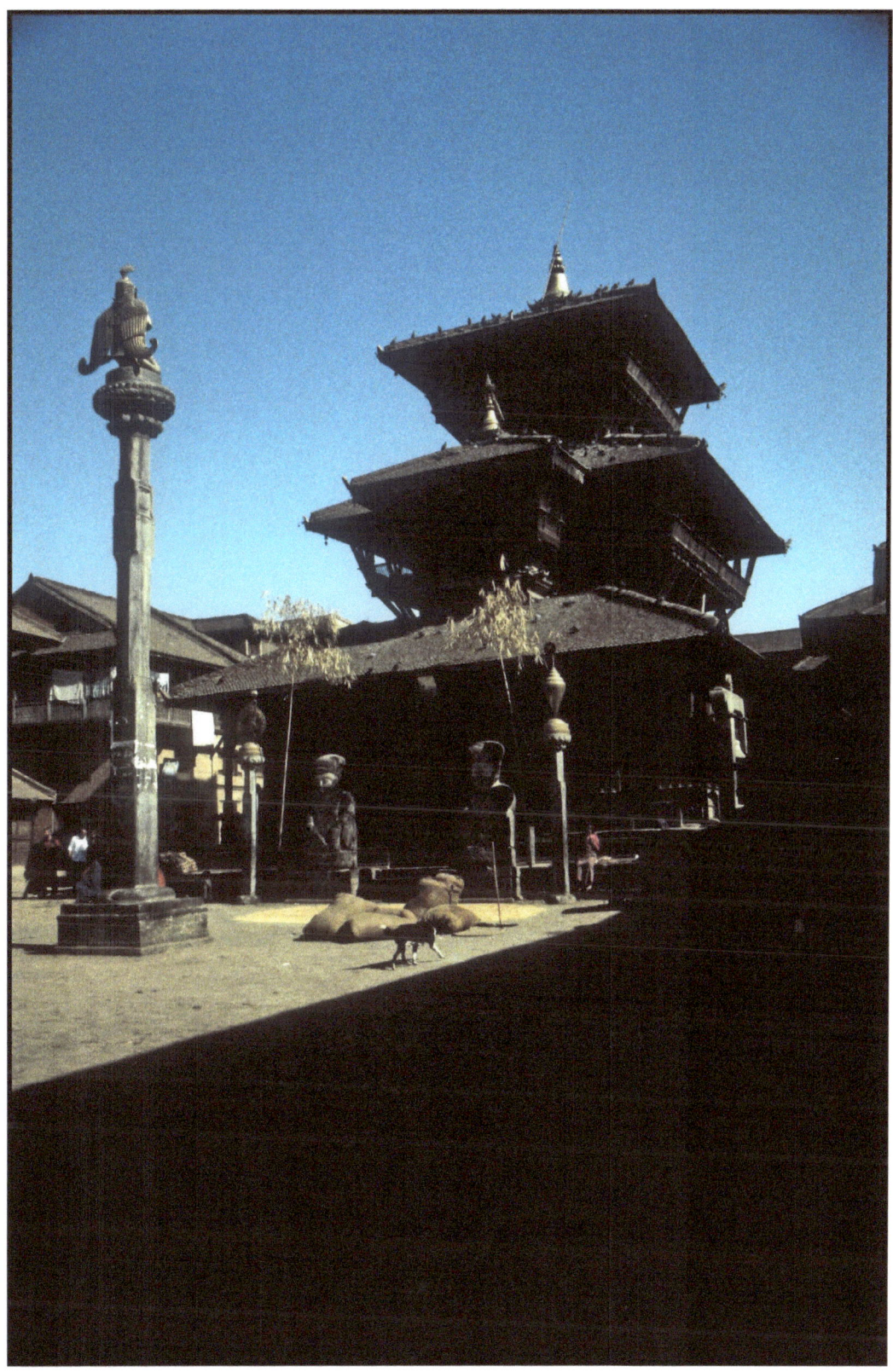

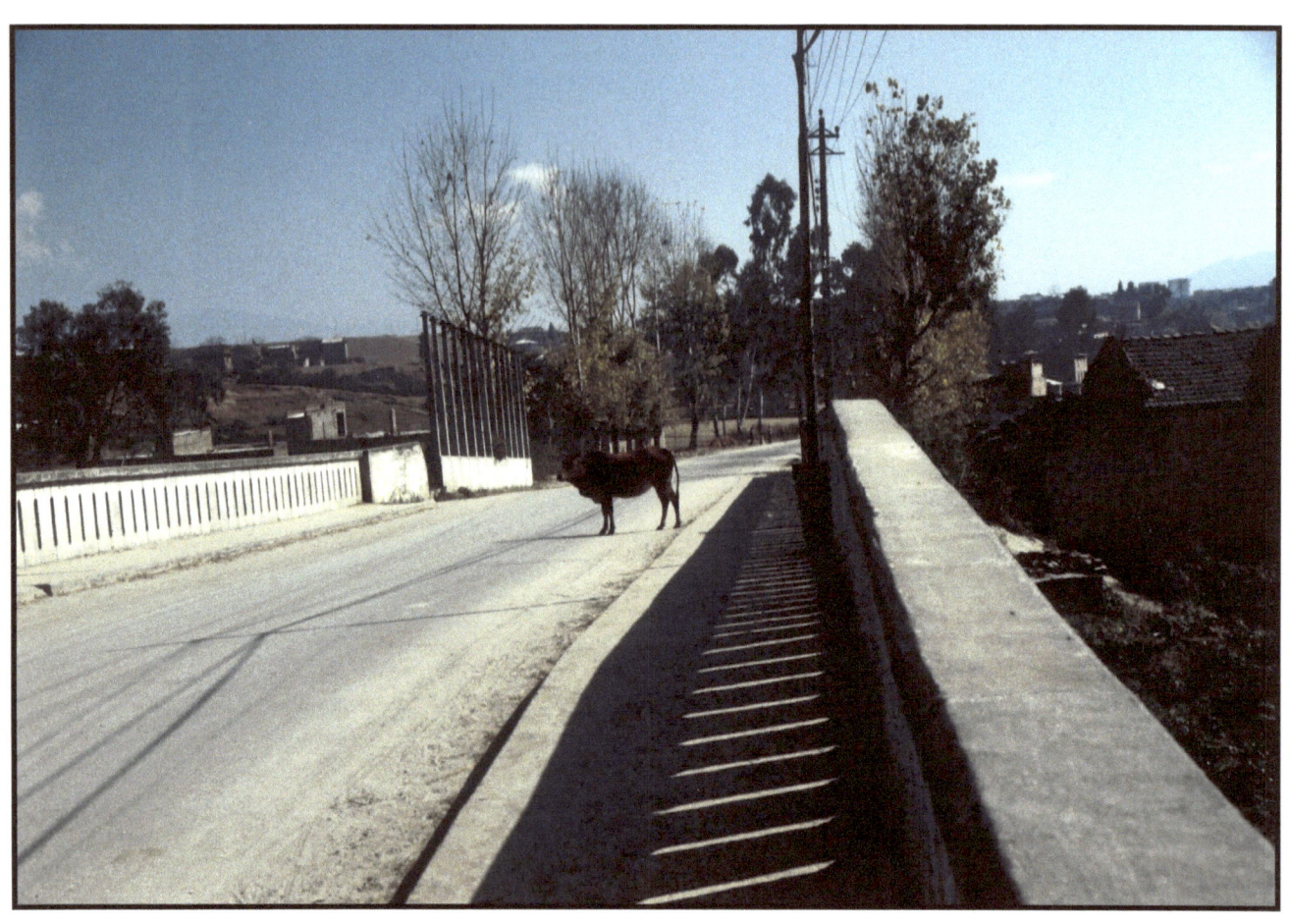

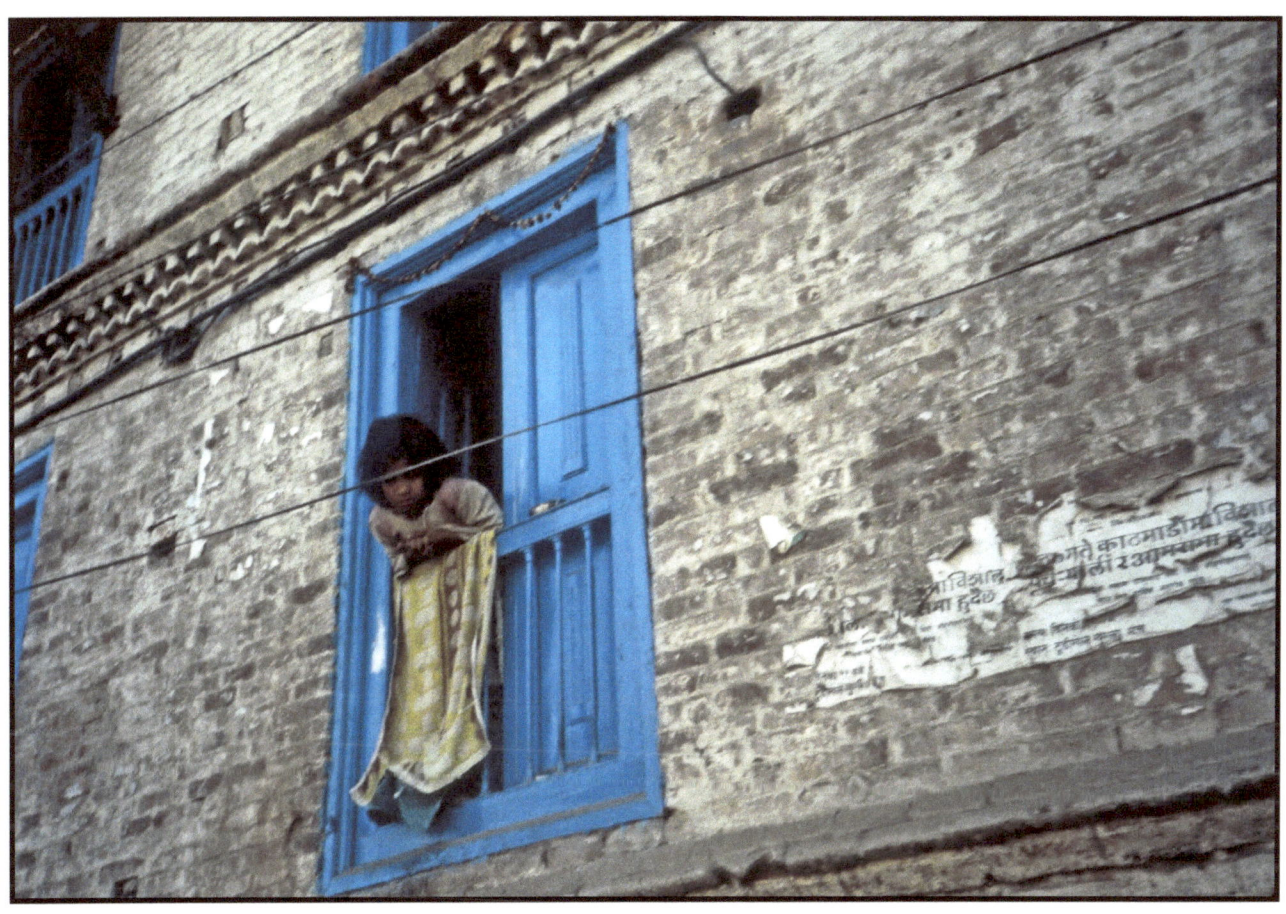

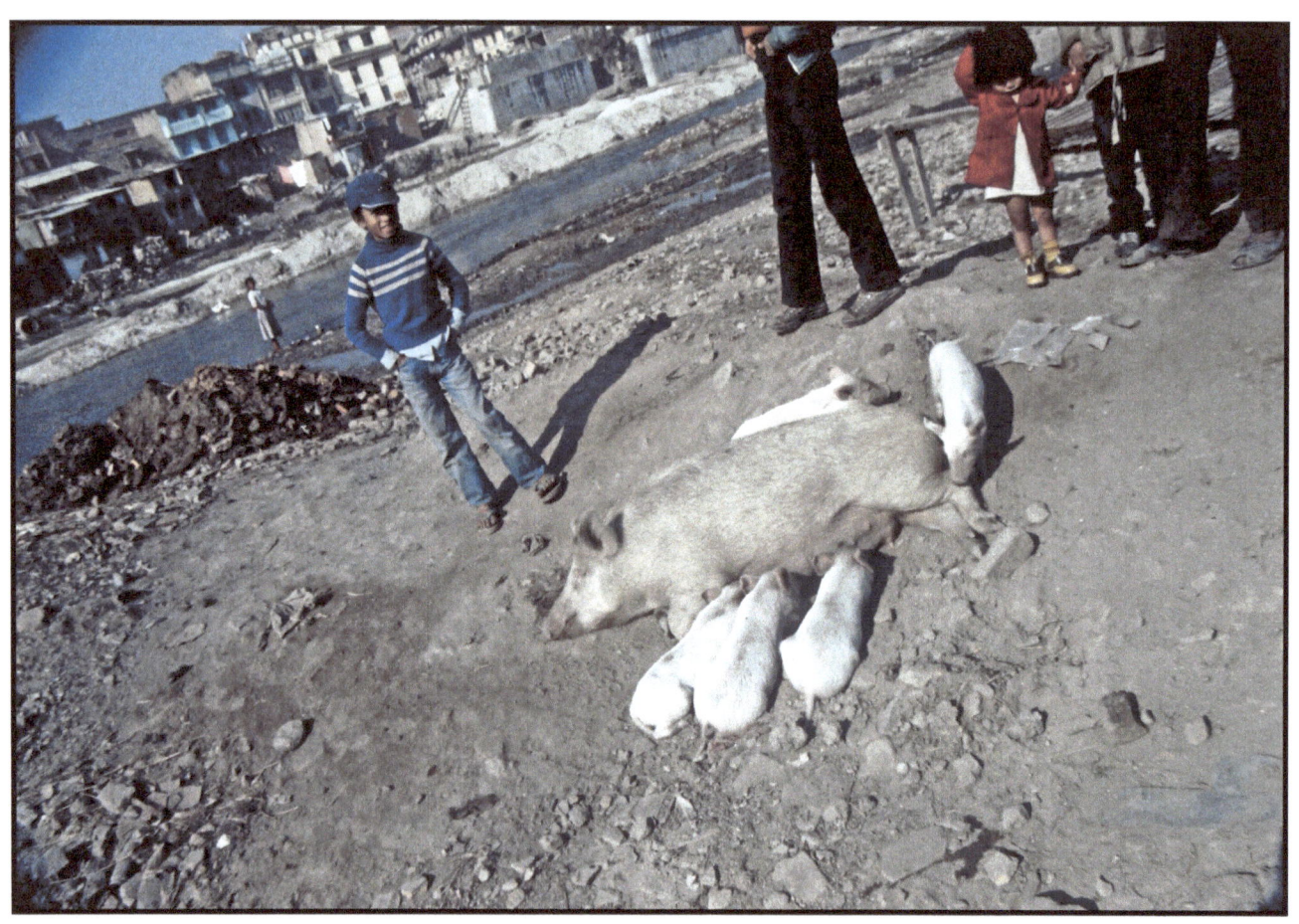

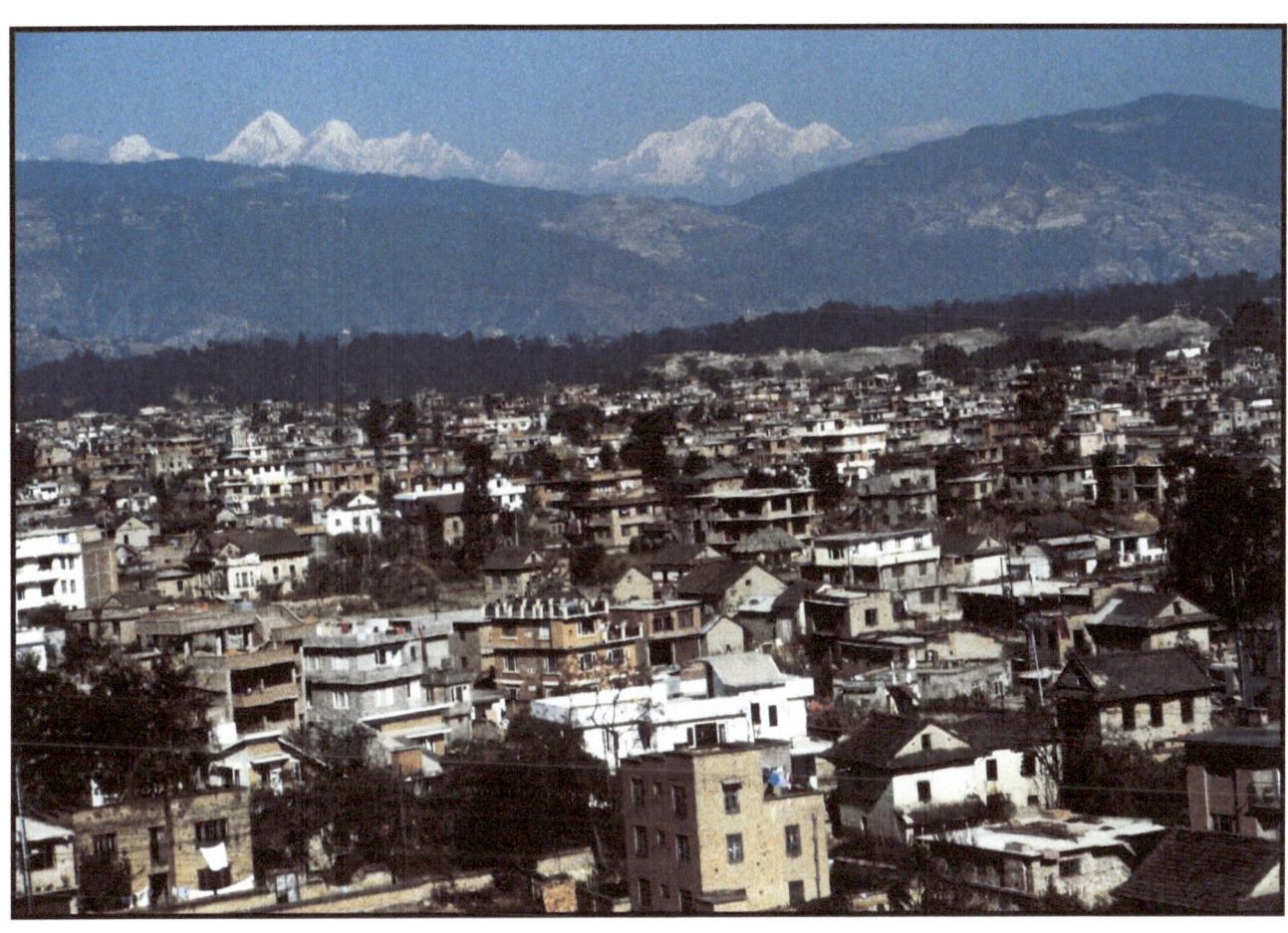

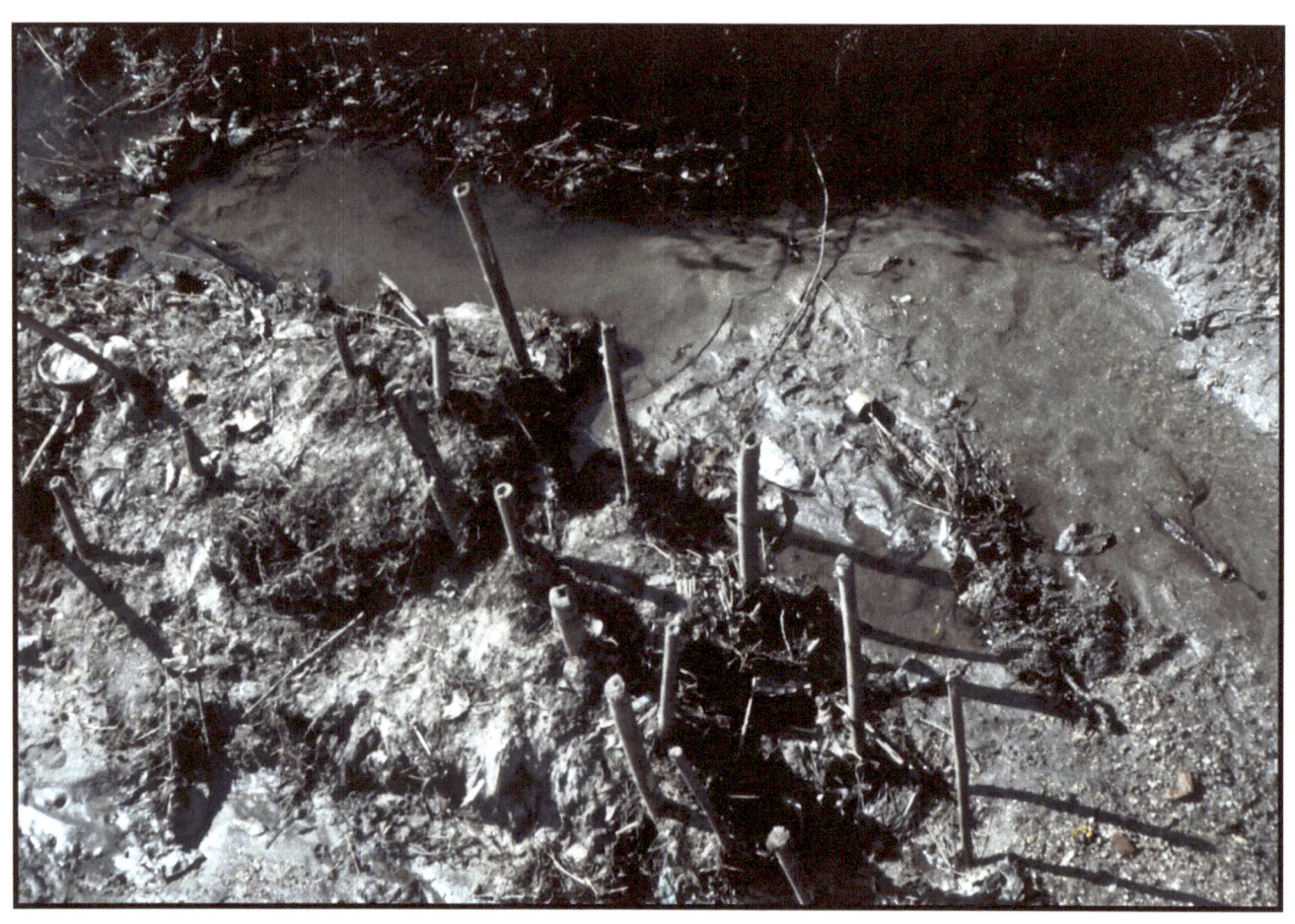

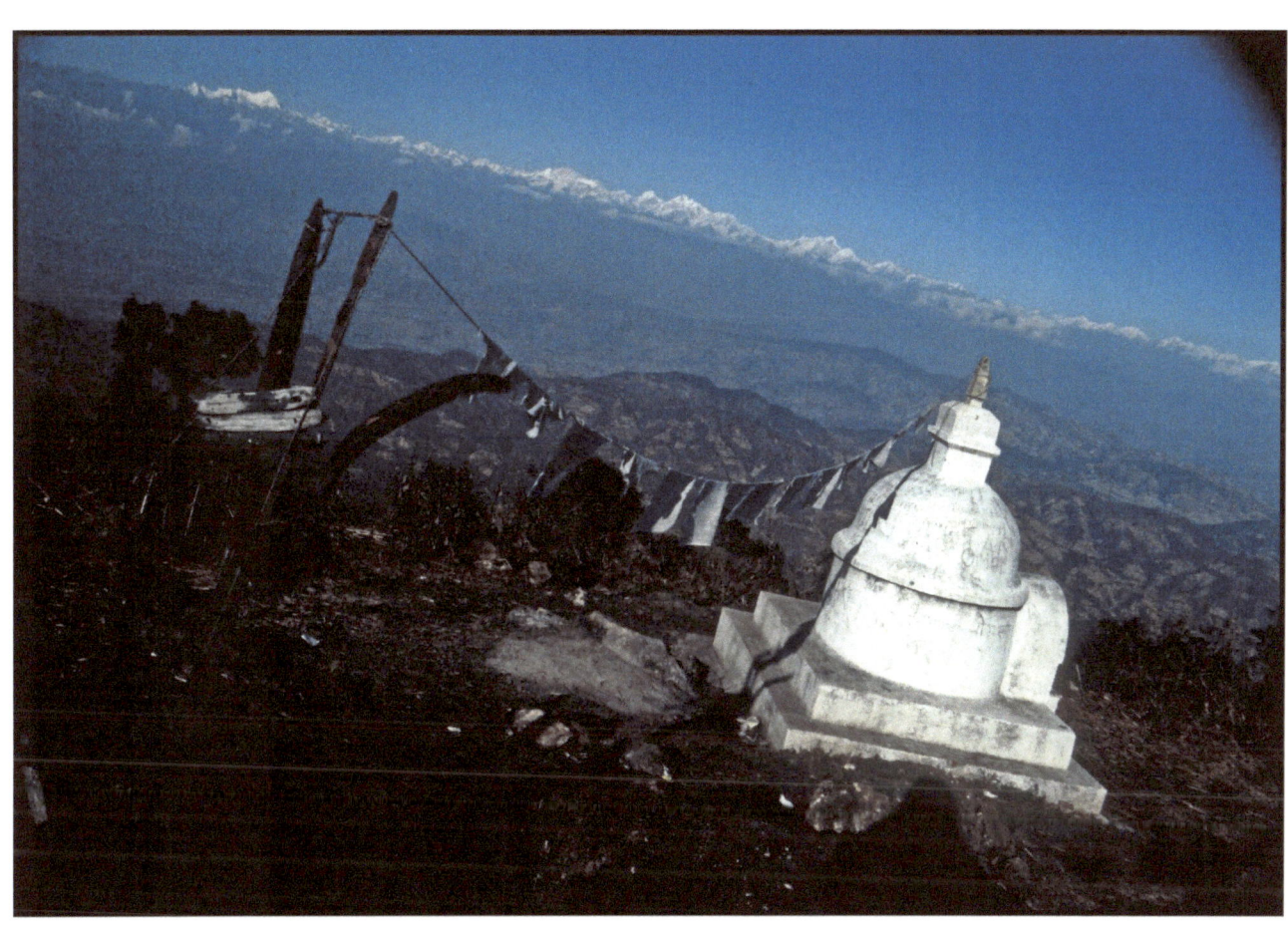

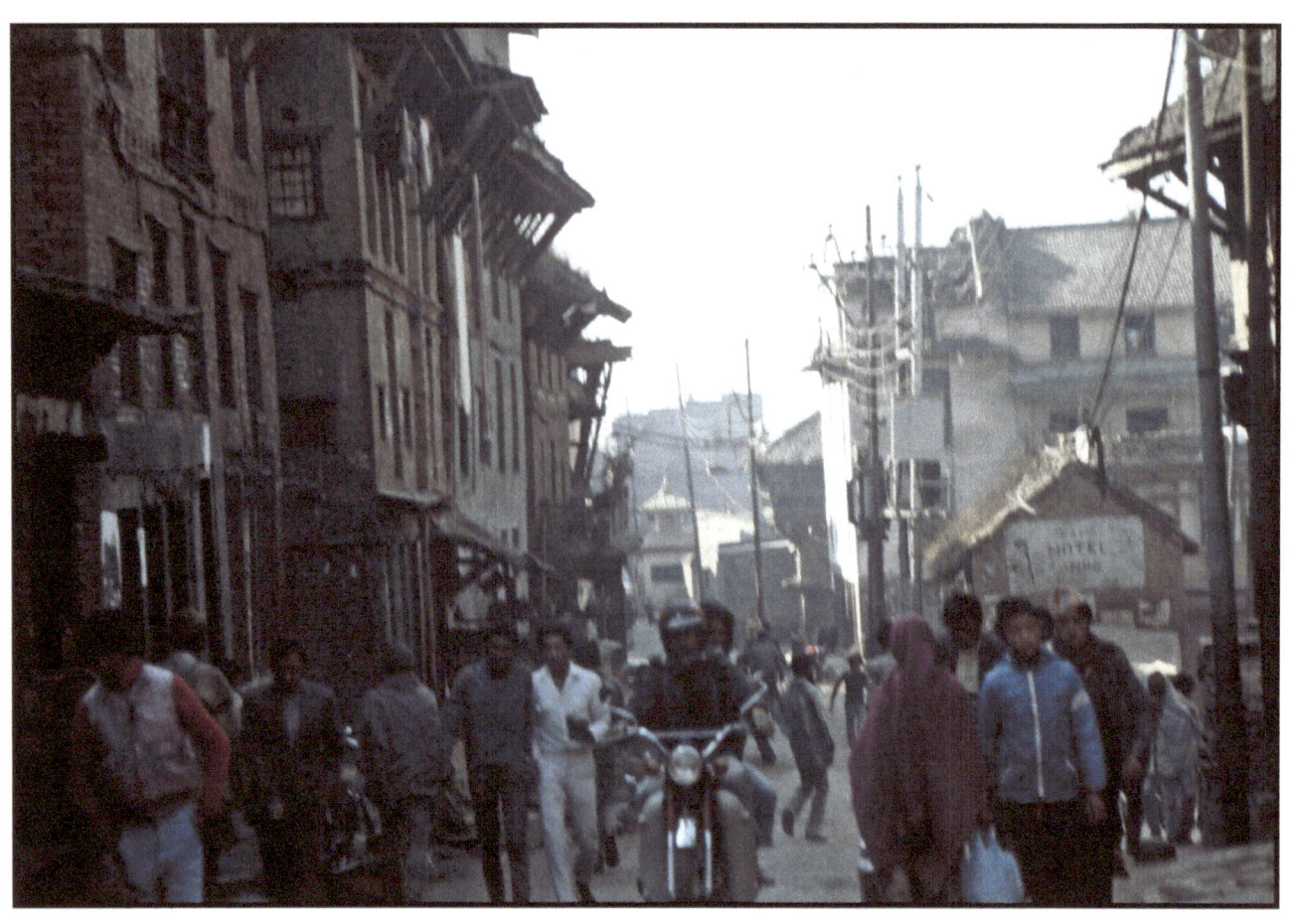

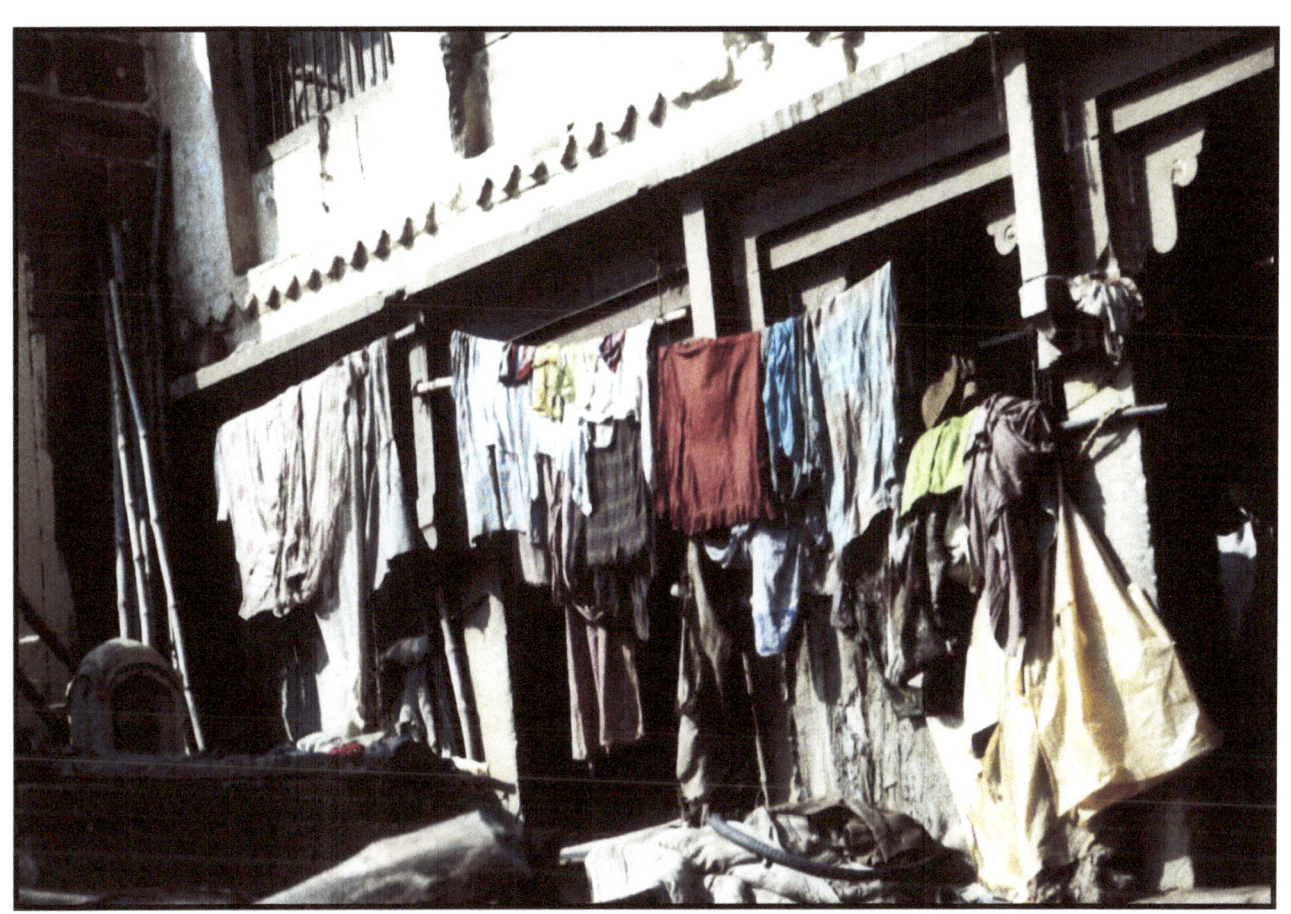

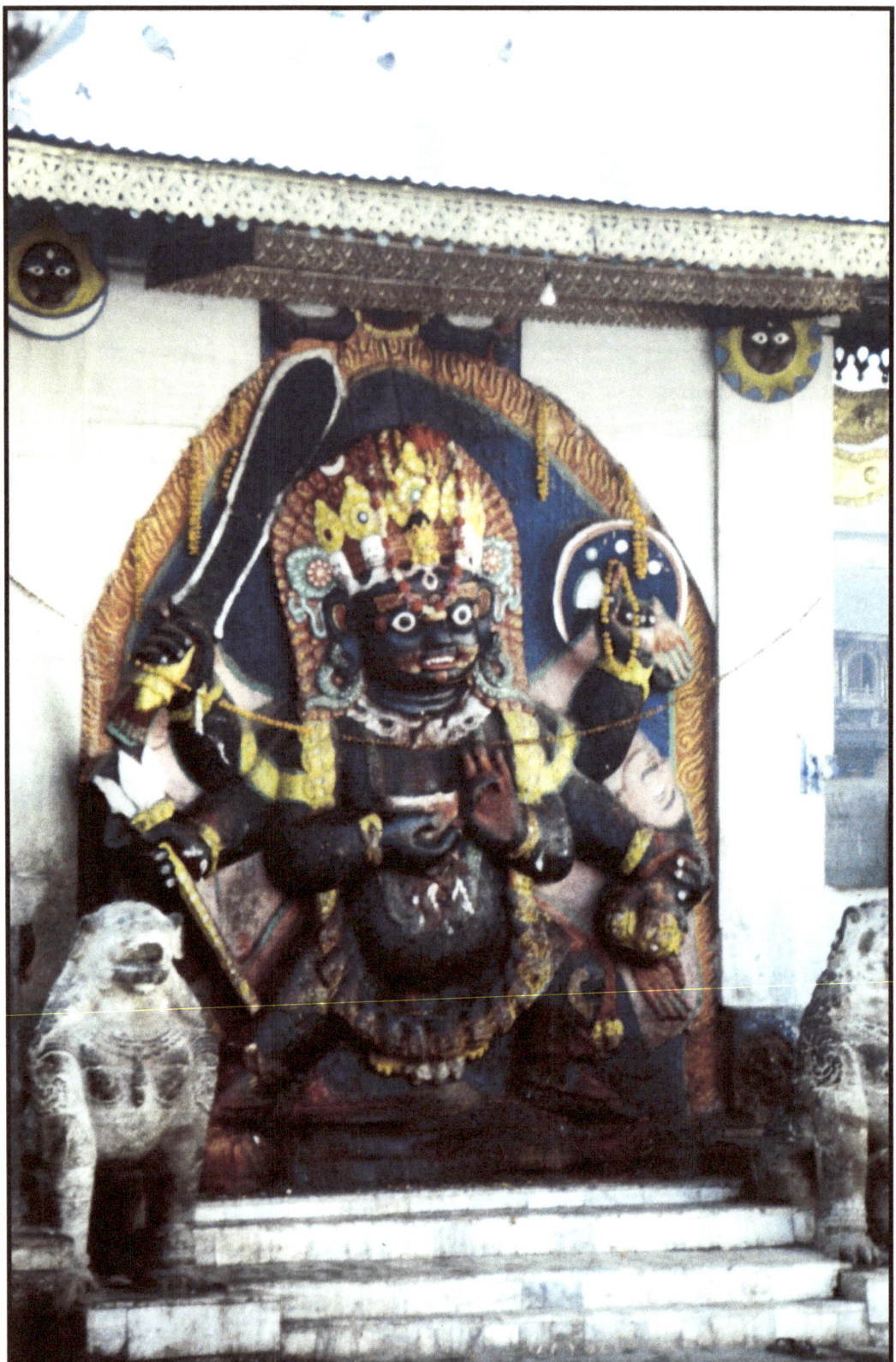

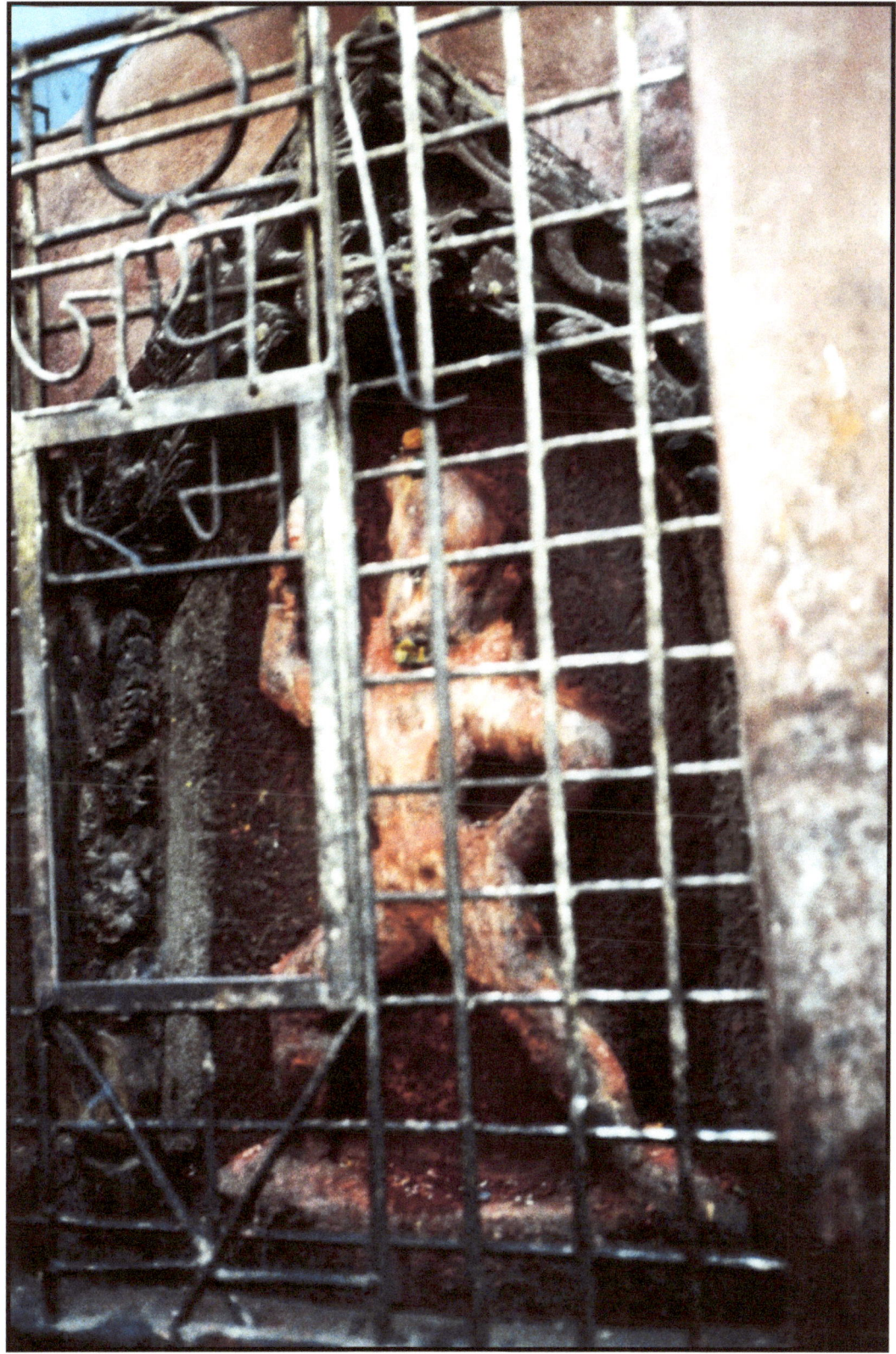

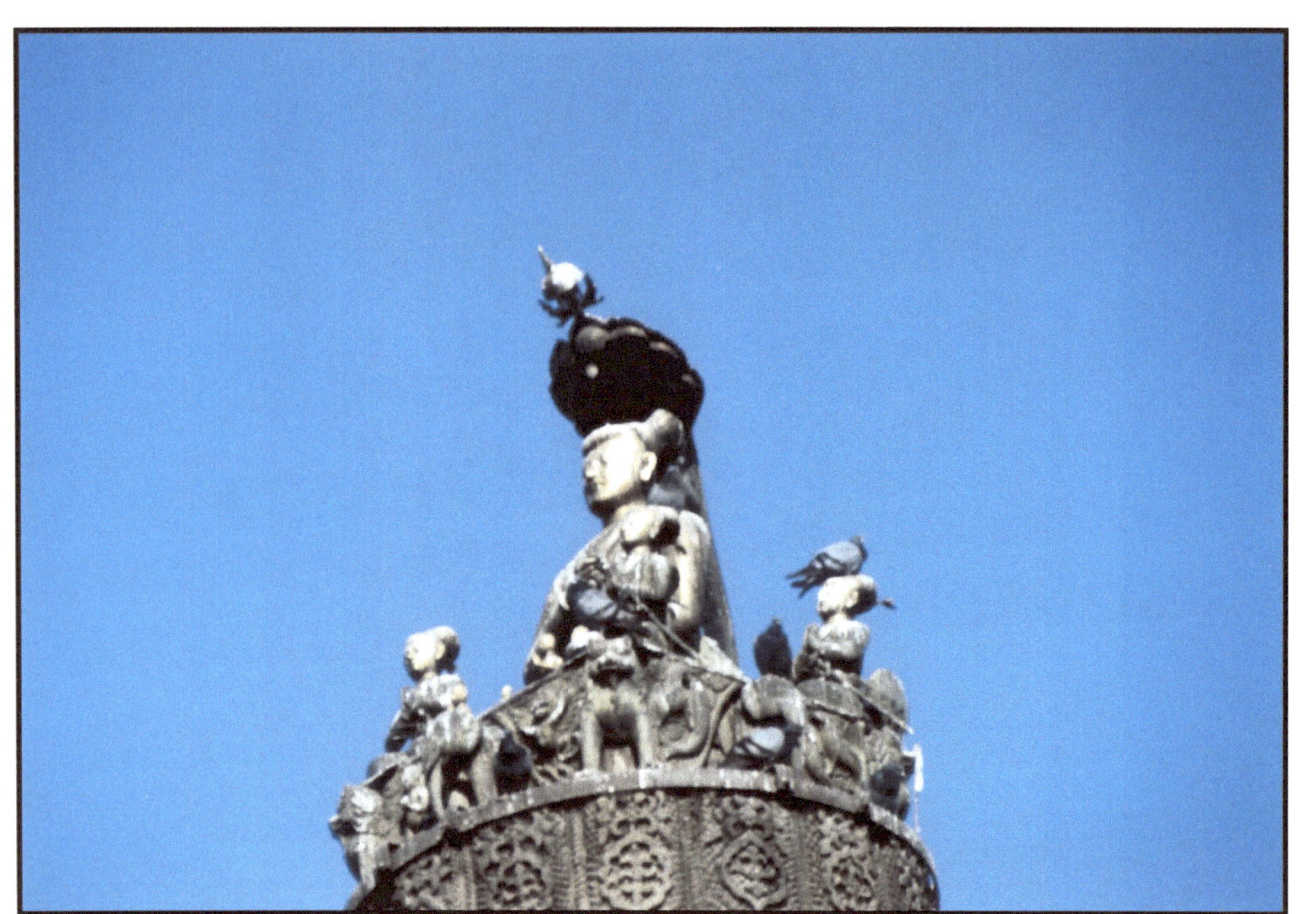

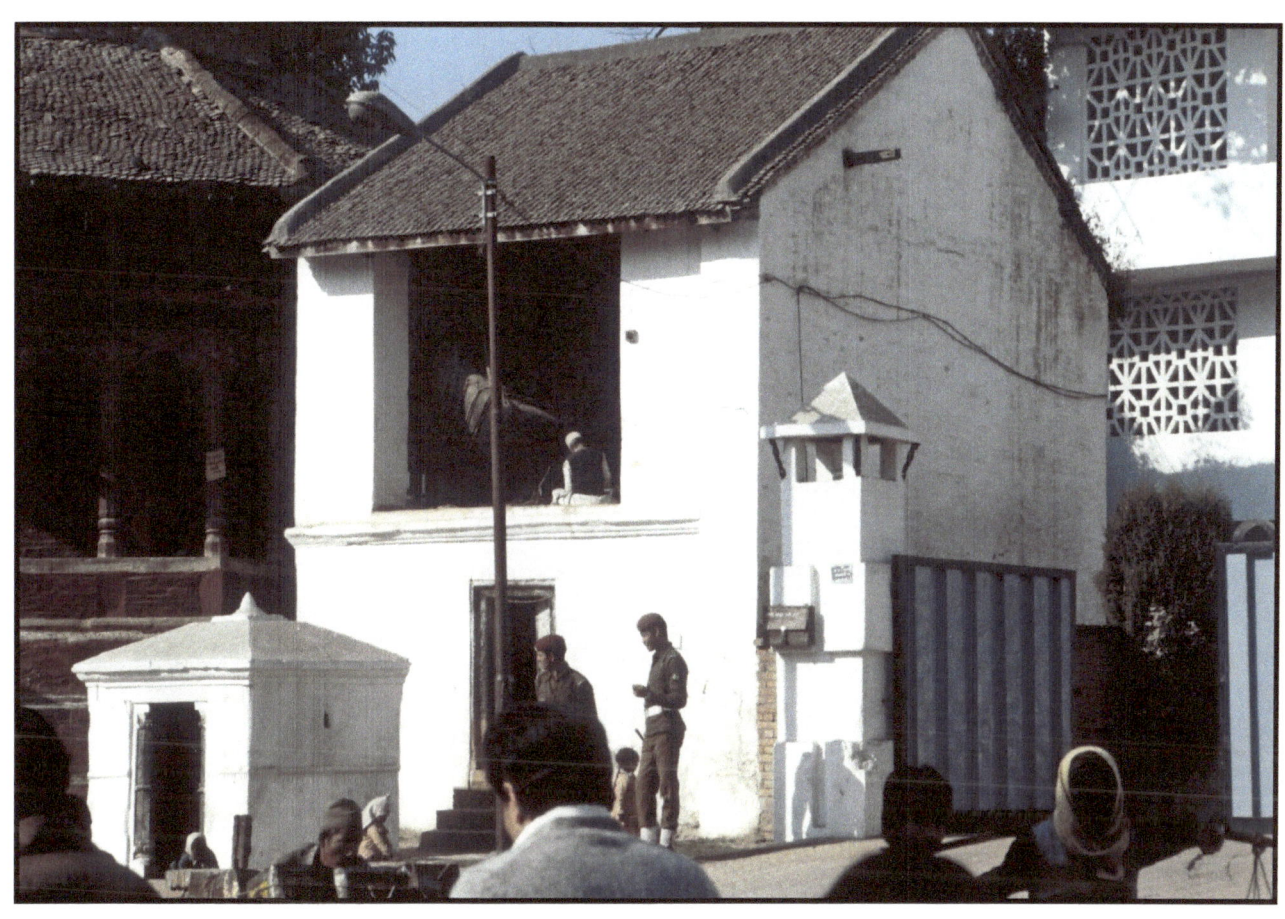

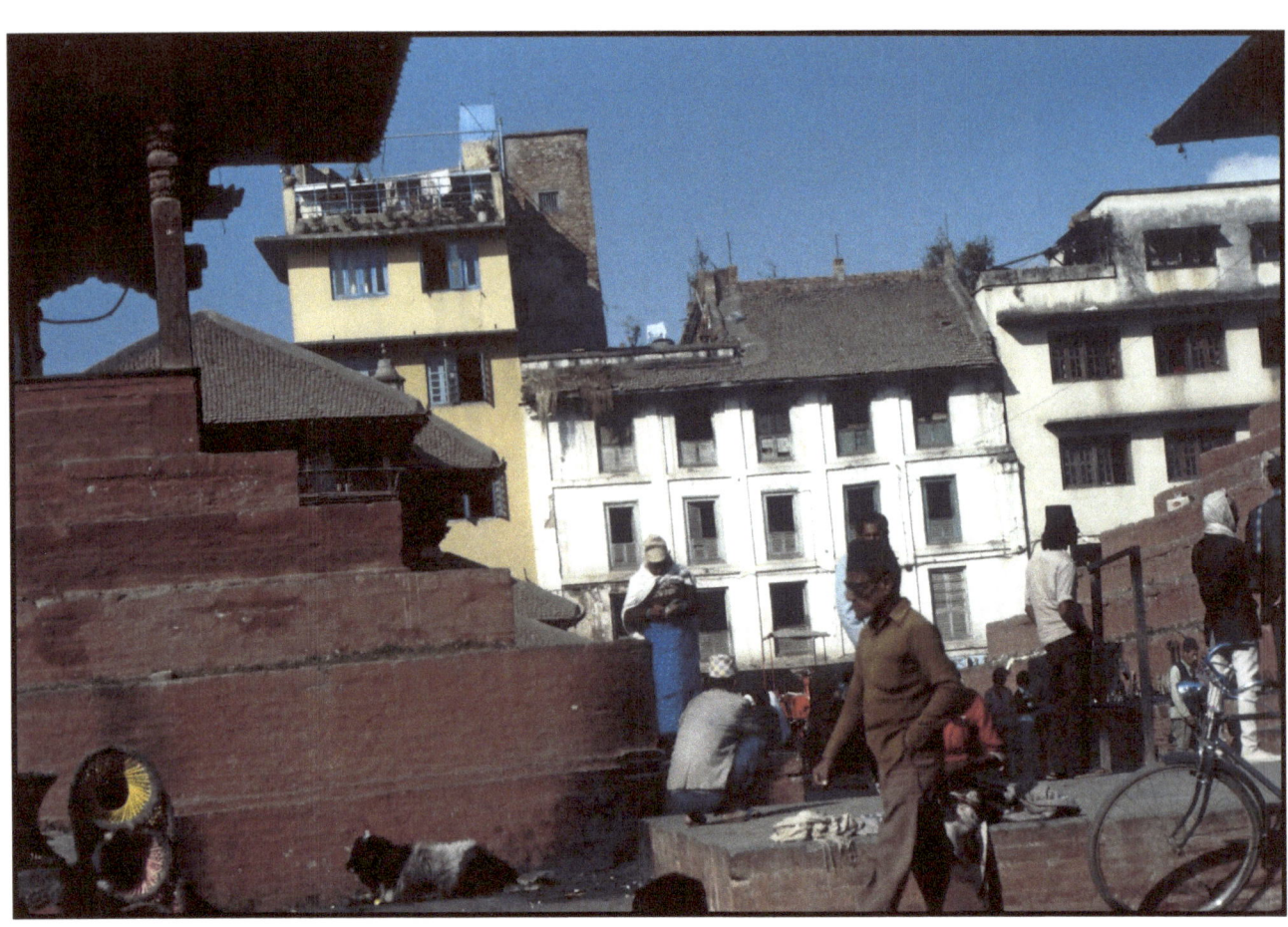

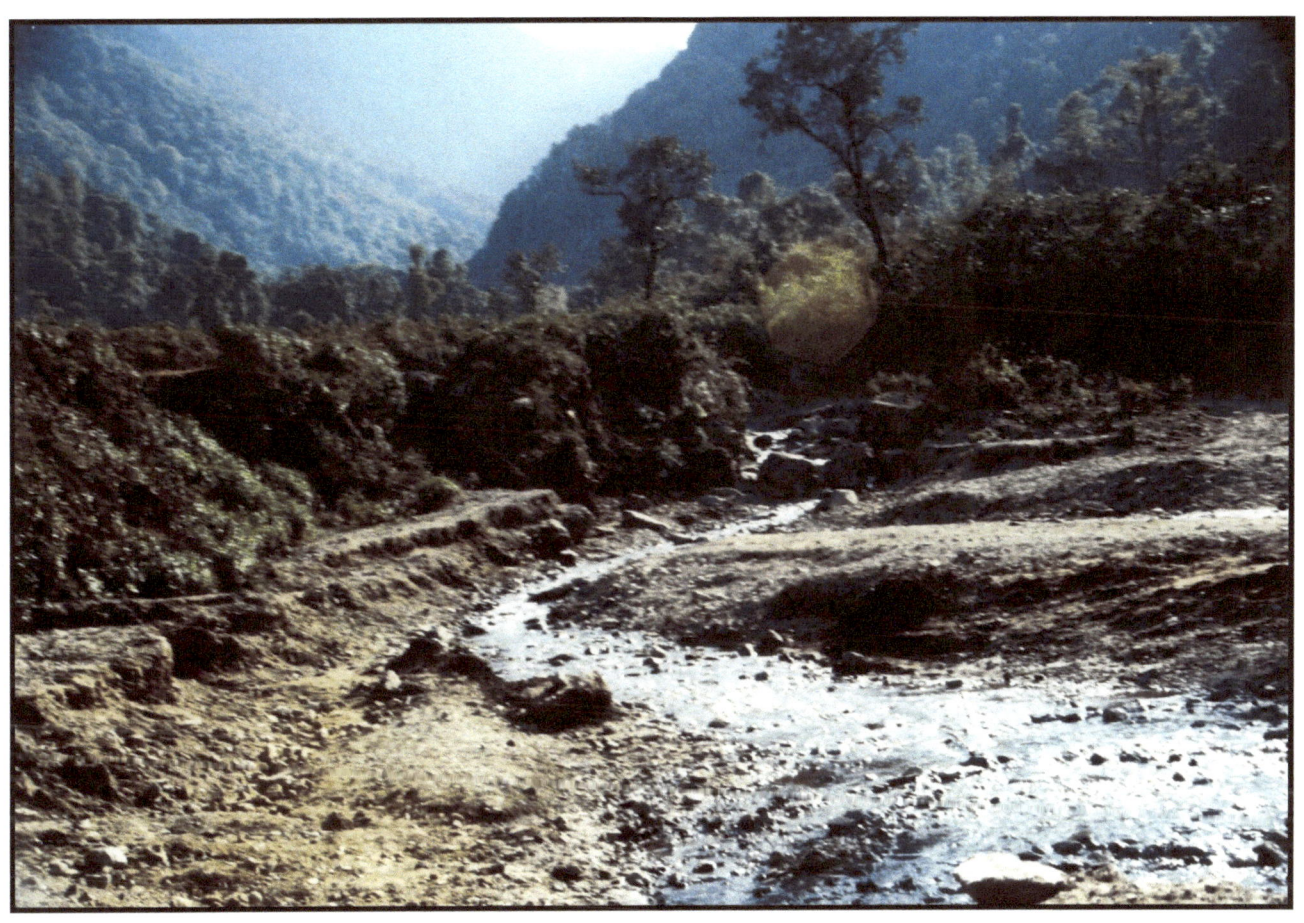

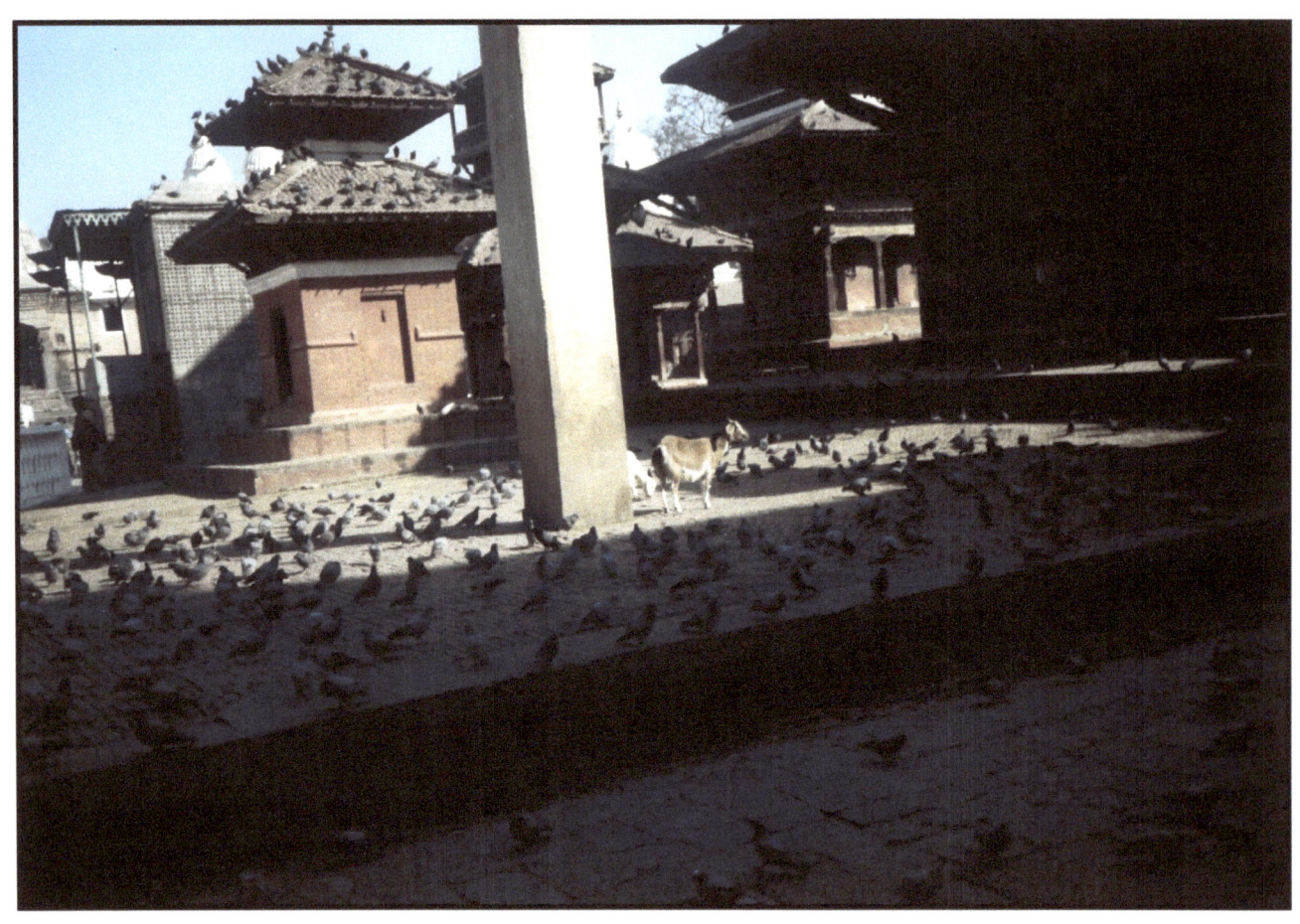

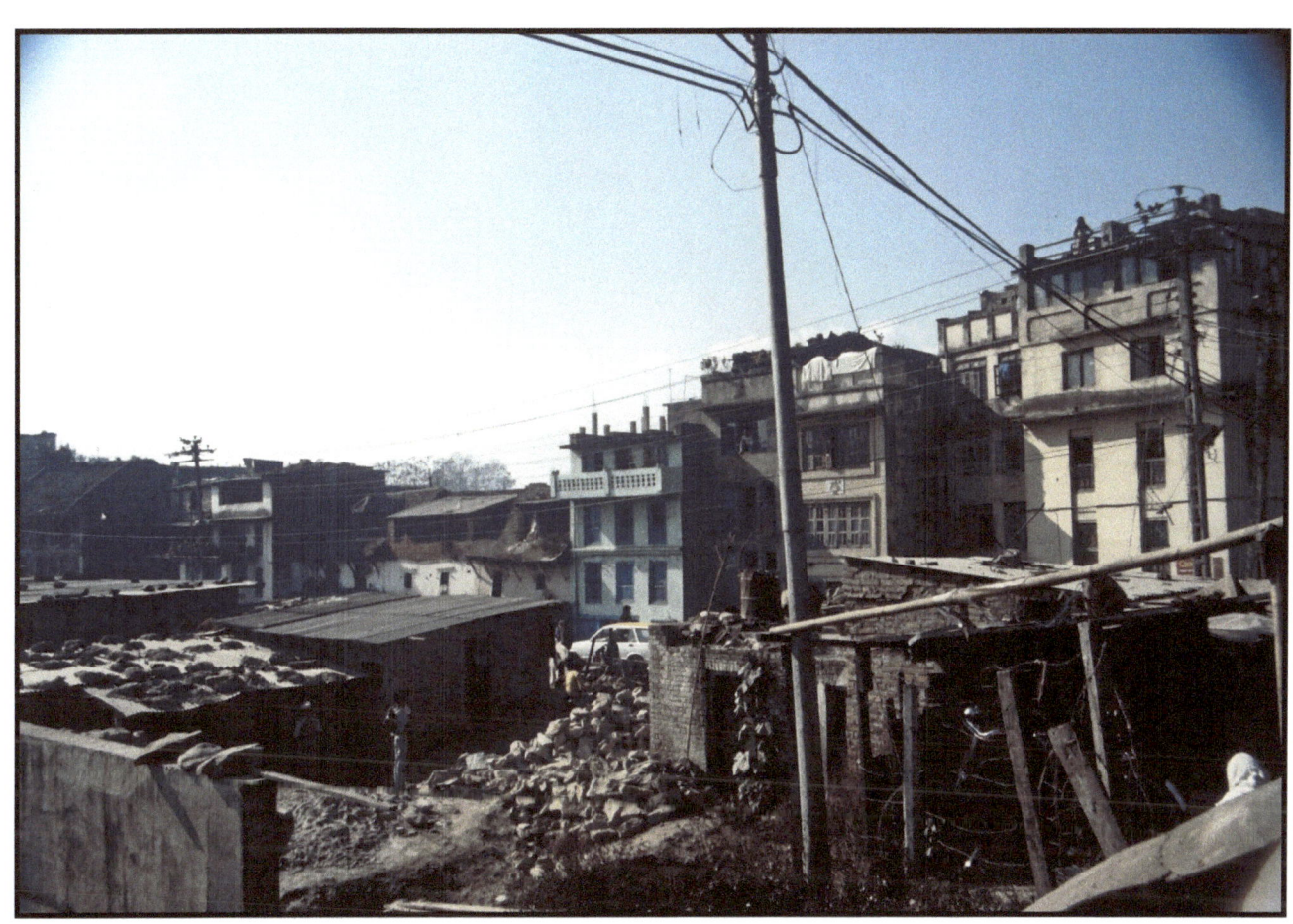

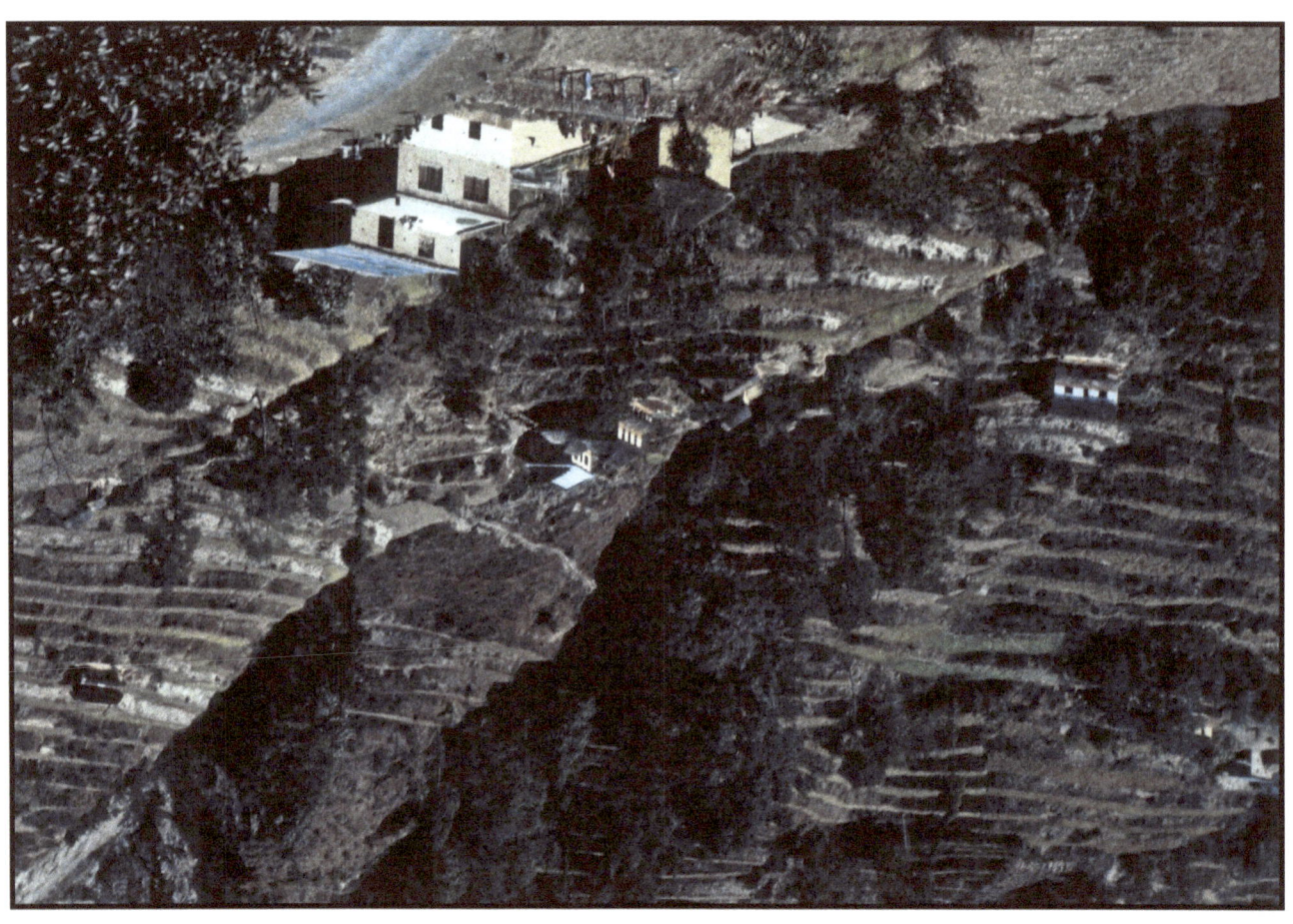

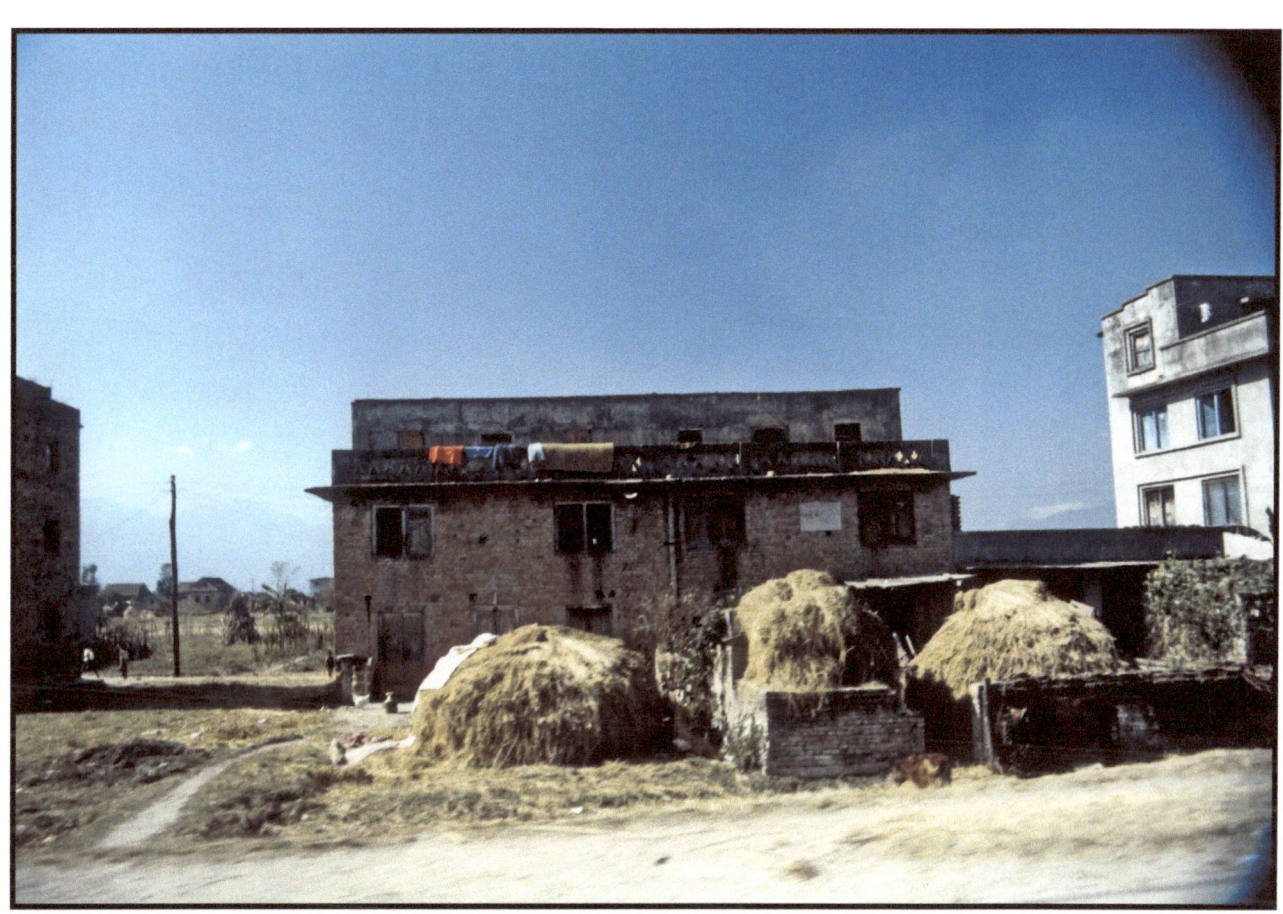

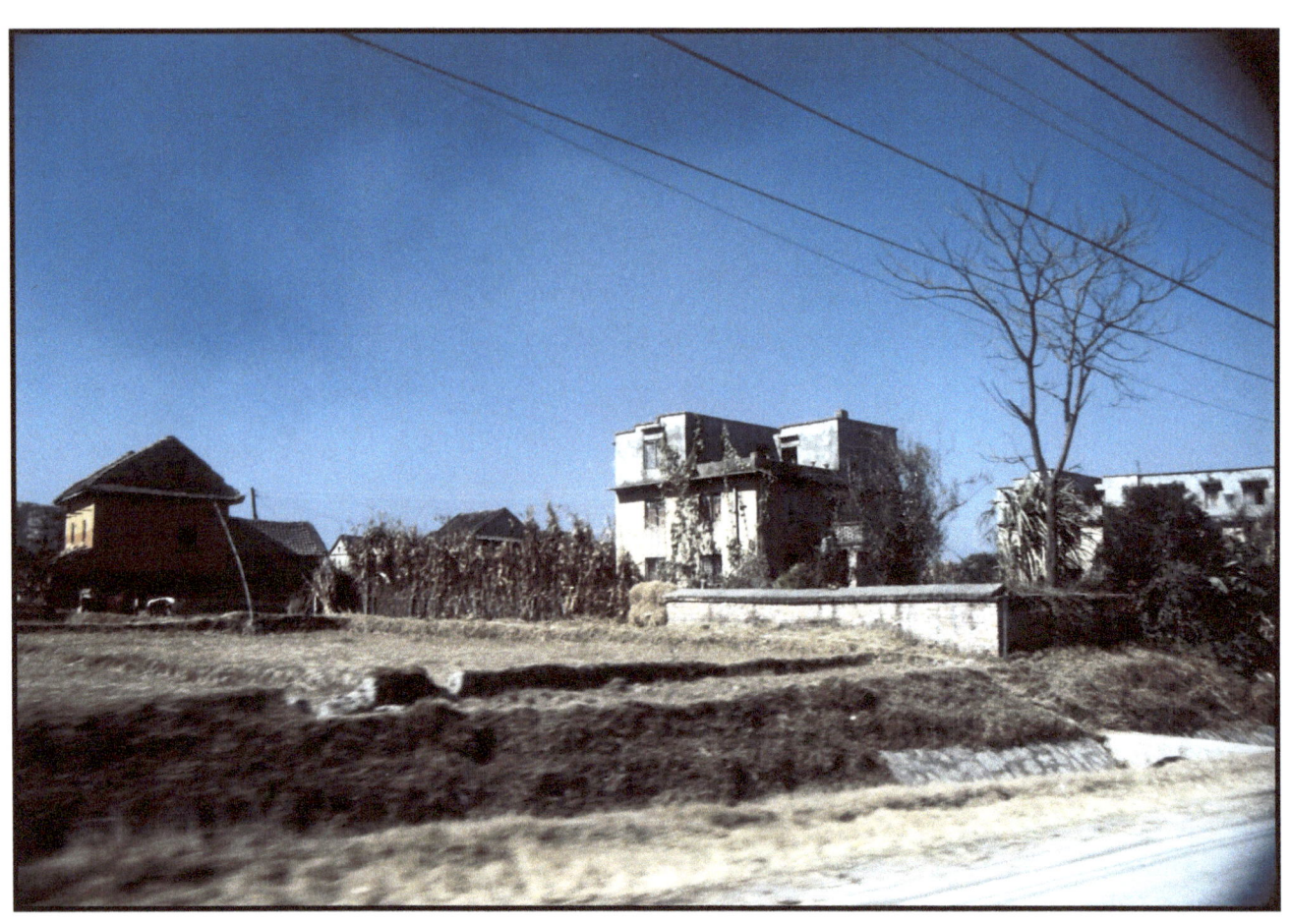

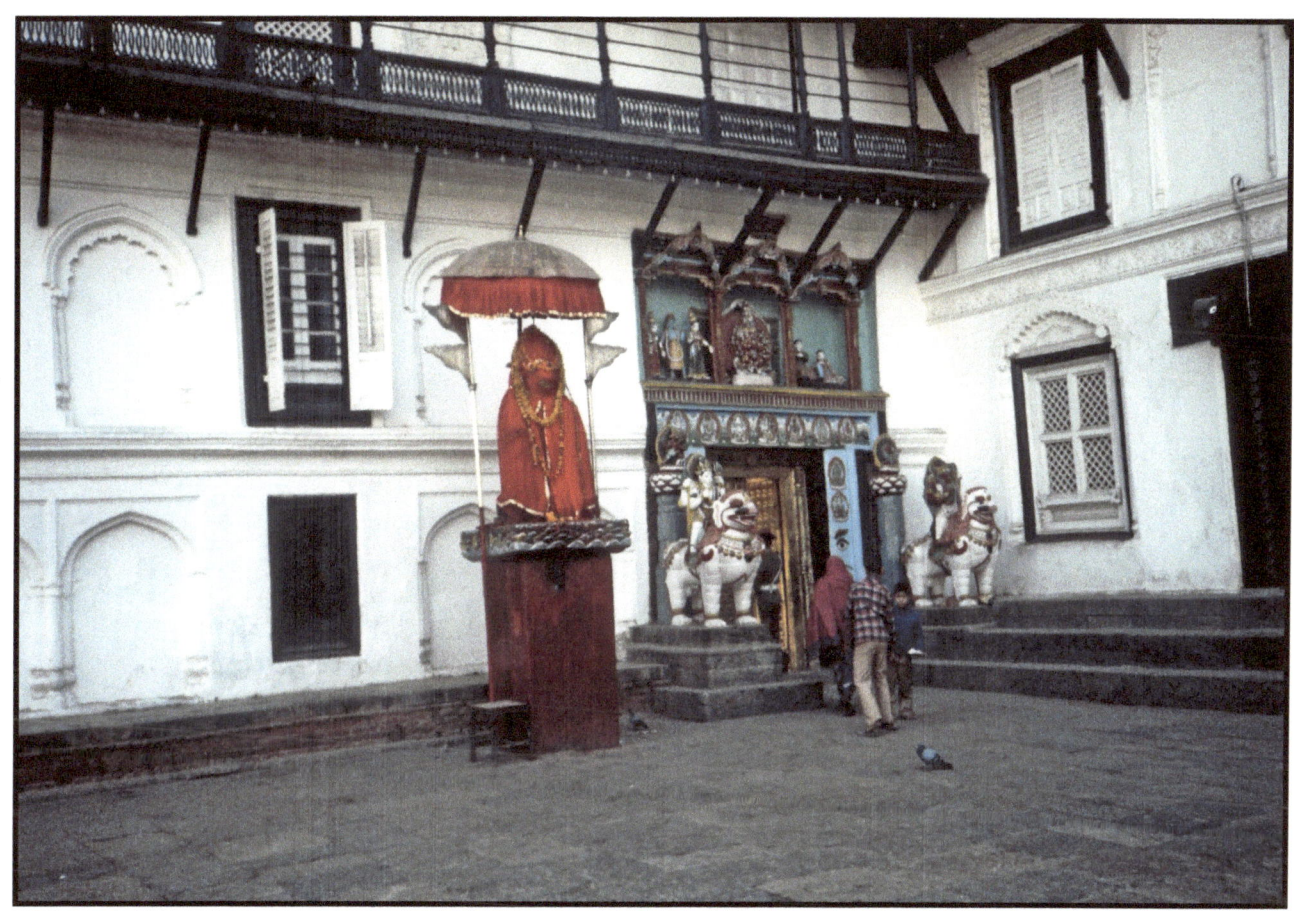

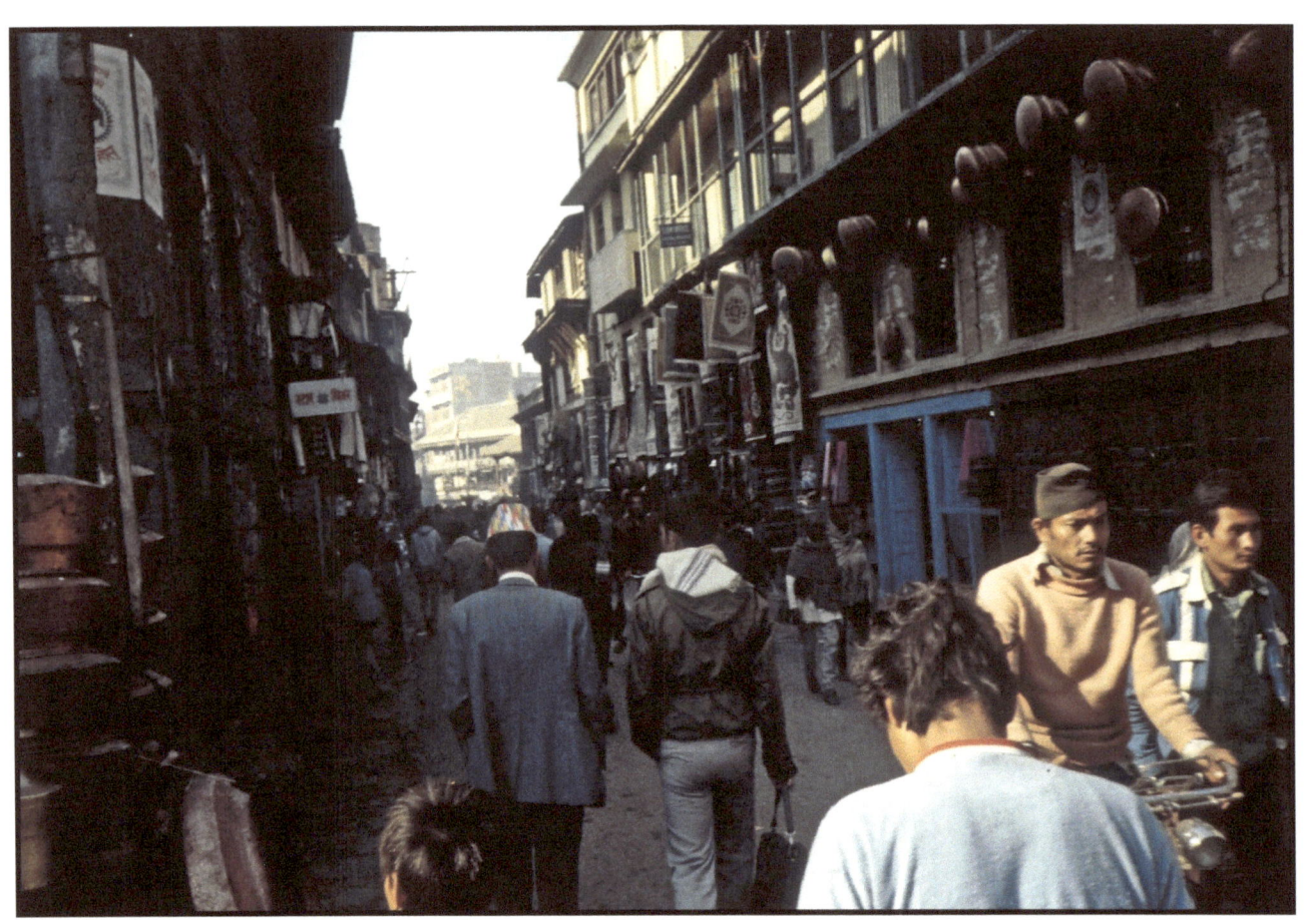

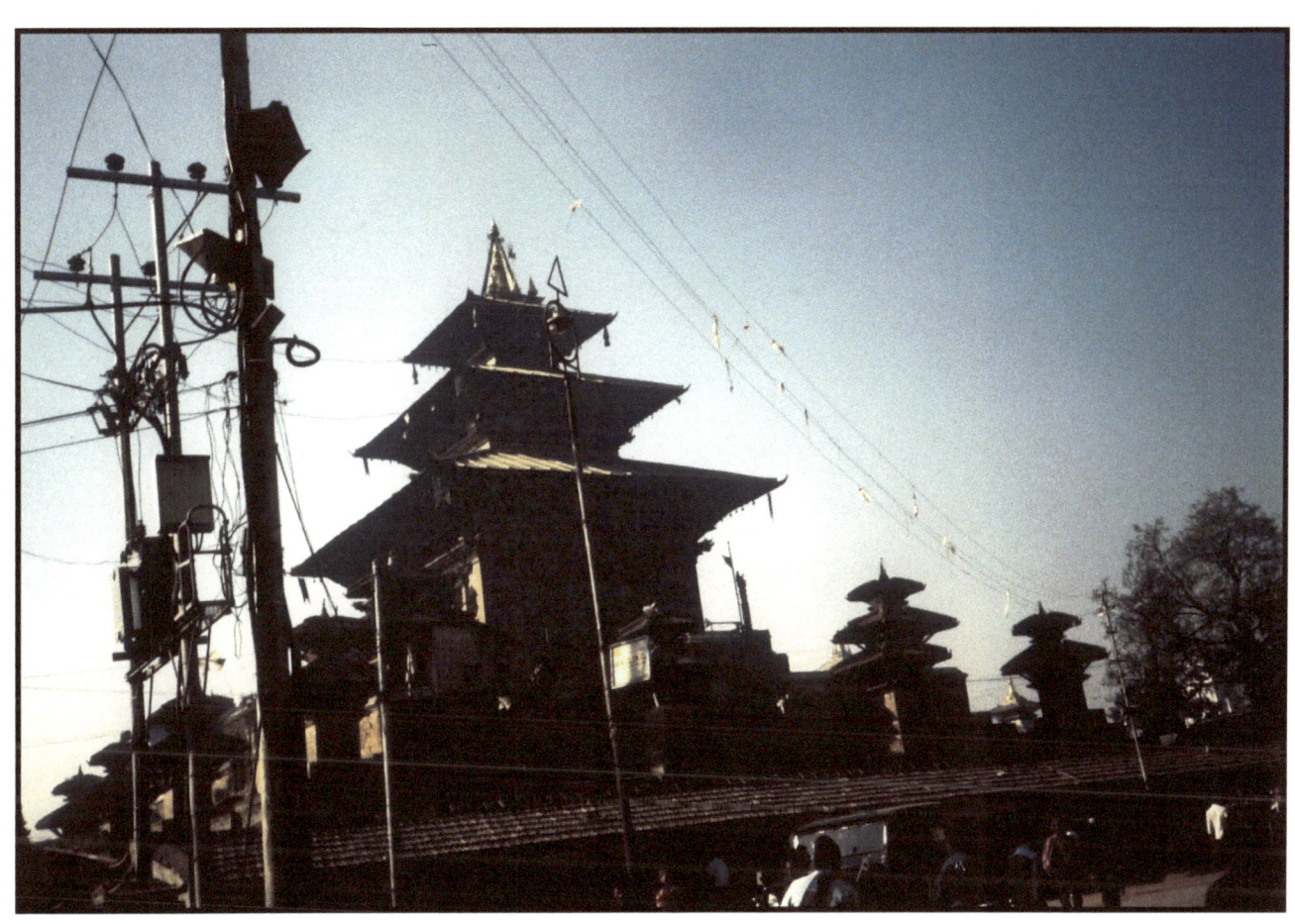

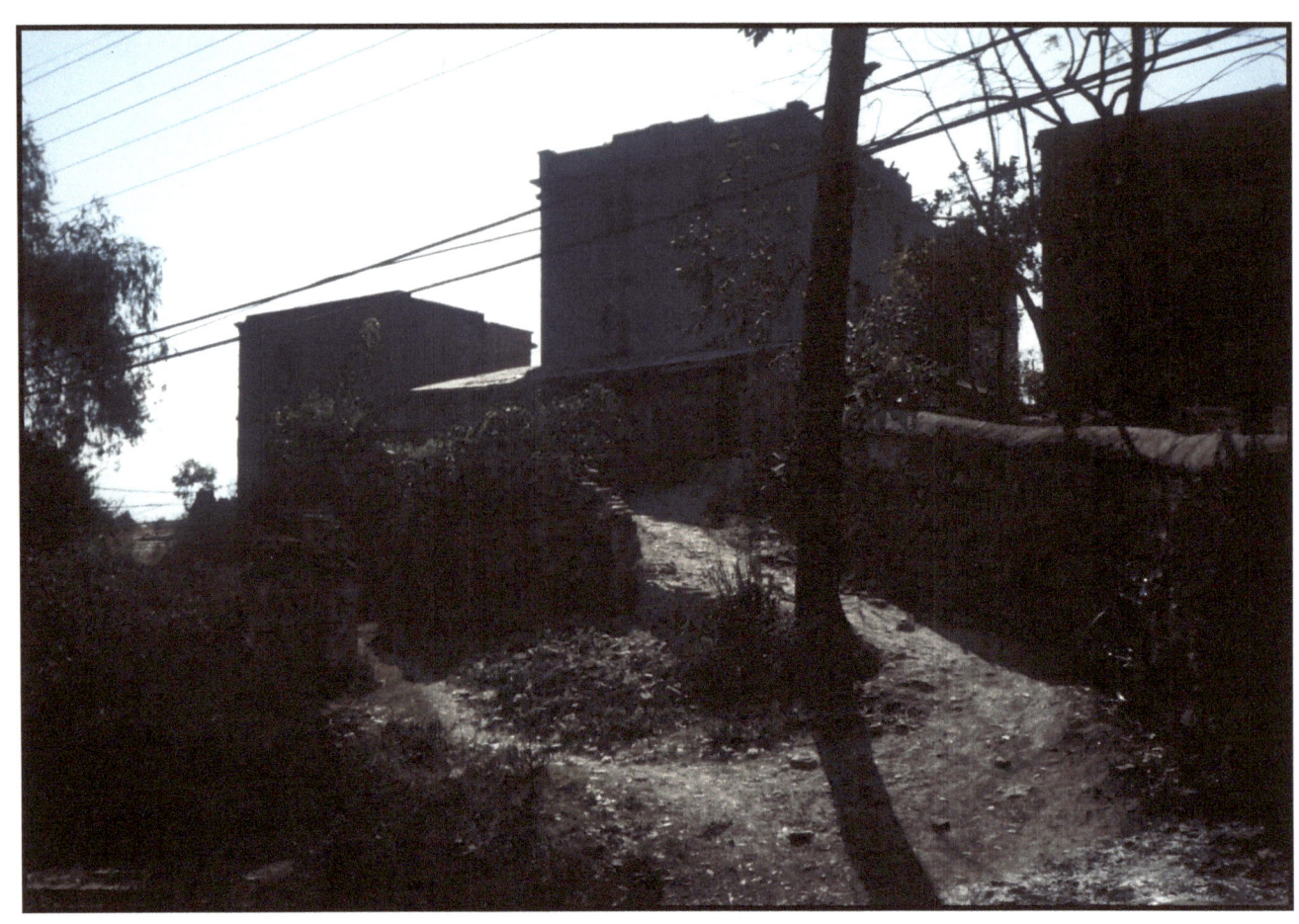

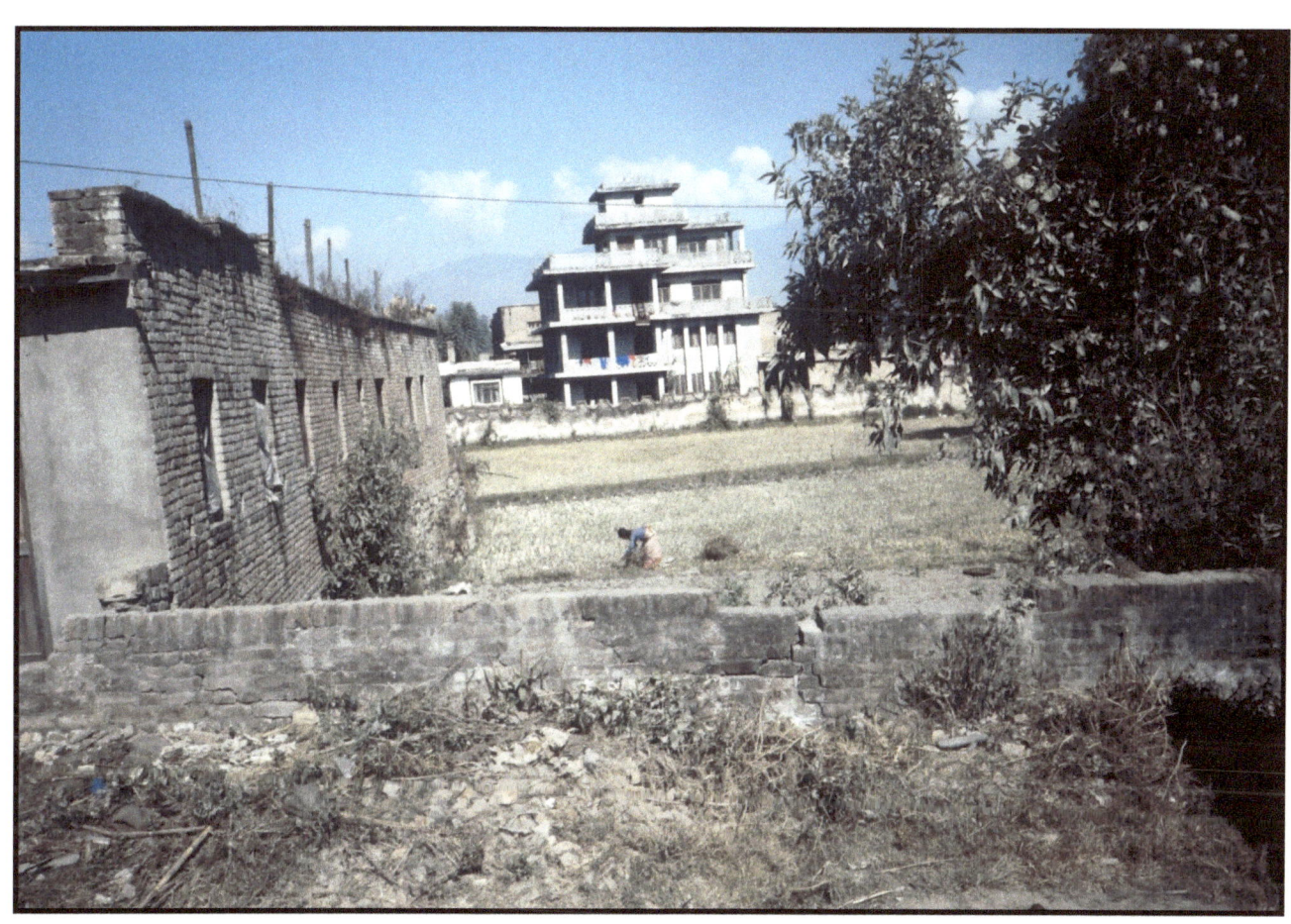

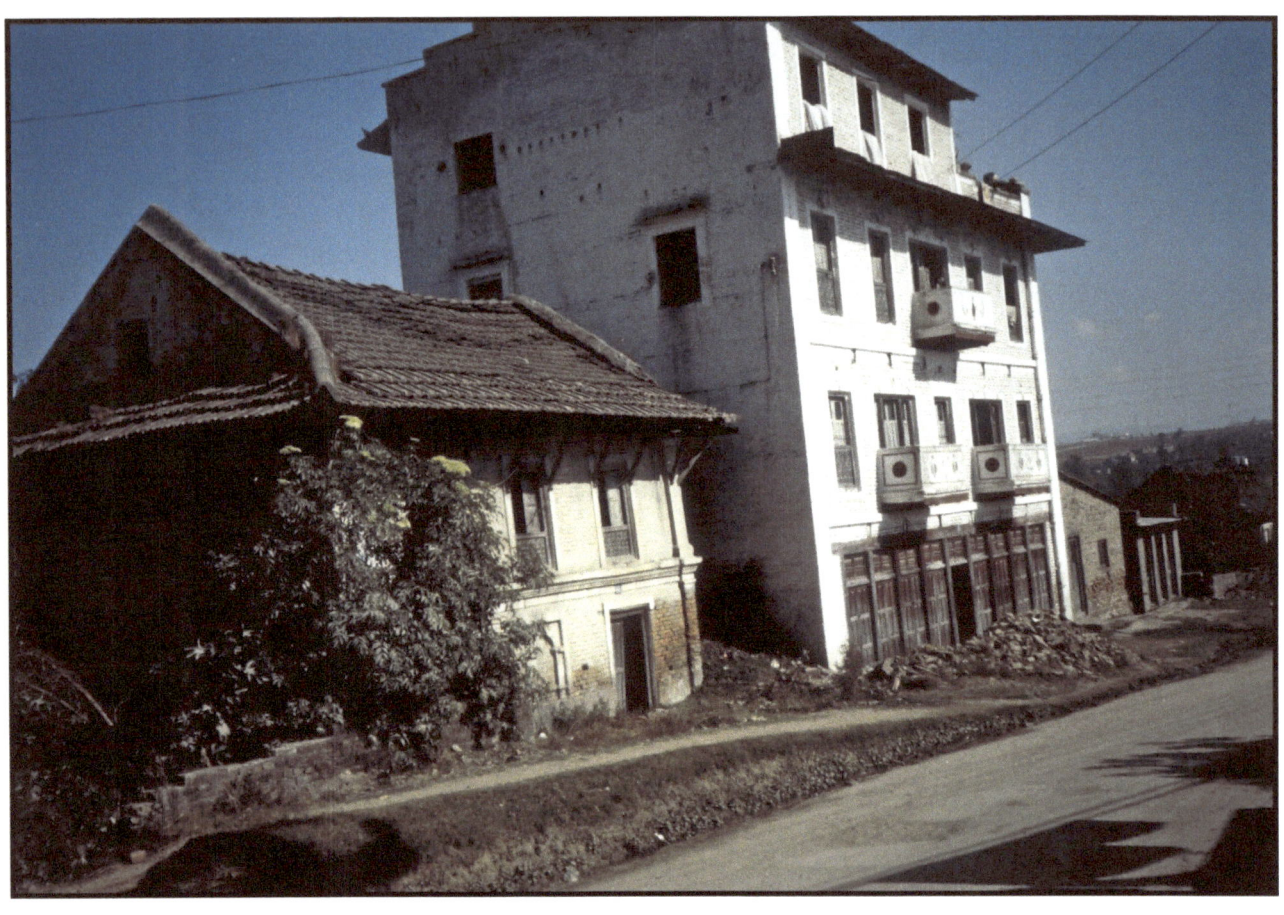

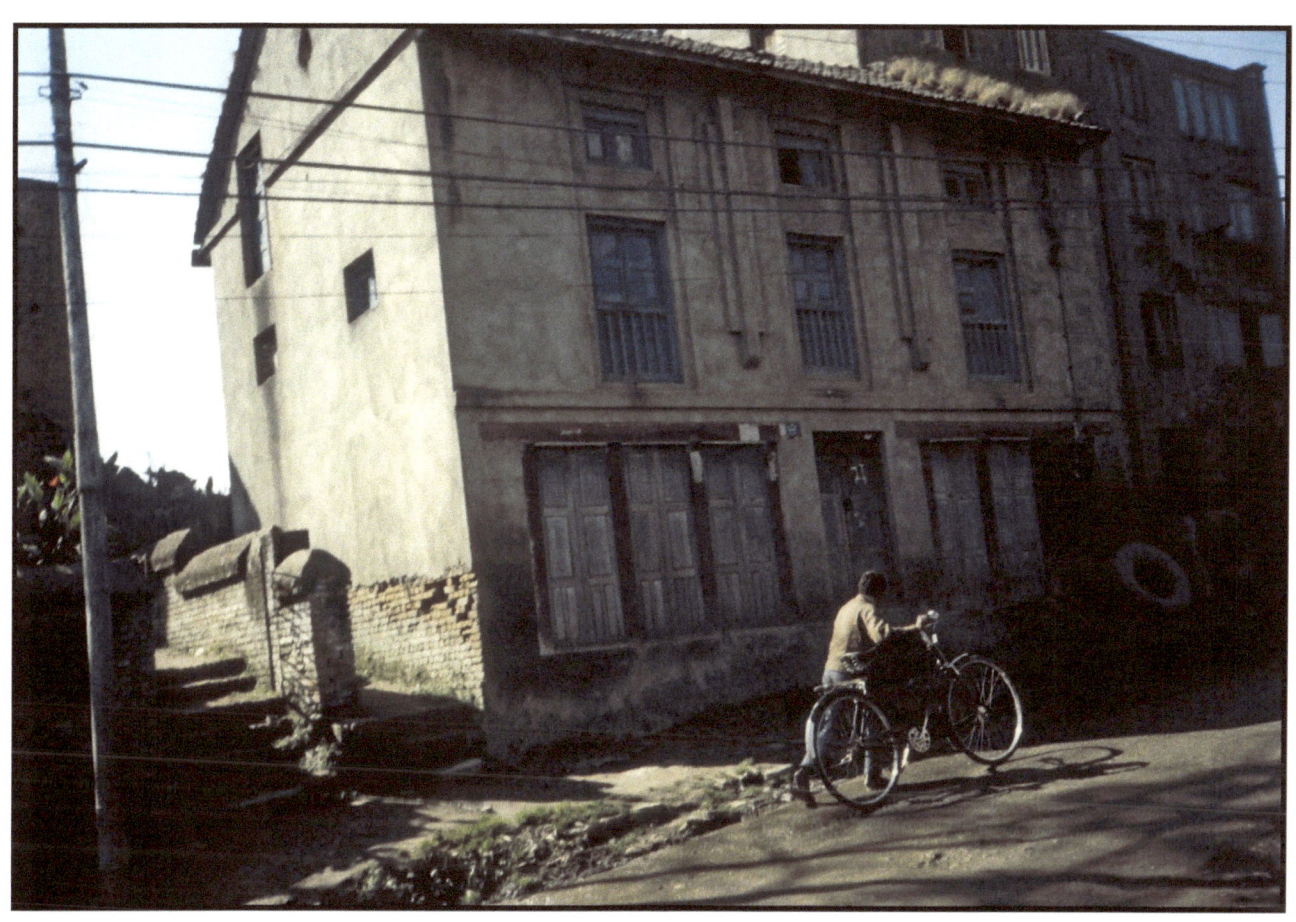

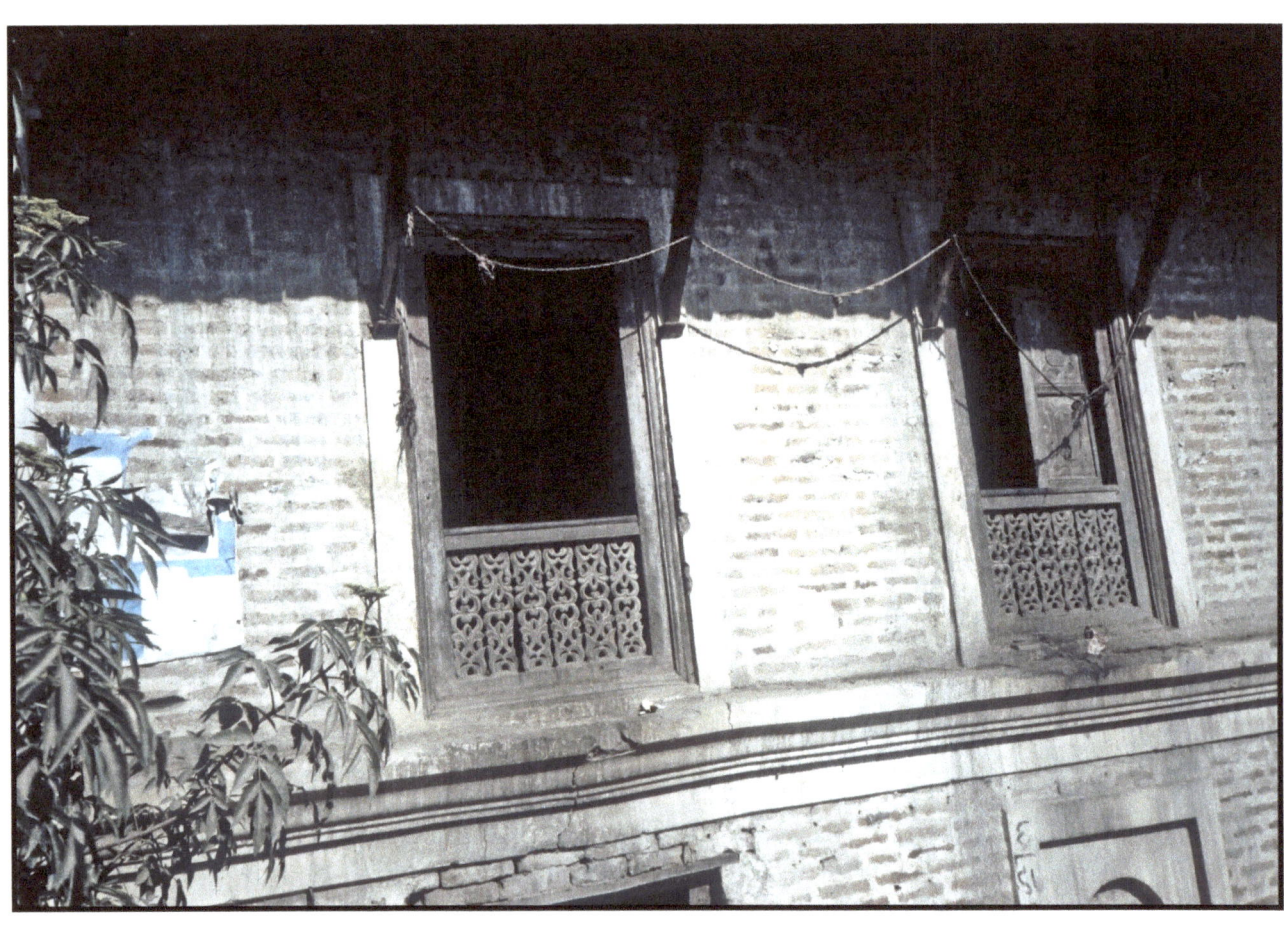

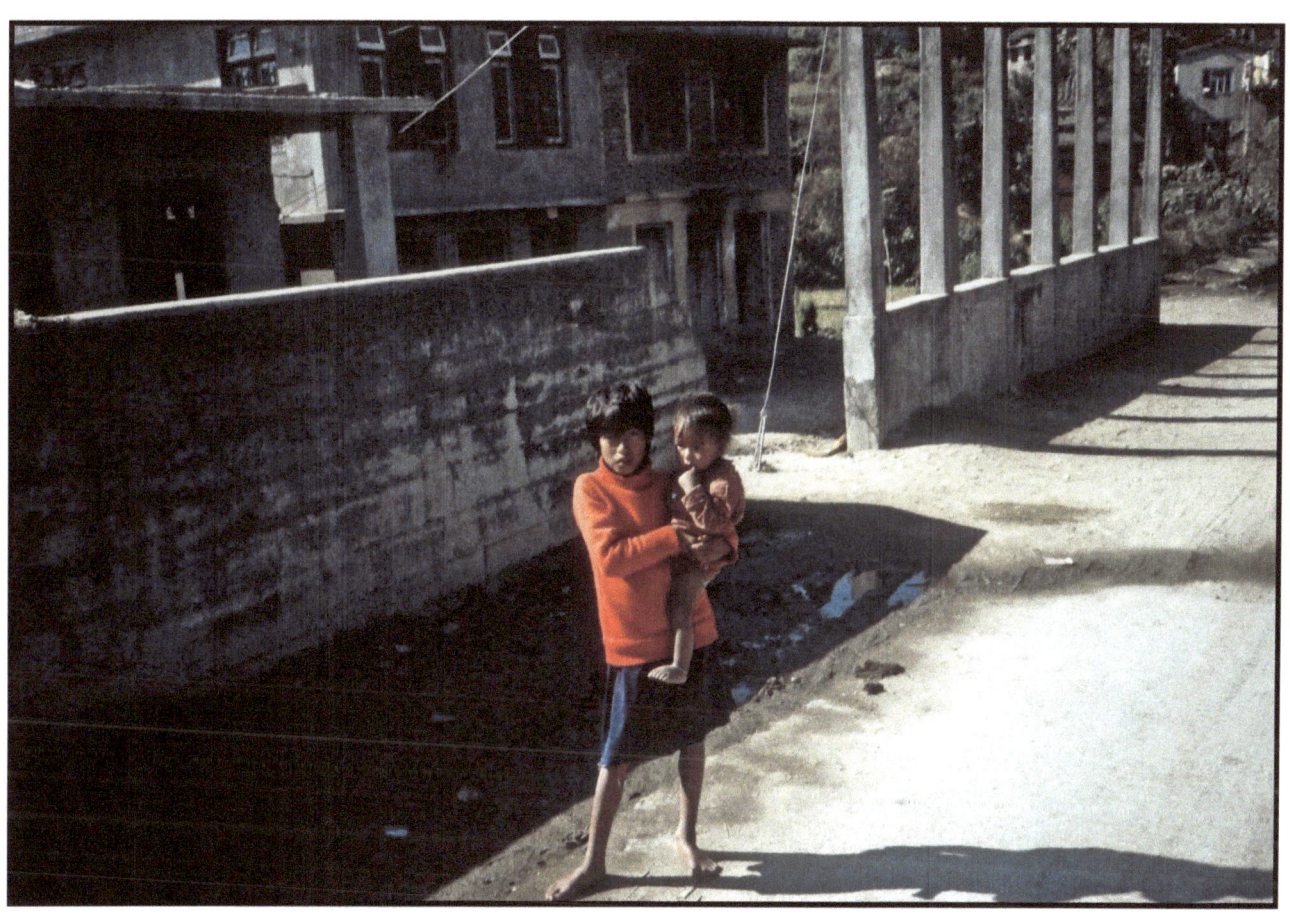

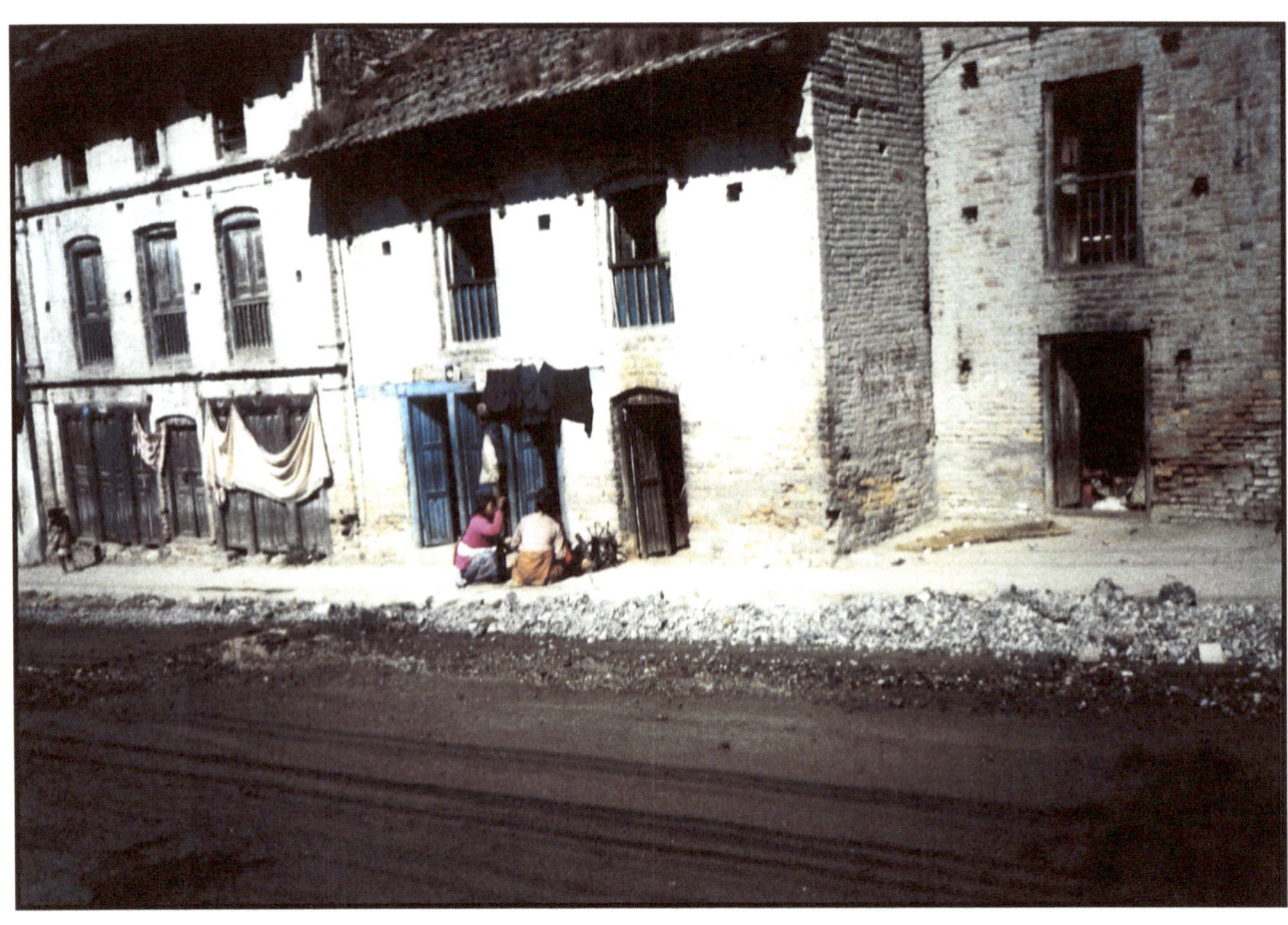

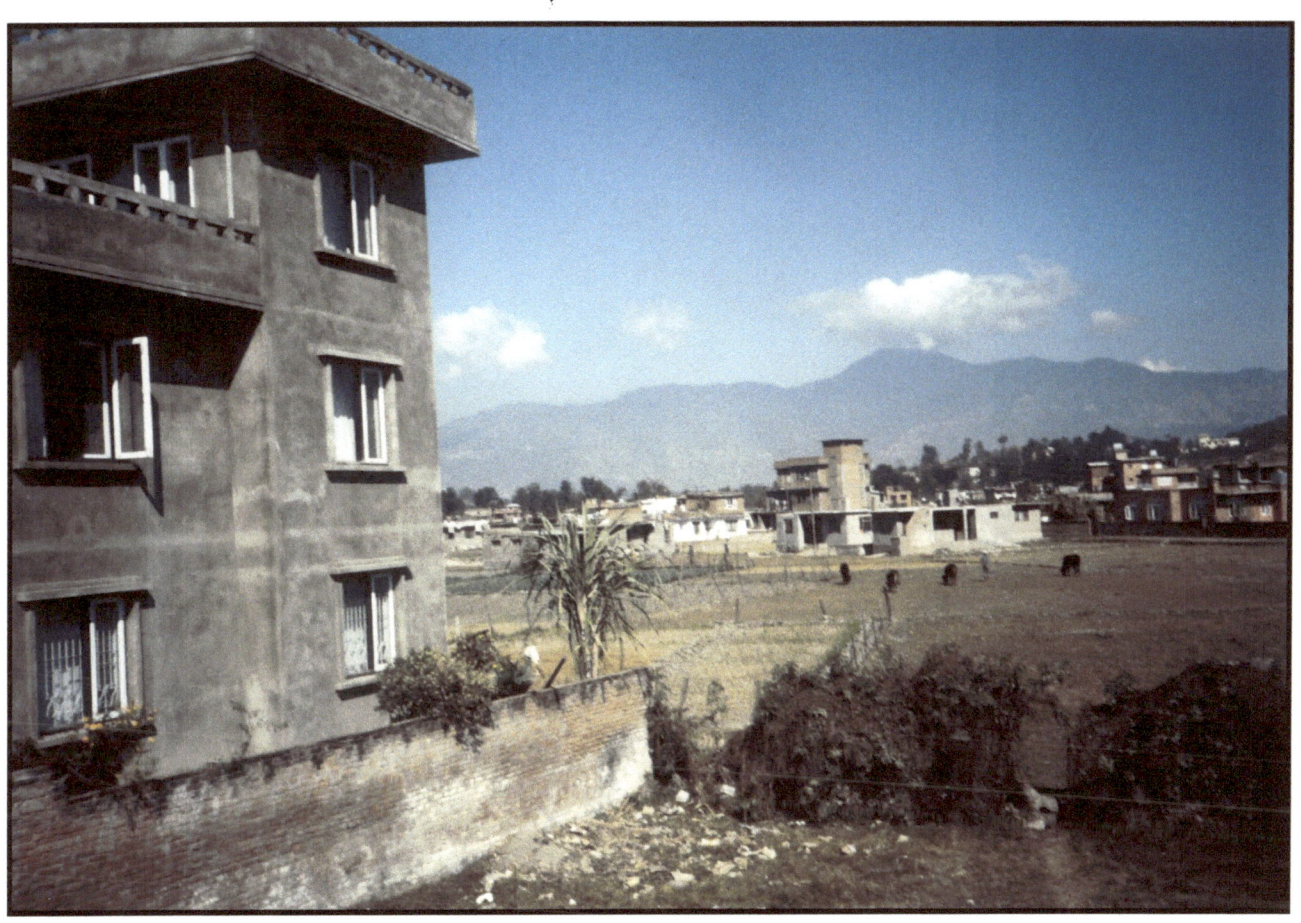

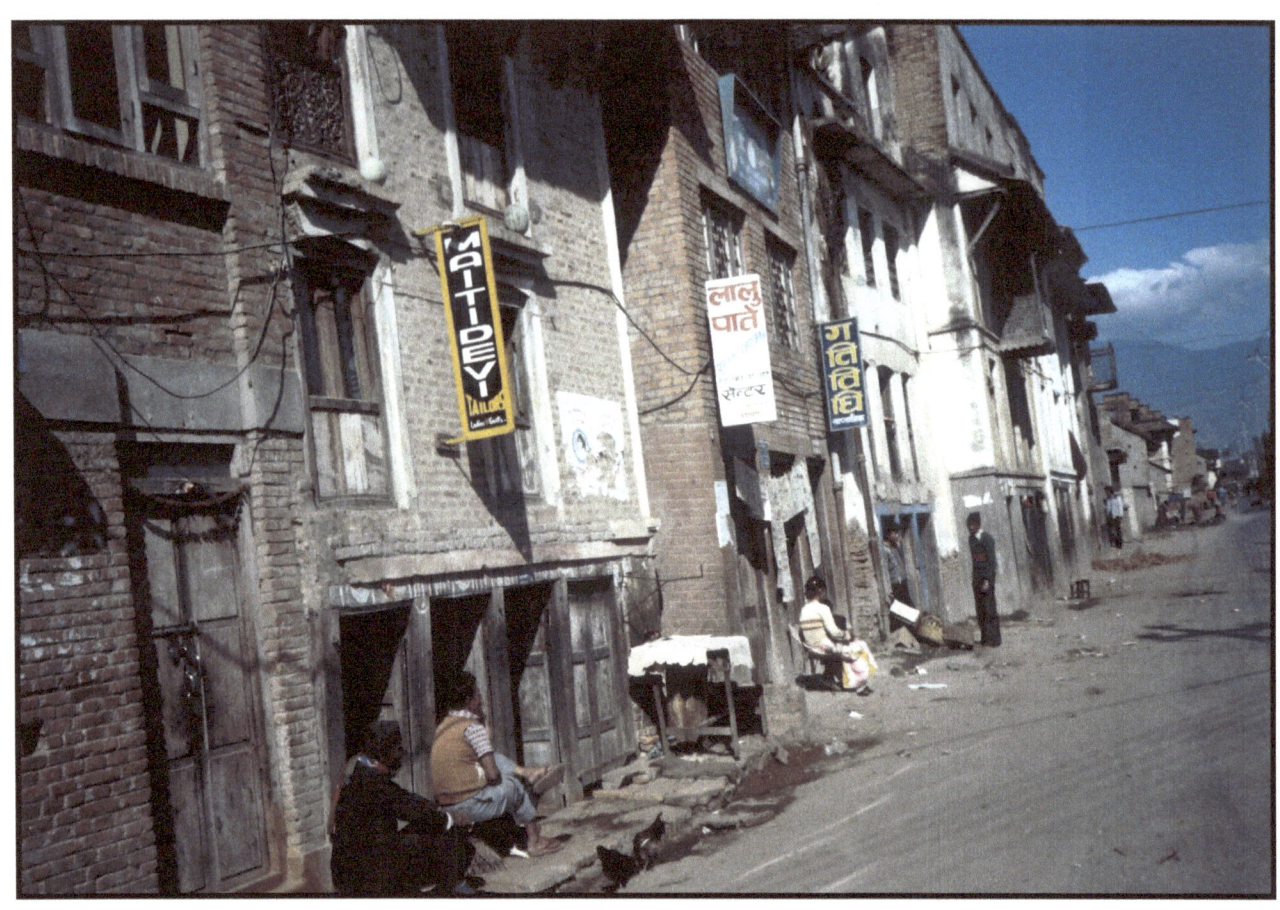

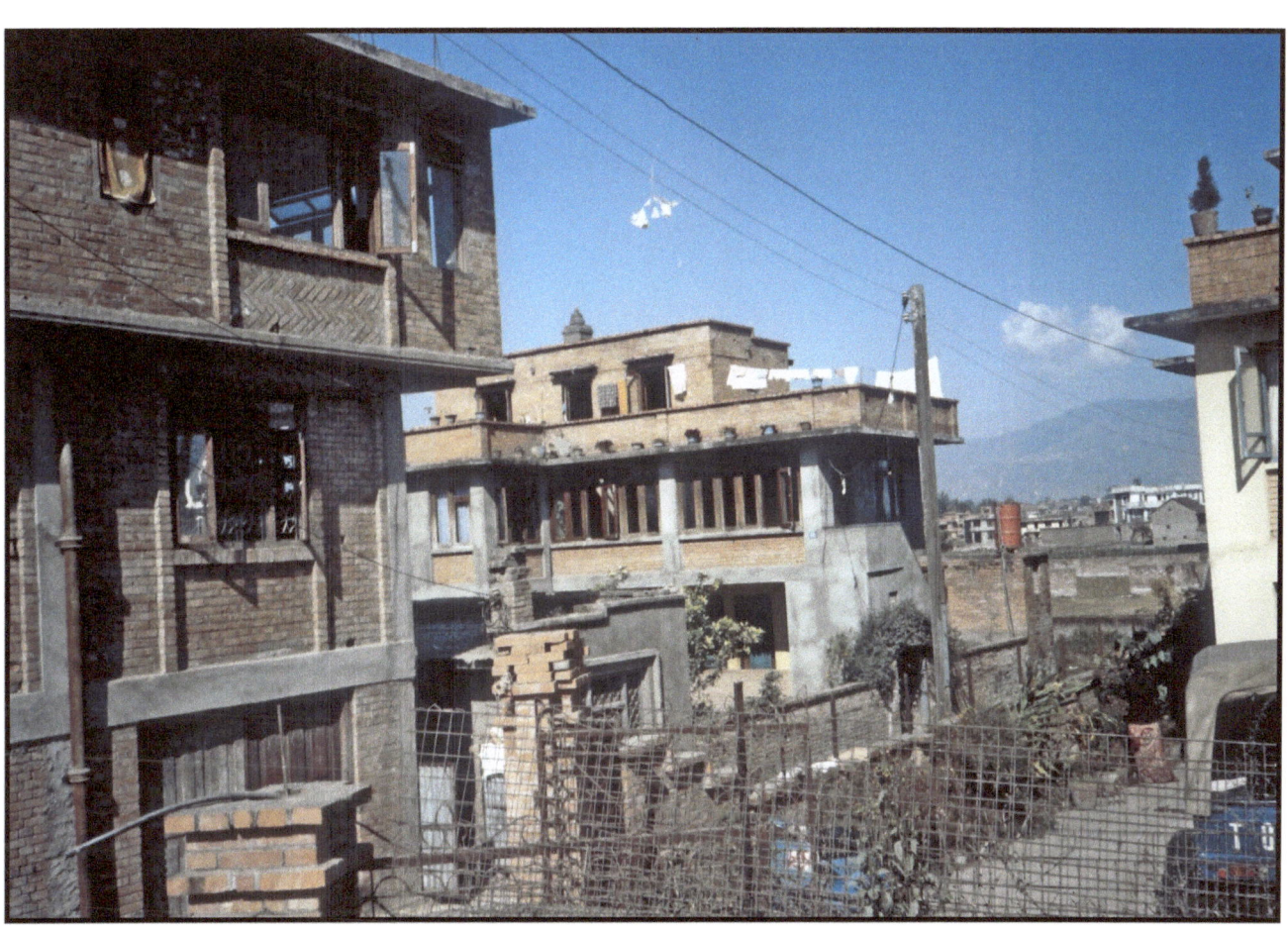

www.ingramcontent.com/pod-product-compliance
Lightning Source LLC
Chambersburg PA
CBHW051147220526
45473CB00003B/690